THE
BERKSHIRE
VILLAGE BOOK

The places, the people and their stories

Berkshire Federation
of Women's Institutes

COUNTRYSIDE BOOKS
NEWBURY BERKSHIRE

First published 2019
© Berkshire Federation of Women's Institutes

COUNTRYSIDE BOOKS
3 Catherine Road
Newbury, Berkshire

To view our complete range of books please visit us at
www.countrysidebooks.co.uk

ISBN 978 1 84674 382 5

*All materials used in the manufacture of this book
carry FSC certification*

Produced by The Letterworks Ltd., Reading
Designed and Typeset by KT Designs, St Helens
Printed by Holywell Press, Oxford

🍁 FOREWORD

The Royal County of Berkshire is not my county of birth, but it is the county I have called home for over forty years. Despite my long residence in Berkshire, reading this special book has widened my knowledge and whetted my thirst for even more stories of local history.

Berkshire certainly is a beautiful county. It has something for everyone; stunning scenic rural areas, bustling urban spaces and everything in between. But, to appreciate the beauty of the Berkshire I love, one has to leave the motorway that cuts the county in half. One needs to get out of the car and find other modes of transport. Cycle, horseback, boat, walking boots, even helicopter or hot air balloon, I have tried them all! This book will take you on a most unexpected journey. Not only into hidden corners of villages and their surrounding areas, but also  back in time to explore our history. It is so easy to see why Berkshire has always been a favourite county for both kings and queens.

I am not only truly proud of this book, I am extremely proud of everyone, especially our Berkshire WI ladies who have contributed to the overwhelming content. Certainly, a wealth of knowledge of family, area and county history. Thank you all.

I sincerely hope when you have this book in your hands, that it will take you on the journey of your life through our Royal County of Berkshire.

Marlene Voke

ACKNOWLEDGEMENTS

The production of this book has only been possible by the enthusiastic research of the contributors and the untiring efforts of Joyce Pack, who helped me to co-ordinate the project brilliantly.

A huge thank you to all who contributed – writers, artists and photographers. You have all played an important part in making this book a picture of life in Berkshire in the 21st century.

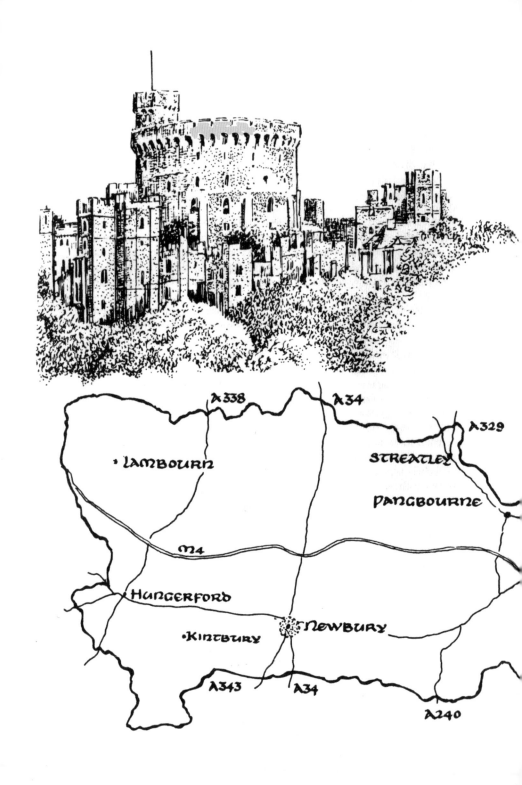

THE ROYAL COUNTY OF BERKSHIRE

🍁 ALDERMASTON VILLAGE

The picturesque village of Aldermaston lies halfway between Reading and Newbury. It is reached turning south off the A4, when the railway station and wharf are almost immediately seen. After crossing the Kennet and Avon Canal, the road runs for 1½ miles, and the village is approached across a bridge which spans the River Kennet.

On the right stands the Old Mill Hotel, a working flour mill until the late 1920s. The recreation ground lies nearby, and in the south-east corner is the village lock-up. This is said to have been last used in 1865, when a drunkard was locked up overnight; he is reputed to have been found burned to death the next morning.

The Street consists mainly of red brick and timber houses, and several Elizabethan cottages with inglenook fireplaces. The Aldermaston Store lies on the left. Years ago this was a saddler and harness-maker's shop. At the bottom of The Street stands the Hind's Head Hotel, parts of which date back to 1650. In 1800, this was known as The Congreve Arms, for, in those days, Aldermaston belonged to the Congreve Family. It boasts a clock tower with a gilt fox as a weather vane. To the right, down Wasing Lane, is the Aldermaston Church of England Primary School. Halfway along The Street is the old blacksmith's, which became The Aldermaston Pottery, exporting its wares all over the world, now converted into a private house. A little further is the Loosey or village green.

In Church Road are almshouses, built in 1706 by the Rev. Robert Dixon 'for the use of four widows of good character'. Details concerning the houses can be found in Aldermaston Church. Fifty yards further on is Cedars School which had previously been the Aldermaston School. Here there is a tablet in the brick wall to John Stair, schoolmaster in 1770, to commemorate the fact that he produced the first Williams pear. On the west wall of the same building can also be seen the Congreve coat of arms.

Up the hill is the church of St Mary the Virgin, whose churchyard is entered through a lychgate, erected in 1920 at a total cost of £270 collected from the parishioners in memory of the men who were killed in the First World War. Aldermaston Church has many items of interest: a Norman west door; 12th-century stained-glass windows; an early 14th-century scratch nail on the south-west buttress of the tower used in the early days to mark the times of services; a 16th-century triptych; a medieval wall painting in the Lady Chapel; a Jacobean seven-sided pulpit with carved panels and sounding board; and a fine alabaster tomb of Sir George and Lady Forster. There is also a peal of eight bells. A large proportion of the church was restored in 1898 by Mr Charles Keyser, who also commissioned wall paintings by Philip Harry Newman.

The history of Aldermaston Court remains mostly unknown. Certainly, a manor house has been there for hundreds of years, the earliest recorded reference being a visit by Edward II in 1321. It is also known that Queen Elizabeth I visited there in 1558 and 1601. An early manor house on a site near the church was rebuilt in 1636, and this building was destroyed by fire in 1843. Two years later, Aldermaston Court was rebuilt as it stands today. The house includes the original oak panelling and carving in the entrance hall, staircase and gallery; it also features the chimneys and much of the stained glass from the 1636 house. The entire Aldermaston Court estate, which included many of the houses in both the village and surrounding area, was sold by auction, in separate lots, on 20th/21st September 1939, just seventeen days after the outbreak of the Second World War.

One other feature to be seen in Aldermaston is Church Acre, in Fisherman's Lane. This is a tract of land which actually measures 'two acres, one rood and 33 poles'. It was bequeathed many years ago for the support of the church, and it is let by the curious custom of the 'candle auction'. Every three years, on or around December 13th, a meeting is called, and a horseshoe nail is inserted into a tallow candle, one inch below the wick. The candle is then lit by the Vicar, who makes the first bid and it is up to him (or her) to keep the bidding going. The church wardens and the Lord of the Manor are expected to smoke church pipes all this time, and everyone drinks hot punch. The candle gradually burns down until it reaches the pin, which then falls, and the last to bid is declared the purchaser for three years. This is practically the only remaining example of this ancient custom in England.

🍁 ALDERMASTON WHARF

Aldermaston Wharf is a small settlement 1½ miles (2.4 km) from Aldermaston Village with direct access to the A4, the railway line and the Kennet and Avon Canal towpath.

The River Kennet was made navigable between Reading and Newbury and opened as the Kennet Navigation in 1723. The canal section through Aldermaston Wharf runs from Frouds Lane Marina to Ufton Bridge, with the original River Kennet continuing approximately ½ a mile south of the canal. With the construction of a wharf a trading community developed. Then, on completion of the Kennet and Avon Canal in 1810, local trade flourished further with exports of timber products, malt and flour, and imports of coal, groceries and manufactured goods. Canal trade continues at Aldermaston, primarily in leisure and tourism. The original Grade II listed Wharf Cottage is now a visitor centre and tea room operated by the Kennet and Avon Canal Trust, and is next to the boat hire business.

In 1770, a brewery was opened alongside what is now Aldermaston Lock. For many years the brewer lived in Bridge House (now Alder Bridge School). Strange's Brewery ceased in 1945 when the site was purchased by Sterling Cables. A factory operated there until 1990.

Aldermaston Station was opened in 1847 by the Great Western Railway. Tragically, the original Victorian station building was mistakenly demolished in the early 1970s by a foreman confusing the names of Alderminster and Aldermaston. Trains run west to Newbury and Bedwyn and east to Reading and London Paddington. Electrification of the lines was completed up to Newbury in 2018.

Since 1995, the area has developed significantly through new housing and is served by the Butt Inn public house, originally built in the 1920s. A new pedestrian and cycle path was constructed in 2012 to provide safe access between Aldermaston Wharf and Village. It also links with the National Cycle Network along the Kennet and Avon Canal towpath.

🍁 ALDWORTH

Aldworth is a small and historic village high up on the Berkshire Downs. It lies in an Area of Outstanding Natural Beauty between Reading and Newbury.

The parish of Aldworth comprises 110 households; some 300 people of all ages and includes the hamlet of Westridge Green: in all an area of about 1,806 acres. Agriculture plays an important role and much land is owned by Yattendon Estates. There are five working farms in the parish. A few villagers are home workers, but most of them work in neighbouring towns or commute to London. There is no bus service, so the car is the primary means of transport.

Aldworth is set in a fold of the Downs where the ancient Ridgeway descends to the Thames at Streatley. At its southern edge there is an intact section of Grim's Ditch. The Domesday Book records Aldworth as Elleorde, meaning Old Enclosure.

In the 13th and 14th centuries the Manor was held by the Norman family of de la Beche. Five generations of this knighted family had a profound effect on the village and their legacy lives on. The church of St Mary is home to the Aldworth Giants: a unique collection of nine life-size effigies of these Berkshire landowners and public officials, who served during the reigns of Edward I, II and III (1272-1377) and were closely tied to the monarchy.

Of the Norman church of St Mary, only the lower part of the tower and the font remain. In the early 1300s Sir Philip de la Beche, then Sheriff of Berkshire, rebuilt the church and his new chancel is still in its original form. The altars were rededicated on 2nd August 1315. The south aisle, commissioned in the 1330s by Sir Nicholas de la Beche, has finely carved monumental effigies under canopied tombs providing a showplace for the family's achievements.

Queen Elizabeth I visited the church to see the effigies on 2 May 1644, accompanied by the Earl of Leicester. A parchment tabling the names of the de la Beche family effigies was removed to show the Queen. This was never brought back, making it now difficult to accurately identify each effigy.

St Mary's is a much loved, visited and used church. The effigies and canopies were recently cleaned and conserved and in 2012 a small extension was added providing a toilet and kitchenette. In 2000, villagers produced a magnificent Aldworth Millennium Tapestry. This depicts historical events, places and people of Aldworth, and hangs permanently in the church. A book about the making of the tapestry also gives a detailed description and history of everything depicted.

The oldest inhabitant of Aldworth is an ancient yew tree, which has been growing in the churchyard for well over 1,000 years. In January 1976 it suffered serious storm damage, but a part of it survives. Many people come to see the Aldworth Giants, the tapestry and the ancient yew tree. Visitors also come to view the beautifully carved gravestone of a past resident of Westridge Green – war poet Laurence Binyon, who, in 1914, wrote the poem *For the Fallen*. Words from this poem are traditionally read at Remembrance services every year.

St Mary's church is open every day and each summer provides delicious Wednesday afternoon teas to many visitors. Concerts and flower festivals help raise funds for its upkeep and the regular services, including a monthly Breakfast Church, offer villagers a welcoming place for worship. In 2015, a full-colour history and guide book, *St Mary's and the Aldworth Giants*, was published.

Aldworth has seen many literary figures living in or visiting the village. Alfred Lord Tennyson loved the village and married Emily Sellwood from Pibworth House. He named his house near Hazelmere 'Aldworth'. Richard Ingrams, author and former editor of *Private Eye* and *The Oldie*, has lived in the village for over 50 years and plays the organ at St Mary's church services. The village's fascinating history was told in a documentary film *Place of Giants*, made in 2016 by independent film-maker Nicholas Brazil.

Life in Aldworth today is relatively peaceful, but there is plenty going on. Country pursuits and leisure activities are popular. The village school closed in 1962 and the much loved shop and post office closed in 2002. However, the old school and shop survive as private dwellings and a community-run Saturday market offers a weekly opportunity to shop and chat.

In 2016 a new village hall replaced the old one on the tree-lined recreation ground. In summer it also serves as the cricket pavilion for the Bell Inn cricket club. Adjacent is a children's playground. The hall is used for activities such as the Saturday market as well as a toddler group, art and crafts, exercise and Pilates classes, meetings, talks, concerts, plays, parties and weddings.

There are two thriving pubs in the village, the Bell Inn which dates from about 1340 and the Four Points Inn, an old, thatched wayside inn. Both pubs are exceedingly popular, having lovely outdoor space and offering villagers, walkers and visitors a good choice of refreshment.

Opposite the Bell Inn, is the attractive village well, which is 370 ft deep. This was dug following an outbreak of typhus in 1860. Water is now supplied from a tank at Bower Farm, and pumped up from nearby Compton.

Aldworth as a village has evolved slowly. In the 1950s a few council houses were built on former church land, then four bungalows for the elderly in a cul-de-sac named The Glebe. In 1998 the English Rural Housing Association built a further six houses, which were officially handed over to residents by the Princess Royal, whose arrival by helicopter was quite an event and is recorded in the Millennium Tapestry.

Some might say Aldworth is in a kind of time warp but this is part of its charm, making it an attractive village to both live in and visit.

🍁 ARBORFIELD

The village of Arborfield is about 5 miles south of Reading and 4 miles west of Wokingham. Arborfield and Newland parish is an amalgamation of two parishes, which were joined together in 1948. The old area of Newland is nearer to Sindlesham and Winnersh.

Arborfield Green is a new development on the old army garrison site and is in the parishes of Finchampstead, Arborfield and Barkham. A great deal of new housing has been built in this area and a bypass around Arborfield is planned for 2022. Reading Football Club is at present building a new training ground on the site of the old Wokingham Borough Golf Course.

A focal point for Arborfield is the cross, which has been a crossroads for many centuries. It gained a new meaning in 1919 when the War Memorial was erected. During 2004, the five-ways crossroads was developed into a roundabout.

The modern village centre is along the Eversley Road, moving south from the cross and centred on the village hall. The heart of the current village is a conservation area and there are many footpaths, bridleways and byways connecting the village to its neighbours. The old Swan Inn has had a variety of uses since closing and may now become residential. The Bull Inn, where Queen Victoria stopped on her way to Stratfield Saye, is now a popular pub restaurant.

Arborfield and Newlands WI still meet in the village hall, where they have met since it was opened in 1931. Among other users of the hall, the local history group keeps alive an interest in the past and a gardening club has extensive links to others in the area.

The local park is owned and managed by the Parish Council where residents have contributed to the tree and bulb planting, and it is a much valued and well-used recreation area. There is an active and expanding primary school in the village and a new children's nursery in the park pavilion. An area of woodland between Arborfield, Bearwood and Barkham called the Coombes is much used by walkers, horse riders and cyclists.

The village has an area of ancient woodland called Pound Copse, which was gifted to the Parish Council and is maintained with the help of Berkshire Conservation Volunteers. There is also an important and historic site which surrounds the old churchyard, and the ruins of a chalk and flint church, circa 1200. The new parish church, St Bartholomew, was built in 1863 and has many links with the local community through its ministry, services, school and social events.

🍁 ASHAMPSTEAD

Some years ago we, the parishioners of Ashampstead, wrote a book about the parish. It started with the following paragraph and I don't think I can improve on it as an introduction.

'Ashampstead has been described as 'the parish where nothing ever happened': no battles, no great houses. Queen Elizabeth I never slept

Ashampstead

here. Nevertheless, for at least six thousand years – and probably for very much longer – people have been born in the parish, have made their living from the fields and woods, have built their homes and raised their families.'

Ashampstead Parish was originally part of Basildon Parish and only became a separate parish in 1847.

Worked flints have been found around the parish dating from both the Mesolithic and Neolithic periods (*c.*10,000 BC – *c.* 2,500 BC). Neolithic people started farming around 4,000 BC, and they and their flocks and herds began clearing the woodlands that had developed after the last Ice Age. However, the parish has no surface water and this made permanent settlement difficult. The neighbouring parishes all have settlements of the Bronze Age, Iron Age and Roman periods, but no definite settlement of any of these periods has been found within Ashampstead.

After the Battle of Hastings (1066), the Norman army marched from Hastings via Winchester to Wallingford, where it crossed the Thames to attack London from the north. Very probably they marched along Ashampstead Road – known locally as Bottom Road. Twenty years later, when the Domesday Book was compiled, the parish was divided between the manors of Hartridge and an unnamed manor, which was probably an unlocated manor called Ashden. The boundary between the two manors was Ashampstead Road and the boundary banks around the manors can still be traced for most of their length. The names describe the sites well. Hartridge means 'the ridge of the stag', and Ashden means 'ash valley'.

The medieval settlement pattern was probably very similar to the modern pattern. The main settlement was around the church at Ashampstead village, but there was also a substantial group of early houses at Ashampstead Common. Medieval arable land was farmed using the open-field system. Farmers, or husbandmen as they were called, held a varying number of long narrow strips scattered throughout large open fields. In addition, there were a number of small, irregularly-shaped paddocks called crofts or closes around each husbandman's homestead. These were used as orchards and gardens, as well as for grazing and holding livestock. Traces of the open-field landscape can be seen on the earliest detailed plan of Ashampstead Parish, the 1844 Tithe Map.

Ashampstead and Burnt Hill Commons were important to the parish as grazing land and as a source of fuel, timber and bedding for animals. They also supplied the many poles and sticks required by pre-plastic farmers. Around 1240, a deer park was created on the Commons for the Lord of the Manor. A substantial bank was raised all the way around the Commons with the ditch on the inside to contain the deer. Most of this can still be traced. The deer park seems to have fallen from use around 1550, when the area reverted to being a common.

During the Second World War, the commons were used as convoy camps as the armies were assembled for the D-Day invasion of Normandy. Some traces remain, particularly at Burnt Hill, where the concrete camp roadways obliterated the old common paths. After the war, the camp buildings were used to house displaced and homeless people. Some families still living in the area had members who lived in the huts before they were finally demolished.

Non-conformity, especially Methodism, was very popular in the area in the 19th and early 20th centuries. There were chapels at Ashampstead Green, at Quick's Green, and at Burnt Hill. The lack of a pub within Ashampstead village is probably due to the Methodists' disapproval of alcohol. The Fleece and Feathers, now the Fleece and Feathers House, was originally the New Inn. 'New' in relation to another pub, the Four Points, further along the Bottom Road nearer Aldworth. It was essential to the drovers and other travellers on the Bottom Road and could not be closed. Another essential pub was the Axe and Compass, now the Nut and Bolt House, at Burnt Hill. This served the brickmakers who worked in the area. Brickmaking was hot and thirsty work.

Another result of Methodism was the demand for education by people previously denied it. Schools were provided by public subscription in villages all over the country. Ashampstead School was built in 1873/75 on land granted by the Hopkins' Estate of Tidmarsh, using money raised by subscription in and around the parish. It served as a school until December 1971 and then became the village hall.

The building of the road to Hampstead Norreys in 1938 gave access to the railway and made it possible for villagers to go to secondary school and to work outside the parish, but it was the widespread availability of cars from the 1950s onwards that changed the village from an agricultural settlement to a dormitory for Reading and Newbury. The village expanded along Chapel Lane and Holly Lane and The Flower's Piece estate was built. As farm mechanisation increased, more and more people took work outside the parish. The village shop closed in 1973, in the face of competition from supermarkets.

Industry is now being brought back into the countryside. The redundant farm buildings at Child's Court Farm on Ashampstead Common have been converted into offices and workshops of many kinds, and a redundant dairy, just outside the village, has been converted into a thriving farm shop at Casey Fields.

🍁 Ashmore Green and Cold Ash

Ashmore Green and Cold Ash are situated approximately 4 miles north east of Newbury in West Berkshire, with a population of around 4,000 and in an area of 7.5km.

There is a village post office/shop, a church, three public houses, a village hall, a primary school, a Roman Catholic school and a private boarding school for girls. There is also an Anglican church and convent.

St Mark's Parish Church was built in 1864 and is in the gothic revival style. In 2000, thanks to a substantial bequest, a parish room was built to include a hall, a kitchen and toilets attached to the church. One of the recent ministers was Rev David Winter who for several years appeared on the BBC Radio 4's 'Thought for the Day'. During his time as minister he arranged two television broadcasts from St Mark's in 1997. The church has solar panels attached to the roof to supply electricity for the church and the national grid.

The catholic convent, which dates from the 1920s, is home to the Franciscan Missionaries of Mary and is a school, retreat and conference centre. Over many years in the past, the nuns farmed the fields around the convent and could be regularly seen in their habits driving tractors, feeding animals and harvesting.

Many villagers helped at harvest time and the local children had much fun chasing the rabbits which ran from the stubble.

St Mark's primary school was originally situated next to the church but a new building was established in 1981 opposite the church. The school has around 150-200 pupils aged between 4 and 12 years. The original school has been converted to two private houses.

The third school in the village is Downe House, a private boarding school for girls. It moved to Cold Ash in 1922 having outgrown its original premises in Bromley, Kent where it was situated in Charles Darwin's former home. Over the years, many girls of note have had their education there including Clare Balding, Sophie and Tessa Dahl, Miranda Hart, Geraldine James, the Duchess of Cambridge and her sister Pippa, and Lady Gabriella Windsor.

The three public houses in Ashmore Green and Cold Ash are the Sun in the Wood, the Spotted Dog and the Castle. The Sun in the Wood is the only pub in Ashmore Green as at least three others have closed down in recent years. The Spotted Dog in Cold Ash was originally a blacksmith's forge in the 1800s – the earliest record of it trading as a pub was in 1869. The Castle, which is situated next door to the Spotted Dog, in the centre of the village, is recorded as a business in the 1800s.

The Acland Memorial Hall is host to many clubs and groups including Ashmore Green and Cold Ash WIs. It is very well-equipped and situated next to the recreation ground, tennis courts and football and cricket grounds. It is home to the Cold Ash pre-school and is hired out on a regular basis for many activities and functions. It was built in 1925 and fully refurbished in 2014. The hall is named after Sir Reginald Acland whose wife donated the land for the site.

Ashmore Green Farm and Thirtover Farm were sold in 1988. Thirtover Farmhouse is now the county headquarters of the Girlguiding Royal Berkshire. Although now gone, the village had its own bakery and village shop situated opposite the Castle and Spotted Dog public houses. It was owned and run by two brothers. On Christmas Day each year over several decades, it was open to villagers to cook their turkeys. Many of the husbands and fathers would carry a tin holding the bird with a large jug for the juices and a cloth to cover, to the bakery ovens. Most would then cross the road to one of the pubs. When notified that the birds were cooked they were then collected and taken back to the homes where the ladies had prepared the rest of the Christmas lunch. This is a memory held dear by many in the village.

Despite the fact that the village is quiet with very few incidents, there have been a number of tragic events. In January 1986, a local woman was found dead in a car in Cold Ash woods. A year later a fire at Cleeve in Ashmore Green claimed the lives of a young mother and her daughter. In February 2000, a young female dentist was thrown from a balcony by her partner, resulting in her death. Late in 2003, a father shot his wife and son at a property in Slanting Hill. In 2006, the landlord of a local pub was found dead in his car.

Ashmore Green and Cold Ash are situated in a beautiful rural part of West Berkshire and feature in the novel *The Unseen* written by Katherine Webb. There have been many changes in the village over the years including the closing of the Children's Hospital and the Children's Home as well as several pubs and shops. There was an Observer Post and a Home Guard Group in the war. The population has increased steadily over the years and it is still a lovely village in which to live. There are many activities including football, cricket and tennis, theatre, fitness, dance and music groups, two WIs and several church and meeting groups amongst many others; something for everyone.

❉ BARKHAM

The Anglo-Saxon name recorded in AD 952 for Barkham was *Beorchamme*. The spelling changed in later records but has remained as Barkham since the 16th century. This means 'birch tree meadow', a clearing made in the woodland for hay.

After the last Ice Age, trees slowly dominated the area. Pollen records give evidence of some tree clearance and the beginning of agriculture in the Mesolithic/Neolithic divide about 5,000 to 4000 BC. However, woodland was always of great economic importance here, right through to the 20th century.

In the late Bronze Age, around 1300 BC, a mysterious 'burnt mound' of charcoal and burnt flints was created beside a small stream in the centre of the parish. Fire was used to heat flints and these provided hot water. The purpose of this is a mystery. It might have been used for feasting, but no mammal bones were found. An alternative suggestion is that it was for a ritual involving the use of steam, like a sauna. Whatever the answer, radiocarbon dates obtained from the charcoal indicate a long period of use over hundreds of years.

The boundaries of the 250-acre (3 hides) Saxon estate in *Beorchamme* are described in a Charter of AD 952. Although attempts have been made to interpret them, their exact course is not completely clear. Some Saxon period pottery has been found in the fields of the parish.

Barkham is also described as being the size of 3 hides in the 1086 Domesday Survey. It was always one of the smallest parishes in the area within the former

Berkshire and Windsor Forest. It lay on the western fringe of the royal hunting preserve of Windsor, between the two medieval administrative 'Walkes' of Bigshotte and Bear Wood. It had a small population, never over about 200, and large areas of common within the woodland.

Hidden away from the busy traffic-filled roads which dissect the village is the church of St James the Apostle and the former moated, medieval manor house now named Church Cottages. Moats were largely created for very personal reasons from the middle of the 12th century into the 15th century; the one here was perhaps for security. The present house was possibly rebuilt at the end of the 15th century and was divided into two dwellings over 160 years ago. Sometime, possibly during the 17th century, the site of the manor of Barkham 'migrated' to a newer substantial house on Barkham Road. This was known then as Barkham House until the mid-19th century, when the name Barkham Manor was adopted.

There are traces of another moated site near the parish boundary with Finchampstead. Biggs Farm house was close to the corner of Biggs Lane and Princess Marina Drive. The house was demolished after the War Office purchased the land in 1911 following the creation of the Remount Depot in 1904. The moat is now a rectangular landscaped grass area beside the road.

In the porch of the church of St James lies the wooden effigy of a medieval lady wearing a long dress. It is thought she may be a memorial to the 14th-century Agnes de Nevill, daughter of Thomas. She is one of only five medieval wooden effigies in pre-1992 Berkshire of which one is in the parish church of Englefield and three in the parish church at Sparsholt. For special services Agnes is given a bouquet of flowers set between her now handless arms.

In the churchyard of St James is a chest grave close to the south transept, dedicated to the Rev David Davies, Rector of Barkham between 1782 and his death in 1819. He was orphaned when young and sent to school in Barbados. He was very aware of, and kept records of, the poorest families of the farm labourers in Barkham. Conditions were the worst in the 1790s during a time of bad harvests, high inflation and war against the French. He wrote of his concern '*at their mean and distressed condition*'. Davies regularly sought charitable aid wherever he could from his wealthier acquaintances and regularly helped with generous donations in kind himself where the need was greatest.

He wrote a social tract published in 1795, *The Case of Labourers in Husbandry Stated and Considered*, which analysed the detailed information he had meticulously gathered from both his Barkham parishioners and elsewhere. Conditions for the poor were worse in the south of England than the north.

The basic diet of a poor family in Barkham was home-made bread, thin soup and a little cheese; meat was usually from pig. Milk was hard to come by and tea was the staple drink whose leaves were used several times. There was insufficient ground around their cottages to grow vegetables. In Barkham in the 1790s, about one fifth of families were regularly dependent on the poor rates for assistance.

Rev Davies argued over many years that a man should be paid a minimum wage to cover the cost of his family's basic needs rather than relying on charity. His work was read and appreciated by many, but it was not until the 1834 Poor Law Amendment Act that more radical change came about.

Near to his grave is one of Rev Peter Hampson Ditchfield, Rector from 1886 to 1930. He was a prolific writer on history, archaeology, folklore and so on. With William Page, Ditchfield edited the four volumes of the *Victoria County History of Berkshire* in the early 20th century. He edited the *Berks, Bucks & Oxon Archaeological Journal* for 28 years and the Notes and Queries column on local history in the *Reading Mercury*. Rev Peter Ditchfield was also fondly remembered by his parishioners.

Both of these Rectors were passionate about education. When Rev David Davies came to Barkham there was no school and he paid 2d a week for up to 8 children to attend a private school run by Dame Payne. An early 19th-century owner of Barkham House, Henry Clive set up a day school shortly before the death of David Davies who left money for several children to be educated there. Mr Clive paid for the building of the schoolroom which is a single storey building in Barkham Street, part of the front of The Gables which used to be named Old School House. The schoolmistress, Mrs Mary Penlington, was the wife of an employee of Mr Clive.

Another hidden aspect of Barkham perhaps, is the greater density of ancient trees. There are more here than in any other parish in the Borough of Wokingham. Apart from a great number of veteran oaks, there is a rare four-line avenue of lime trees planted across the landscape. Although the winter winds and other storms have taken their toll, about 88 lime trees remain today.

🍁 BASILDON

The settlement of Basildon has existed since the early years of the first millennium. Many years ago the remains of a Roman villa were found in Lower Basildon, though sadly almost all evidence of this was destroyed when the Great Western Railway was built in 1839. The railway bridge built at that time is thought to be the one included by Turner in his famous painting *Rain, Speed and Steam*, which is now in the National Gallery.

The church of St Bartholomew, Lower Basildon, was built in the early 13th century. The nave, chancel and south doorway survive to this day, and the church is well worth visiting. In a sealed vault under the church lie the remains of Basildon's most famous citizen, the agrarian reformer Jethro Tull, whose ideas were to revolutionise agriculture in this country. Tull was born in Basildon in 1674 and baptised in St Bartholomew's church. The memorial stone to Tull, near the south wall of the church, was erected in 1941.

Basildon has its share of ghosts. The Grotto, in Lower Basildon, was in the possession of the Fane family, and reputedly it is haunted by a Lady Fane who committed suicide by throwing herself down the well. It is said that her ghost used to appear in a certain room in the house in the 1890s. More recent sightings have been of a silvery figure brushing past residents on the stairs or drifting across the lawn. As well as the ghost of Lady Fane, since 1943 there have been sightings of the ghost of a serving girl with red hair and a tattered green dress. She appears between October and January, between nine and eleven in the evening. The witch, Nan Carey, is said to haunt a corner just outside the village.

The Palladian-style house of Basildon Park was built in the late 18th century by Sir Francis Sykes, known as the Nabob. His son, the second baronet, is probably best remembered as the owner of a Berkshire sow called Slut, who was adept at retrieving game! The profligate third baronet, also called Francis, was forced to sell the estate in 1838 to James Morrison, a wealthy former MP. The estate remained in the Morrison family for almost a century, and in the early years of the 20th century James Morrison, grandson of the original owner, commissioned the famous architect Sir Edwin Lutyens to design houses for the estate, many of which survive in Basildon to this day. They are some of the most attractive houses in the village.

During the First World War the house served as a fifty-bed hospital for the Guards Regiments. Basildon, like nearly every other village in the United Kingdom, lost a high number of men during the war. Their names, together with the names of those men from the village who died in the Second World War, are recorded on the war memorial outside St Stephen's church, Upper Basildon. The church of St. Stephen is a modern building which recently celebrated its 50th anniversary. There is a community centre attached which is used not just for church events but also for a once-a-week café and post office, besides Bridge Club meetings, exercise classes, and WI meetings and the WI Craft Group. The Basildon branch of the WI was founded in 1937.

At the outbreak of the Second World War Basildon House was requisitioned by the government, and a TA regiment occupied the house for the first three years of the war. It subsequently housed a battalion of the US Army. At the end of the war the house was, unsurprisingly, extremely dilapidated, but it was bought by the second Lord Iliffe. He and his wife Renee restored the house with care and love. Since 1978 it has belonged to the National Trust, and is well worth a visit. The house has been used several times as a location in films, firstly as Netherfield Park in the 2005 film *Pride and Prejudice* with Keira Knightley and Matthew Macfadyen, in the 2006 film *Marie-Antoinette*, as Lord and Lady Radley's house in *Dorian Gray* (2009), and most recently in *Pride and Prejudice and Zombies*. It also served as Lord and Lady Grantham's London house in *Downton Abbey*.

After the war Basildon continued to grow, though the designation of a substantial part of West Berkshire as an Area of Outstanding Natural Beauty has meant that development has, for the most part, been confined to the village envelope. At the end of the 1960s there were still two shops, three pubs and a garage in the village, but over the following forty years all of these except the Red Lion pub closed. Basildon today is largely a commuter village, with only one pub and no shop, but our excellent primary school continues to flourish, as do many village societies and clubs.

A new village hall was built in 2004 next to the recreation ground and it is much used by local organisations including The Basildonians, our amateur dramatics society, the Folk Dance Group and the Badminton Club as well as for yoga classes and private functions of all sorts. The monthly Village Market is held there and the WI is one of the groups that provide refreshments. Every September the Horticultural Society holds a summer show on the recreation ground at which the WI always provides the ever-popular cake stall.

❧ BEECH HILL

The village of Beech Hill, thought to have formerly been Beche Hill after the de la Beche family, has little easily discovered history, because a fire destroyed most of the archives prior to 1860.

Originally part of the parish of Stratfield Mortimer, Beech Hill became a parish in its own right in 1886 with its own Parish Church of St Mary the Virgin.

Beaumys Castle was a manor in the parish of neighbouring Swallowfield, given to Sir Nicholas de la Beche in 1335. De la Beche received a licence to crenellate, so in 1338 he fortified the manor house. The castle was protected by earthworks and surrounded by a moat. Sadly, a copse surrounded by a moat is the only evidence left of the Castle of Beaumys.

Beech Hill House was built in the 17th century by the Harrison family, who owned it for many years. In 1739 it was purchased by the Lodden merchant, Henry Hunter, whose descendants lived there until 1950. After that it was for some years a home for refugees run by the Ockenden Venture but has since been turned into flats. At the other end of the village is Trunkwell House, originally the Tudor home of the Noyes family, now a well-known hotel, restaurant and wedding venue.

The Jubilee reservoir was built in 1897 to commemorate Queen Victoria's Diamond Jubilee. The original pump had broken down and the well was full of muddy surface water. Donated by Mr J. J. Ratcliffe, the reservoir held 16,000 gallons of water, thus giving the village a magnificent supply. However, in 1905 the tap would not work, and nobody seemed to know whose responsibility it was to repair it – eventually a 1d rate was charged to villagers for its maintenance. In 1937 a severe drought dried up the reservoir, and water from an imported tank had to take its place. The mains reached Beech Hill just in time for the outbreak of war, and the ornamental railings that had adorned the reservoir were turned in as 'war effort'.

For the Millennium, Roland Joy, who was born in Beech Hill, was commissioned to design and build a bas-relief sculpture depicting some of the village's history. This now stands opposite the parish church.

🍁 BEENHAM

The village of Beenham is situated on the crest of a hill about 350 ft above the Kennet valley. 'Ham' is Old English for place, or home; 'Been' could have come from 'Benna', an important person from whom Beenham is derived.

The older part of the present village dates from the 17th century, and is found around the Six Bells, an inn taking its name from the bells of the parish church, although there are several much older dwellings, notably White Cottage, whose barn is of 'cruck' construction dated 1500 or earlier, and other farms and cottages built in the 16th century.

There has been a church on the site of the present Church of St Mary since medieval times; this was destroyed by fire in 1794. An estimate for new bells, frame etc was £393.7.2d but parishioners managed to collect 21cwt of melted bell metal in the churchyard and so reduced the bill to £154.4.0d.

The church built to replace it was also destroyed by fire, except for the brick tower which survived and is now the west tower of the modern church built in 1859.

Inside there is a memorial to Sir Charles Hopson, who was responsible for much of the woodwork in St Paul's Cathedral. He was knighted by Queen Anne and lived in Beenham House. There are other memorials to families who have lived in the Manor House, such as the Carters and the Warings. The inside walls have been painted with a New Testament theme by an amateur artist, Miss Sharp, in 1900. Outside the south porch stand some interesting carved tombstones.

The first school was built in 1840, a church school 'for the education of children in the principles of Christian Religion'. It consisted of one big classroom divided into two by a curtain, two small cloakrooms and two small playgrounds, one each for boys and girls. Each child paid a few pence a week and donations were made too. However, by 1892 the church could no longer afford the upkeep so it was handed over to the Board of Education and renamed Beenham Council School. It was 18 years before improvements were made to the facilities. The children still sat on long benches without backs, and learned to read by using the same book in turn.

On 9th March 1948 the school burned down during the night. The children were taught in the Victory Hall while a 'temporary' school was built – this was kept in use for many years until a new school was finally built on another site.

St Mary's Farm is a lovely 18th-century house which used to be the parsonage house for the church. One of its vicars was Thomas Stackhouse, author of *A New History of the Holy Bible*, written in 1733 when he was a famous theologian; today he is perhaps better remembered for his heavy drinking, patronising the Three Kings Jack's Booth, a coaching inn on the Bath Road, a convenient horse-ride away!

The Manor of Beenham existed in the 16th century and was held by one Henry Parkyns, who probably built a house on the site of the present one, quite likely a timbered and gabled mansion, no trace of which now exists. The present fine, large house, originally red brick, now painted white, was built by Sir Charles Rich, and is an impressive landmark seen from the Bath Road.

Henry Waring, the Victorian owner, improved the house, built racing stables and enlarged the gardens. In the 1920s the house became the home of the Waddell family. The last member to live there was a Miss Majorie Waddell.

The Stocks inn, a rectangular house of grey and red brick built around 1729, closed in 1999 and was turned into residential housing. It is one of four small country houses of similar design, the others being the vicarage and two on Beenham Hill, The Malthouse and Hillfoot House.

The old inn sign was rare, suggesting that the inn was built on the site of ancient stocks, but this is not so. It was called after its first landlord, Donald Stocks. There is strong evidence to suggest it had been the local bakehouse. In the grounds was a 17th-century barn, and stocks erected in deference to the inn's name, but which are not the origin of it.

Men working for Major Waring of Beenham House could claim a mild or bitter at the bar if they attended church on Sunday mornings. A famous regular was Old Charlie, an intelligent poacher who had his own special place in the bar. He had trained his dog to hide in his bicycle basket and to bark only at the approach of a policeman!

Beenham today is a vibrant village, happily including many young families, and the school is thriving. Most of the houses enjoy views over the rolling farmland of the North Wessex Downs, a designated Area of Outstanding Natural Beauty. It even includes a vineyard within its boundaries.

🍁 BINFIELD

Binfield derives its name from the coarse grass in this clearing or 'feld' in Windsor Forest. At one time the forest was divided into 16 Walkes, or administrative areas. The Binfelde Walke was mentioned in the 16th century under Sir Henry Neville, the keeper, who lived at Billingbear. The village runs along a ridge and gives a view of the Chiltern Hills to the north-west. Windsor Forest covered all this area and was well stocked with fallow deer for the King's hunting. The severe game laws pressed heavily on poacher and peasant alike to maintain the royal prerogative. Said to mark the centre of Old Windsor Forest, the Stag and Hounds inn on the Forest Road, part 14th century, was converted to an inn in 1727. William Cobbett once visited the inn for 'an excellent breakfast'.

The busy A329 and A329M roads run through the south-western part of the village from Bracknell to Reading, providing adjacent and heavily used access points to the M4 and south to the M3. From the north, the B3034 is a slightly quieter route from Windsor to Binfield that runs through the centre of the village. This is the old turnpike road created in the 18th century so that wheeled traffic could travel more comfortably along the forest tracks. The formation of the Turnpike Trust to build the Forest Road is commemorated by an oval stone set up by the roadside at Bill Hill.

Of the local historic manors and houses, Binfield Place is said to be the oldest house in the village with a history that goes back to Henry VII. It has

16th-century moulded beams and a chimney marked 1702. Tradition has it that bad luck will befall the owner if a 17th-century bas-relief of a lady's head is moved. Binfield Lodge, one of James I's hunting lodges, claims that Elizabeth I slept there and boasts that Cecil Rhodes was also a visitor. Elm Grove in Monk's Alley has a raised bowling green which may have been the site of ancient earthworks. White Hill, the erstwhile home of Alexander Pope, is now called Pope's Manor. The beautiful grounds and lake are accessible to the public.

The northern part of the village houses the old parish church of All Saints, much restored but with the main part dating from the 15th century. There is, however, a record of a priest of Binfield as early as 1174. The unusual open wooden porch with different carvings on both sides is 14th century, and there is some fine 15th-century glass. A unique hourglass stand of hammered ironwork beside the pulpit dated 1628 is notable, as is the half-length brass memorial to Walter Annefordhe, the oldest in Berkshire, to be found in the chancel under the red carpet. Beside the south door there is a medallion memorial to Catherine Macaulay Graham (1731–1791), who spent her later years in Binfield. This lady was of Republican persuasion and an ardent feminist whose views were in advance of her time and not always well received in polite company. Nevertheless, she had conversations with Dr Johnson, and was a guest of George Washington whilst in North America in 1785. The mansion behind the church is the former rectory, enlarged in the 19th century. The artist John Constable sketched All Saints' church in 1816, whilst spending his honeymoon at the rectory. The churchyard at All Saints has become a wild flower sanctuary. At least 23 different species grow here.

St Mark's church, a Chapel of Ease built in 1867, has in recent times been mainly used for church groups, meetings and events. The church provides overnight shelter and meals for homeless people in turn with other churches in the district. Further to the south of the village is the area of Amen Corner, its name taken from the congregation of a Dissenting Chapel built in 1875, who used to say to each other as they left after a service 'God be with you, Amen.' In this corner also, there formerly existed a brickworks employing 60 craftsmen making fine, wire-cut bricks. Beehive Lane clearly takes its name from the old brick kilns with their beehive shapes.

Binfield is located only two and a half miles from the centre of Bracknell and the small, quiet village was affected by the designation of Bracknell as a New Town in 1948. Residential development of the new town proceeded largely within its own borders from the 1950s but by 1980 the expansion of Bracknell and desirability of rural life at such close quarters led to pressure on

Binfield's green fields from building development. That has proceeded apace, with multiple developments on three sides of the village, so that there is no longer a wide green boundary between Binfield and Bracknell to the east or to the west to Wokingham. Only the northern side remains rural. There is always an upside however. The regenerated Bracknell town centre is within minutes on the bus service. Similarly, employment opportunities are easily accessed in the new town industrial areas.

The increase in population, now over 8000, has ensured that Binfield is a thriving community with a Parish Office and GP surgery. A modern primary school, library and small shopping precinct form a central village hub, along with the adjacent Memorial Hall (1920) and Working Men's Club (1906) each of which hosts many social activities.

Popular in Binfield are the annual 10K Charity Run, keenly supported, and the Scarecrow Trail, when families hunt throughout the village for the scarecrows 'in hiding' during the school Autumn half term.

Neighbourliness is all in Binfield. The Working Men's club hosted the Women's Institute scarecrow, Wilhelmina, in 2017, but alas the bar became too much of a nightly temptation for her and she had fallen over by the end of the week.

🍁 BISHAM

Bisham village is of Saxon origin and in the old days was known as 'Bustleham'. It was originally the home of the Knights Templar.

Situated as it is on the Berkshire side of the Thames, one mile upstream from Marlow towards Temple, it has a beautiful location, some 4 miles from Maidenhead, and with the backcloth of the famous Quarry Woods.

The main road to Marlow runs through the village between picturesque brick and timber cottages, some as early as Tudor in origin, and these together with a local inn, the Bull, now enlarged and modernised, make up a delightful model village setting.

The main part of Bisham's history lies in the famous Bisham Abbey and Estate, which at one time extended to 5,000 acres and which is now one of the leading sports centres in the country. Bisham Abbey was the Manor House in the past and has the reputation for being one of the most haunted houses in England. It also has many connections with royalty. Queen Elizabeth I stayed here and Queen Victoria was reputed to have called whilst out driving her carriage. She found no one at home to greet her and was so indignant she ordered her coachman to drive back to Windsor Castle immediately!

The Abbey has been the family home of two great families since the 16th century, the Hobys and then the Vansittart-Neales. As in so many sad instances, the male side of the family was completely wiped out by the deaths in military action of the two heirs to Sir Henry Vansittart-Neale's estate in 1942 and 1944, namely Berkley Paget and Guy Paget, his grandsons. In 1947 their aunt, Miss Phyllis Vansittart-Neale, in answer to a letter to *The Times* by the last Lord Astor, on behalf of the Central Council for Physical Recreation, offered Bisham Abbey to be used by the young as a memorial to her nephews, and on her death her sister, Mrs Elizabeth Paget, sold the Abbey to the Sports Council. New buildings have been erected and the new blends with the old reasonably well. It is well worth a visit.

The 12th-century Church of All Saints stands on the banks of this superb reach of the Thames. Within are interesting memorials to various local residents of the past, including the Hoby chapel, commemorating the family who resided so long at Bisham Abbey from the 16th to the 18th century; and of course the Vansittart-Neales. The Williams Chapel is in memory of General Owen Williams, former resident of Temple House, now demolished, and aide-de-camp and friend of King Edward VII, who used to visit him there.

Bisham is a well scattered community, stretching up to Quarry Woods and Cookham Dean and to the south as far as the Henley Road and Burchetts Green;

All Saints church, Bisham, 1985

also to Temple Island upstream, where there is now a modern development of houses and marina on the island, which was once a paper mill.

Bisham Woods consists of several woods including Quarry Wood, Fultness Wood and Inkydown Wood. The area covers nearly 400 acres and is considered 'the richest ancient woods in Berkshire'. Other features in the wood include an ice house constructed in the 1760s and used to store ice for the preservation of food at the Abbey, and Bisham Quarry which provided the stone for Windsor Castle.

Running through Temple Park Farm is a stream which continues its way past Town Farm out into the Thames by Quarry Wood below Marlow Lock. In close proximity to this stream is a spring which is known as Queen Elizabeth's Well, and the tale goes that during her three-year stay at the Abbey with the Hobys, the Queen used this water for her bath for it was reputed to have healing properties.

A further interesting feature of the village is the War Memorial, which was designed by the famous sculptor, Eric Gill.

Despite many changes, Bisham has preserved its character throughout the centuries and is still one of England's most picturesque villages.

🍁 BOXFORD

The Parish of Boxford is attractively situated in the Lambourn valley in the North Wessex Downs Area of Outstanding Natural Beauty with two conservation areas; one for Westbrook and the other for Boxford. The hamlets of Hunts Green, Ownham, Coombesbury and Wickham Heath are also in the parish. The village lies four and a half miles north-west of Newbury dissected by the M4.

The Parish is characterised by open chalk downland fields running down to the rich soils of the wooded river valley. There are large woodland plantations to the south-west of the parish, through which the Roman Road of Ermin Street runs. The River Lambourn, a famous chalk stream, is designated as a SSSI and an SAC in recognition of its pristine water quality and wildlife. The water meadows between Boxford and Westbrook provide open countryside in the centre of the village and are designated as a SSSI for the rich flora and fauna.

The village shop and the Post Office have reverted to private houses. However, the parish retains a substantial number of historic buildings, including the Mill House, St Andrew's Church, Boxford House, the Bell public house and many listed thatched properties.

A Millennium Project saw the restoration of the war memorial and the building of a lychgate at the entrance to the churchyard under which a Boxford Millennium time capsule was buried. After the First World War, residents tried unsuccessfully to raise the funds to build a memorial lychgate, the Millennium Project was therefore a fitting tribute to those lost from the parish in both wars.

Boxford's Parish Plan, completed in 2008 with an 80% response rate, confirmed a strong desire to preserve the special landscape character of the parish and identified the wishes of the residents. Many items were carried forward to an Action Plan. As a consequence, the Parish Council successfully lobbied the Highways Agency for quiet tarmac on the M4 round the village; the Boxford History Project (BHP) researched and published a simple history of the parish, and was instrumental in building and using a Heritage Centre in 2015 on the site of the collapsed Parish Room.

The renovation of St Andrew's church was carried out in 2010. This project provided a social space within the body of the church, with a kitchen and a disabled toilet. This space has been used for Parish Council meetings, workshops, lunches and coffee shops. Work was also carried out to improve damp by removing the Victorian render to the external walls. This revealed an attractive flint wall construction and more importantly a rare Saxon window with a shutter in the chancel's north wall. This confirmed the Saxon origins of the church, built most probably by Abingdon Abbey and the finding completely overturned its known history. Following the retirement of the Rector Nigel Sands in 2009, Boxford became part of the nine-church East Downlands Benefice.

Also as a result of the Parish Plan, a thriving new "eco" Village Hall was built at the Recreation Ground in 2014 with a purpose-built section for the pre-school. This was funded by the sale of the old Village Hall site, now a place for two homes. Also included in the Action Plan was a new children's play area in the Recreation Ground; this too has been completed.

Boxford is as ancient as it is attractive. It seems off the beaten track but people settled here from the period of the Stone Age, attracted by the pure waters of the River Lambourn and the productive soil. From 2012 BHP volunteers from the village and surrounding area have been exploring three Roman sites with the assistance of the Berkshire Archaeological Research Group (BARG) overseen by professional archaeologists. This culminated in a three-year archaeological project funded by the Heritage Lottery Fund, which was completed in 2017. During the three-year project, two villas with bath houses or suites and one farmstead were uncovered and recorded. However, most amazing of all was the discovery in 2017 of part of a Roman mosaic pavement which experts considered to be the most important Roman mosaic find in Britain for over half a century because of the remarkable choice of subjects depicted.

There are a number of new clubs at the Village Hall but sadly there is no longer a WI in Boxford. Boxford Open Gardens, a regular attraction in previous years has been discontinued for the moment. However, the inaugural match of Boxford Cricket Club called The Boxford Boars was held in 2017. The Boxford Masques, originated by Charlotte Peake who lived at Westbrook House in the early years of the 20th century, is flourishing once more. The productions are no longer held at the open-air amphitheatre on the side of Hoar Hill in Boxford but are now staged at Welford Park and are run by Boxford volunteers in co-operation with the Watermill Theatre. The considerable and recent changes in demography with many young professional couples and their families making Boxford their home, has reinvigorated the community and the parishioners of Boxford appear determined to enjoy the delights of the attractive place in which they live.

🍁 BRACKNELL

We ladies from Bracknell Wick Hill WI and Harmans Water WI would like to tell you some interesting facts about our town of Bracknell.

The area known as Old Bracknell (just south of the railway line) is where the ancient parishes of Warfield, Winkfield and Easthampstead meet. The first reference to it is in a Saxon charter dated AD 923. The derivation of the name is unknown but it is likely that it means a corner of land covered in bracken.

Until 1815, Bracknell was part of Windsor Forest and for hundreds of years kings and queens of England enjoyed hunting in the area. Edward III built a hunting lodge at Easthampstead Park, which still stands and is now a conference centre, and Catherine of Aragon, the first wife of Henry VIII, spent time there following her divorce.

The area was a favourite haunt of highwaymen and the Old Manor pub, which is now a restaurant and pub, once housed Dick Turpin's cottage. A secret passageway could be accessed behind a painting above the dining room fireplace which led to the Bull Inn and a preserved priest hole can still be seen today.

In 1948, following the end of the Second World War, Bracknell was

Easthampstead Manor House, Bracknell

designated a 'New Town' to accommodate the London overspill. People were encouraged to move here with the promise of homes and jobs. The first estate built was Priestwood.

Today Bracknell is a suburban town which is home to 83,000 people. It is in the Borough of Bracknell Forest. Our symbol is a deer of which there are many in the woodland that surrounds the town.

Since the long awaited shopping centre was completed in September 2017 Bracknell has jumped from 247th best place to shop to 33rd and rising. The new shopping centre was named The Lexicon. At first this did not seem to fit with local people but the shopping centre is certainly a conundrum of words with shop names like Flying Tigers, Smiggle, Tangs, Seasalt, Barkers, Joules and many more. Now you hear people saying that they are going to The Lexicon instead of just into town. So it does now seem to fit and we are very proud of The Lexicon.

Although we are a new town our history has been preserved with many listed buildings, of which South Hill Park is probably the most iconic. It is rich in cultural history and home to our arts centre and theatre, which we all try to support by visiting it as often as we can to take in a show, cinema, meal

The Old Manor pub, Bracknell

or to do a course, or even just to sit on the terrace with a drink and take in the wonderful grounds.

🍁 BRADFIELD

The original village of Broad Field with church, mill and manorial Bradfield Place, stands around the Pang chalk stream, noted for its Blue Pool a mile or so upstream. Springs keep the sandy bottom fuming with miniature volcanoes, while a trick of light in the transparent depths produces an intense blue. These springs have never failed, even when droughts have dried out the upper reaches of the Pang. Sadly, this is now privately owned.

Elias Ashmole, whose collection formed the nucleus of the Ashmolean Museum at Oxford, came to Bradfield in the 17th century. He was bent on marrying the rich widowed lady of the manor, despite the attempts of one of her sons to murder him. The couple soon moved up to London, leaving Bradfield Place to decay. All was sold to a London merchant, who built himself a brand new mansion which has now totally disappeared, leaving its name to Great House Wood and its site carpeted with snowdrops.

The vital history of Bradfield began when the manor came into the possession of Henry Stevens, whose great-grandson, Thomas, was to change its face completely. Thomas Stevens inherited the parish from his father in 1842 and dominated the local scene for nearly half a century. He set about rebuilding and restoring the 14th-century church, as a tribute to his father. With the idea of founding a choir school for the enlarged church he opened a school in 1850, in what remained of Bradfield Place. The school grew rapidly and new buildings were added year by year. Thomas Stevens was an authority on the English Poor Law and a contributor to its reform. He was also instrumental in establishing the local workhouse. Only the central part of the building remains, having been developed into a private house surrounded by other housing in its grounds. Sadly, Thomas Stevens' many activities led to him being declared bankrupt. Being the largest landowner and employer in the parish a great deal of hardship ensued. His school, Bradfield College, however, had been taken over by a governing body and continued to grow in size and reputation. It is famous for its Greek theatre which has been restored. Sadly, the impressive St Andrew's church is now closed due to diminishing congregations and the enormous cost of its upkeep.

However, the parish has increased and prospered, developing away from the old village on to the higher ground at Southend. The great majority of the present inhabitants are employed outside the parish. Bradfield Southend has a church, a primary school, a village hall, playing fields with a cricket pavilion, a pub, and most importantly, a shop and Post Office. There is an impressive war memorial, tidied each month by the WI. A service is held there each year followed by WI tea and cakes in the nearby Social Club.

In the old village, the outstanding addition has been the restoration of care homes by The Riverside Group – a great photographic opportunity!

The most notable recent inhabitant of Bradfield Southend is Catherine Middleton, now the Duchess of Cambridge. She spent her early years here, was baptised in St Andrew's church, and was a member of the local Brownies pack which met in St Peter's church, before moving to Bucklebury.

🍁 BRAY

Bray is situated at a bend of the Thames, a mile from Maidenhead and within easy access of the M4 motorway. The name 'Bray' was generally taken to mean 'a marsh', and it is certainly not a 'dry' village.

The pubs and restaurants are flourishing. Bray contains two of the five three-Michelin-starred restaurants in the United Kingdom. The Fat Duck opened in 1995 on the site of the Ringers pub. The owner, Heston Blumenthal, has also taken on the leases of two pubs, the Crown and the Hind's Head, which are pubs and restaurants.

Waterside Inn continues to thrive. It has not changed much and its fabulous location and wonderful menu continues to attract people, as ever. It is now under the management of Alain Roux. The Albion, a pub in Mill Lane, has changed hands three times and is now an Italian restaurant called Caldesi in Campagna which holds cookery courses from time to time.

Just off the banks of the Thames lies Monks Eyot, originally the property of the Abbey of Burnham. This was acquired by Charles Spencer, third Duke of Marlborough, who built a fishing lodge there in 1739. This has been extended and modernised over the years and is now the Monkey Island Hotel. It is now under the ownership of a Malaysian company, and once more undergoing renovation, but its position on the river is stunning and should remain successful.

The Parish Church of St Michael is the dominating feature of the village, and dates from Edward I. It was built in 1293 on the site of the original Norman church, and has many beautiful and elaborate examples of 14th-, 15th- and 16th-century brasses. Simon Alwyn, who changed his religion rather than give up his parish, is believed to be the vicar made famous by the song *Vicar of Bray*. His tombstone lies in the middle of the nave. The church has recently undergone major repairs including to the tower, windows, and the organ, which has been totally renewed.

In the high street stands Jesus Hospital, a Grade I listed building. It was founded by the Worshipful Company of Fishmongers pursuant to the will of William Goddard in 1609, a statue of whom stands over the entrance to the hospital gardens. The name hospital is rather confusing, but in bygone days it meant almshouses, schools, etc. The original 34 almshouses, built in a quadrangle between 1623 and 1628, comprise around 6 acres. Jesus Hospital is now owned by the Donnington Hospital Trust and provides beautiful accommodation for elderly people.

The River Thames, of course, runs through Bray and flooding has been greatly reduced by the building of the Flood Relief Scheme, now known as Jubilee River, which is a seven-mile river course running from above Maidenhead to below Windsor. It is an attractive addition to the Thames Valley, but it is not navigable. There is a swimming event held on this waterway from time to time.

Bray has changed over the years with the closure, in the 1990s, of the post office and the village shop which supplied all groceries, meat and alcohol.

Bray

There has also been an increase in road traffic – which of course is happening everywhere. Locally this is partly due to a new access road into Maidenhead and the station. There is also a new school in Maidenhead on the Bray Road, but this has not caused as much disruption as was anticipated.

The population of the village has not increased much and the only new houses are a small complex in the centre of the village where the garage used to be – many years ago – called West Court. A successful hairdresser has opened in the High Street, and also a gift shop called 'Story'. Bray performs well in the Britain in Bloom contest and has reached the final three times since 1985.

The 400-berth marina remains a popular part of the village with an active boating club and a good parking area for cars.

🍁 BRAYWOOD

According to most maps Braywood doesn't exist! Yet it has a very long history. As might be expected from its name, the first mention of it as Bray Wood (the last remnants of which were cut down in 1917 and auctioned) occurs in the Domesday Book and for centuries it, and the villages or hamlets of Oakley Green, Fifield and Water Oakley, were part of the Manor of Bray and then in more recent times the Parish of Bray. It is difficult to separate these hamlets as for about 50 years almost all the land in them belonged to one family and for nearly a century this area constituted the Ecclesiastic Parish of Braywood.

Sylvain Van De Weyer, the first Belgian Ambassador to England and a great friend of Queen Victoria, built New Lodge on the Drift Road, high above the villages and bought most of the land from New Lodge right down to the river and covering most of Fifield, Oakley Green and Water Oakley. He built cottages for his workers in various places on the New Lodge Estate and each cottage had the Van De Weyer crest built into its wall. The crest can still be seen on many houses in the area – it is not unlike the Volkswagen emblem. One of the houses, now called Braywood Linn, used to be called Braywood Inn so it seems he provided for his employees' leisure time as well.

As part of the New Lodge Estate, Braywood church was built on the hill known locally as Sparboro, and Queen Victoria agreed in 1871 to create the new Parish of Braywood. This was virtually an Estate church and all the employees and their families were expected to walk up the mile-long drive from the Lodge Gates on Oakley Green Road to the church. This was also the route taken by the Van De Weyer family to New Lodge, and the children of employees were expected to line the drive and curtsey or bow as their coach went past.

The New Lodge Estate was broken up and sold in 1911 and the report of the sale made the front page of the *Maidenhead Advertiser*. After this New Lodge became a clinic and wounded soldiers were taken there during the First World War. Amongst other owners have been Dr Barnardo's and British Rail.

In the late 1950s the Rev Daniels, the Vicar of Braywood, died and Braywood church was deconsecrated. A new wooden church was built next to Braywood School and the Parish was reabsorbed by Bray. The attendance at the new church was poor and now it is used as the school annexe.

Braywood Church of England First School, was opened in 1857, and is typical in design of the schools of that period. Originally all the local children were taught there from 5-14 years old, but now children leave at 9 years old and go to school in Windsor. Before the M4 was opened, the children at Braywood School had the four days of Royal Ascot off, rather than the whole of Whitsun week, because of the volume of traffic going to Ascot. Now there is no need, as few racegoers use the village roads.

The School House, which for many years was the home of the Head of Braywood School, is now a private house. Along the Oakley Green road visitors will find Braywood Cottage, Braywood Lodge, Braywood Cottages – these are all, according to road signs, in Oakley Green, Windsor. Braywood

Memorial Hall is in Fifield, Maidenhead, and Braywood House is in Windsor Forest, Windsor. So, if you're ever asked to visit anywhere in Braywood, make sure you get clear directions.

🍁 BRIGHTWALTON

Brightwalton is made up of a series of scattered hamlets with the village, church, hall and school at the centre.

In the 1860s G.E. Street designed a new All Saints' Church, a large brick rectory with a school house. The church bells are regularly rung by visiting teams and a new vicar has just been installed to minister the seven churches of the West Downland Benefice.

The Domesday Book has a reference to our old church, but there are very few traces of it in the new All Saints' Church. A single, framed painting, hanging on the south wall does provide an idea of what the Saxon church once looked like. It seated 120 parishioners and had a square tower which was so soundly built, its demolition required explosives! Within the old churchyard there are still traces of the brick and flint walls and there is a quaint footpath leading through the middle. The old churchyard was restored in 2005 and those memorial stones that could be deciphered were catalogued and noted in the book *Brightwalton, a Downland Village*. The burial ground was used until 1893.

Brightwalton War Memorial was recognised in April 2016 on the Local Listing of Heritage Assets by West Berkshire Council in partnership with West Berkshire Heritage Forum. The listing states that "It has been recognised as West Berkshire's oldest Great War memorial, erected in 1916 and standing at the junction of Common Lane facing down towards the church. Built largely from locally found materials in 1916 it commemorates the fourteen young men from the parishes of Brightwalton and Catmore who fell in World War 1".

In 1985, an indignant village community prevented the closure of Brightwalton C of E Primary School. There are now over 100 pupils and the school run brings a flurry of activity to the school gates; after which the street relapses back to peacefulness.

Opposite the school, sits Brightwalton Village Hall, which enjoys a beautiful outlook across the playing field and Spray Wood. These days the hall is used by the nursery school during the day with the Young Farmers, Local Gardening Club and Keep Fit making use of the facilities in the evening. The original timber-framed village hall is first mentioned in the Parish Council minutes in 1926. Over the years it has been used as a travelling cinema in the 1930s plus there was a social club with snooker table. The village football team, cricket teams and ladies' hockey club also all used the hall facilities. In the 1940s, the Americans from the Welford base would often come over and use the hall for dances.

The annual May fete raises funds for the hall and despite the hard work involved, the village enjoys coming together to welcome all the visitors. "It's just like villages used to be," is often overheard.

Farming shapes the landscape around the village and recently Manor Farm introduced cattle for beef, milk heifers and calves on to the arable farm. Visiting sheep graze the pastures, the autumn pheasant shoots, and visits of a metal detecting club, remind all that we are on an ancient settlement. There are several studs in the village breeding racehorses and eventers.

Manor Farm is also home to the Saddleback Farm Shop on the B4494, whose tea rooms draw customers from far and wide. Cyclists especially enjoy the breakfasts after a challenging cycle up from Wantage. Deer can be seen grazing the fields and there are often owls, and red kites are spotted soaring above. Visitors marvel at the bluebells in our woods, where there are woodpeckers.

Our village pond sits alongside the playing fields, known as 'Dunmore Pond'. It is fed by a mysterious spring beneath and is also mentioned in the Domesday Book. Villagers get together every year to help maintain the pond and surrounding land for the benefit of the local wildlife and villagers alike.

Brightwalton Holt lies to the east of the main village, on the busy B4494 road between Newbury and Wantage. Historically it was an important stopping place for travellers, with a pub, a farm and several cottages. In the 19th century there was a grocery shop and a bakery within the Holt, plus a garage and petrol station near to where the electrical sub-station is now. The Marquis of Granby pub stood in the centre of the Holt and dated back to the middle of the 18th century. It was a popular place for Brightwalton villagers, who lacked a public house in the main village. It ceased trading in the 1980s and was sold and divided into two houses.

In 1887 a dozen skeletons were found in the Holt, these were believed to be soldiers from the fighting that occurred near this spot during the Civil War in the 17th century.

🍁 BRIMPTON

The village of Brimpton lies on the Berkshire-Hampshire border, bounded on the north by the River Kennet and for some distance on the south by the River Enborne. The greater part of the village lies on the end of a ridge. There are separate communities based on Brimpton Common and at Hyde End/West End. Each community once had its own public house, the Pineapple on Brimpton Common, the Horse and Jockey in Hyde End Lane, and the Three Horse Shoes in the village centre.

Evidence of early inhabitants is provided by a Bronze Age round barrow cemetery on Brimpton Common, while the fragmented cremated bones of an adult and a neo-natal baby in a funerary urn of the Middle Bronze Age (1600-1001 BCE) were discovered at Hyde End in 2001.

Brimpton was first mentioned in an Anglo-Saxon charter of AD 994, the boundary markers described are still visible in many places.

In the 12th Century the Order of Knights of the Hospital of Saint John of Jerusalem held Manor Farm where the oldest existing building in the village remains. This is the deconsecrated Chapel of St Leonard, much altered, but on the northern side a 12th-century doorway and window can be seen. The tympanum over the door contains the carving of a cross patty which has been adopted as the symbol of Brimpton in publications and on the WI banner.

The Brimpton Story: History of a West Berkshire Parish AD 2000, researched and written by residents, was published in 2000 to mark the Millennium. It was reprinted in 2017.

Once an agricultural community, over the past fifty years Brimpton has become the home of many people, mainly employed in the technical industries of the local 'Silicon Valley' or at the Atomic Weapons Establishment at Aldermaston. Classified as a small rural settlement by the planning authority, unlike many villages it has not been subjected to major housing development, with only a few small infilling developments of executive homes. The growing of willow and osiers was important in the past and this has been reflected in the names of the new developments. A number of older houses have been extended and converted and are now second homes. The population is still fewer than about 600 people, less than the census figures for 1901 and 1911. This has had an effect on life in Brimpton and over the years we have lost the village shop, Post Office, the garage, and the last dairy farm. Only one public house remains and there is a very limited bus service. On the other hand, Brimpton has gained a very elegant hairdressing establishment and a resident magician.

The village is still completely surrounded by agricultural land although at the time of writing there is a threat of major gravel extraction to the south and west of the village. This proposal has met a very strong protest from villagers and has created more community spirit than has existed for many years. One of the objections to the gravel extraction to the south came from the Atomic

Weapons Establishment. Their seismic monitoring station, the Blacknest site on Brimpton Common, is responsible for monitoring underground nuclear tests under the terms of the Comprehensive Nuclear-Test-Ban Treaty of 1996, and large scale gravel extraction within a few hundred metres could seriously affect their monitoring equipment. The outcome of this major threat to the village is still unknown.

St Peter's church stands in the centre of the village and its spire can be seen for miles around. It stands on the highest point in the village and, when it was rebuilt in 1869, a third storey and a steeple were added to the existing 18th-century brick tower. The Lord of the Manor, Mr James Blyth, paid for the new church along with the building of a new public house to replace the old inn and skittle ground, which stood in close proximity to the church, something he thought unsuitable.

Brimpton Baptist Church in the northern part of the village dates from 1843. It became very popular with American servicemen stationed at the nearby Greenham Common air base when cruise missiles were housed there in the 1970s/80s. It became part of the Southern Baptist Convention with an American pastor, and still attracts worshippers from a wide area who appreciate its evangelical approach.

The village school is now thriving, with some 50 pupils, the maximum it is allowed, and with good Ofsted ratings. Its small class sizes and lovely rural situation make it popular with parents both in and outside the village.

The Village Hall has been completely modernised and is much used by organisations both in and outside the village, including the very active WI. One of the more unusual users is the pole dancing class. This is actually a type of gymnastic exercise hoping for acceptance as an Olympic sport, and not what many people think when it is first mentioned.

Past residents of the village in the 20th century have included Victor Gollancz, the publisher of detective and science fiction novels with their bright yellow book jackets; Aneurin Bevan, famous for spearheading the establishment of the NHS, and his wife Jennie Lee who played a leading role in the founding of the Open University; and the Sieff family who ran Marks and Spencer when it was still a family business. Israel Sieff and his son, Marcus, were both created life peers and both took the title Baron Sieff of Brimpton. A more recent resident was composer Ron Goodwin, whose film work includes the music for *633 Squadron* and *The Trap*. You may not have heard of the latter but will no doubt recognise music used from it every year as the theme for the London Marathon on television. His other works included the *Brimpton Suite* written for a jazz combo.

❧ BUCKLEBURY

Bucklebury was recorded as Borchedeberie in the Domesday Book and there were several variations in the spelling before Bucklebury became the accepted form in the 18th century.

King Henry I granted the manor to Reading Abbey and the abbot built a house just above the village. Five fishponds ensured a fresh supply of fish for his table and that of Reading Abbey. Being fed by a spring, the ponds also supplied safe drinking water for the household and they remain to this day.

There are signs of pillow mounds on the Common. These man-made rabbit burrows were built at the request of Reading Abbey, probably in the 13th century after the fishponds were dug in the 12th century. The rabbits were caught using ferrets and nets. Rabbits were very valuable animals as the fur was used to line winter clothing and the flesh was considered a delicacy.

Additions to the early Norman Church of St Mary include the beautifully carved south doorway, built in the 12th century. A chest brought from Reading Abbey still remains in the church.

At the Dissolution of the Monasteries the manor was bought by John Winchcombe, son of the famous clothier, Jack of Newbury. He replaced the abbot's house with a fine Elizabethan mansion but died before it was completed. His son, another John, finished the house in which he is thought to have entertained Queen Elizabeth I. The Winchcombes left their mark on the church – an oak beam above the chancel records '*1591 Francis Winchom Esquire Build This*'. In 1701 Sir Henry Winchcombe extended the chancel and added the manor pew above which can be seen the 'fly' window. Its sundial and realistic fly remind us that time flies.

Unfortunately, the Elizabethan manor house was extensively damaged by fire in 1830 and was later demolished, apart from one wing, the kitchens and dovecot. The house has been restored in recent years and the present owner once again lives in the house of his ancestors, now called Bucklebury House. The Tudor dovecot still stands in the courtyard.

Other houses of note are The Manor, previously called The Cottage, the residence of Mrs Webley-Parry, Lady of the Manor in 1906, and standing next door to Bucklebury House. Bucklebury Place, built by Mr A.W. Sutton, who founded Sutton Seeds of Reading, and which became a convalescent home during the Second World War, is now divided into flats. Mr Sutton also founded The Fireside Club for working men. The Rt. Hon George Palmer, of Huntley & Palmer of Reading, acquired the Marlston estate in the late 19th century and built Marlston House, now a school. He also founded The Marlston Club to provide recreation for his employees. Another house of note is the 18th-century Old Vicarage adjacent to St Mary's parish church.

Before the Second Battle of Newbury in 1644, the Earl of Manchester and his parliamentarian army camped on the western end of Bucklebury Common. Despite a skirmish with very strong Royalist outposts, the parliamentarians marched to and captured Bucklebury Common, where they began laying out a large encampment. Bucklebury Parish Records show that three soldiers were buried in the churchyard, but no trace of their graves remains. The burials that took place in April 1644 were from a skirmish at The Forties, just south of the Bladebone Inn.

Bucklebury is proud of its fine oak avenue. The first oaks were probably planted to commemorate the visit of Elizabeth I, others to celebrate the victories of Marlborough, and, a century later, either the Battle of Waterloo or Trafalgar. It is recorded in a diary written by Robert Bedding that; *'December 18th 1821 the 1st oake Tree wase planted of the Row that Goes Down the Common to Wood Gate by Joseph and Thos. Nailor'*. In 1972 young trees were planted when Queen Elizabeth II visited Bucklebury, and eight years later Princess Anne planted a tree to commemorate the 80th birthday of Queen Elizabeth, the late Queen Mother. Another row was planted on the edge of Chapel Row Green to commemorate the wedding in 2011 of Prince William to Catherine Middleton, whose family, at the time, lived nearby.

At the end of The Avenue, in Chapel Row, stands The Bladebone Inn, so called because its copper sign is said to encase the blade bone of a mammoth found in the Kennet Valley in the 17th century. Chapel Row, named after the Chapel of St Mary Magdalen, now demolished, was famous for the Chapel Row Revels and back-swording, which was discontinued many years ago.

In Upper Bucklebury there is the Cottage Inn, previously the Three Crowns, which dates from at least the 18th century.

Travelling west along the Pang Valley is Marlston with its 13th-century church built by Geoffrey Martel to serve his family and dependants, although they were obliged to attend the parish church at Bucklebury on all major festival days. The church still retains its Norman doorway, its Norman holy-water stoup and an ancient bell. This was cast by Peter de Weston, a bell founder of London in the early 14th century. The churchyard is circular, perhaps indicating a much earlier place of worship.

The Parish of Bucklebury is reputed to have more footpaths than any other parish in England. Many were made by men trudging to work at the village foundry and manor timber yard, once the two principal places of employment.

Other tracks were worn by commoners taking their animals to graze. Parishioners were grateful to John Morton, a local farmer and preacher, who travelled to Westminster in 1834 and successfully opposed the enclosure of Bucklebury Common. He eventually became the first pastor of the Congregational Chapel erected in 1840 on Turner's Green. The common has not been grazed since the Second World War, when it was cleared for the repair and storage of vehicles prior to the D-Day landings and to house troops. Much of it is now covered by birch trees and scrub but some areas have been returned to heathland and are home to nightjars and tree pipits.

Bowl turners once worked at their ancient craft on Bucklebury Common. When George Lailey, the last of the local turners, died in 1958, Bucklebury lost a great character. His lathe, tools and some bowls can be seen at the Museum of English Rural Life in Reading.

Times change – the building of the Memorial Hall in 1961 and All Saints' Church a year later provided for the needs of a growing population, especially in Upper Bucklebury. However, the extensive common and thriving farmlands of Bucklebury should ensure it remains a rural parish.

BURCHETTS GREEN

Burchetts Green is a small village which stands rather uneasily astride a busy main road connecting two even busier trunk roads, the Maidenhead-Henley and the London-Bath roads. The houses edge the common and the green, or straggle along the main street, and are surrounded by woodlands, fields and farmsteads. It has no parish church, divided as it is between the three ecclesiastical parishes of Stubbings, Hurley and Littlewick.

The manor house of Hall Place is now taken over by the Berkshire College of Argriculture. It is approached by a magnificent avenue of limes. It is recorded that Hurley Priory owned Hall Place until the Dissolution in 1535. In 1728 it was purchased by William East, a wealthy London lawyer of the Manor House, Kennington, who pulled down the old house and built the one standing today. It remained in the family until after the Second World War, when it was sold to the Berkshire County Council. The old mansion stood in a great deer park of some 130 acres. Descendants of this herd now roam wild on Ashley Hill.

Stubbings Farm, in the centre of the village, boasts a barn reputed to be more than 400 years old, and old maps mark Stubbings Heath to the south. It is believed that the road through the village was made by Lord Salisbury, for his personal use. As his health was poor he journeyed from his home at Hatfield to take the cure at Bath, and went this way to avoid the highwaymen lurking on Maidenhead Thicket. The milestones on this stretch give the distances to these two towns. Alleyhill Coppes, now Ashley Hill, dominated the scene then as it does today.

Woodlands Cottage, built in the 17th century, was formerly a Quaker Meeting House. Stubbings House, half a mile to the east of the village, was the home of Queen Wilhelmina of Holland during the Second World War when her country was invaded by the Nazis.

Among the legends and ghost stories of the neighbourhood is that of Claude Duval, the famous highwayman who is said to have carried out his expeditions in this area. Both Woodlands and Burchetts Green House are said to be haunted, the latter by Druids! Hall Place is no exception and students claim to have seen a coach and horses crossing the lawn at the back of the house. The ghost of a servant has also been seen at Black Horse Lodge. It is said that the Clayton East family would drive to Ascot in their horse-drawn carriage and, if the day had been profitable, scatter their winnings to the servants lining the drive, on their return.

Much has changed since the days of the well in the centre of the village supplying villagers with water but there is still plenty to recommend the village. Burchetts Green C of E Infant School is still thriving and the Michelin-starred pub, the Crown, was also recently voted 10th in Estrella Damm's top 50 gastro pubs in the United Kingdom.

🍁 BURGHFIELD

The community of Burghfield comprises the village and the common, and is situated approximately 5 miles south-west of Reading, to which it is connected by a regular bus service.

The original Anglican church in the village was mentioned in the Domesday Book, with the current building being built in 1843. The church of St Mary the Virgin famously houses the wooden effigy of Roger de Burghfield, which was stolen in 1978 and later reinstated in the church in 1982 after £10,000 was paid to recover it. The recent addition of the Parish Centre offers valuable meeting rooms for the use of the church and many other village organisations, including a thriving playgroup.

Whilst the village has seen relatively little development over the years the popular village school (infants and juniors) has been enlarged recently and now has its own playing field; however, sadly the Post Office and village store have been lost. There are two pubs, the Six Bells and the Hatch Gate with its adjacent Indian restaurant.

At the centre is the village green, known as The Hatch. Used for sports and play, it also famously hosts a hockey match every Boxing Day, as well as the May Fayre, which brings people from far and wide to enjoy stalls, competitions and fun activities for all the family while raising money for local good causes.

Opposite the green is the Old School House. This is now a private residence which proudly sports a plaque recognising it as the first meeting place of Burghfield WI in 1917.

When The Old Rectory was in the ownership of Mr and Mrs Merton, the garden was of particular note. It was often open for the public to enjoy and offered the opportunity to buy rare plants raised in the garden, as well as to enjoy tea and cake provided by the local WIs. It was also often the setting for fundraising garden parties for local organisations.

Another landmark of the village was HMS *Dauntless*. Originally, the collection of wartime huts was built in 1942 to accommodate munitions workers, but from 1945–81 it became the new entry training establishment for the Association of Wrens. After its closure, new houses were built on the site for service personnel and their families.

Travelling up the Reading Road, or Burghfield Hill as it is more commonly known, you will find Hillfields. Formerly the home of the Willink family, then the Dent family, this imposing building with its extensive grounds was sold in 1992 to become the headquarters of the Guide Dogs for the Blind Association. Burghfield Hill is steep in parts and this lends itself well to the running of the annual Burghfield Box Kart race from the common down to the village.

Burghfield Common has seen much more development over the past 50 years. Extensive housing estates were built on either side of the Reading Road in the 1980s and 1990s and these were heralded by the arrival of a roundabout. Created out of the road-building spoils, it was quite a challenge for WI members to plant daffodils in such little topsoil, but the flowers have thrived and are enjoyed every spring. Another benefit of the new housing was that the builders were responsible for bringing the mains gas supply to the village.

Situated near the roundabout are a doctors' surgery, chemist, dentist and veterinary practice. Also nearby are the greengrocer and bakery along with other larger convenience stores. Sadly there is no pub now in Burghfield Common, but it is well served by a number of takeaway shops and a Bangladeshi restaurant.

Run by members of the combined churches of the area, Café B has become a welcome addition for many people of all ages to meet and enjoy a chat over a drink and maybe something to eat. Currently this is held in the Methodist church hall, situated on the main road through the village, opposite the Post Office. Following the Rio Olympics the postmaster decorated the post box in gold to celebrate Chris Mears' gold medal in the diving event. Local boy Chris attended the Willink School which together with Mrs Bland's Infant School and Garland Junior School makes Burghfield popular with families.

On the Willink School site there is a leisure centre with a swimming pool and large sports hall situated on the Hollybush Lane entrance and at the School Lane entrance is the library. After much campaigning the library now has only one paid member of staff with volunteers making up the rest; a real show of commitment to keeping open this valued service in the community.

At the heart of Burghfield Common is a large recreation ground and a village hall. The "rec" has excellent facilities including a children's play area and a pavilion for the football teams of all ages who regularly use the two football pitches both for matches and training. In addition, it hosts regular fun days and also the new but increasingly popular Burghfest.

The village hall is in constant use by local organisations such as toddler groups, dance classes and dog training in the daytime and regular users during the rest of the time. With a large hall and smaller hall attached and an excellent kitchen it offers an adaptable and comfortable space for all occasions.

Burghfield Common is close to Wokefield Common which is a popular place for walkers with or without a dog. Another outdoor activity involves growing your own on one of the two allotment sites.

All in all, Burghfield is a busy and growing village. Good facilities including schools, churches, shops, a leisure centre, medical facilities, Post Office and library mean that this is a busy and vibrant place to live. It has the feel of living in the country, but has the benefit of being set within the Reading, Newbury and Basingstoke triangle.

❦ BURNT HILL

A mile from Yattendon is the hamlet of Burnt Hill, an 18th-century brick-making settlement. There is a nucleus of old cottages and a chapel, built in 1864, and later additions of more modern houses. It has a small, friendly community – many of whom enjoy walking the lanes and ancient woodland which surrounds them, especially at bluebell time!

❧ CALIFORNIA

California is a community within the parish of Finchampstead which creates a good local spirit with many clubs available and the opportunity for exhilarating country walks. The area still retains some of the feel of Windsor Forest with some wonderful woods and rural areas. However, there has been much development. A neighbouring area was the Arborfield army garrison which was closed in 2017, giving the potential for many dwellings to fulfil the government criteria for housing.

A jewel in the crown of the village is California Country Park, a lovely 100-acre nature reserve with the scenic Longmoor Lake and its water birds and species of wild orchids – a pretty and peaceful place to frequent. John Walter III had the lake dug out to provide the clay from Longmoor Bog to make 4.5 million bricks to build Bearwood House. Additions to the Park include a scout hut, children's play area and paddling pool, plus a licensed café serving homemade food managed by a local family. A motorcycle speedway track opened in 1932, which became a popular pastime for riders every Sunday until 1958. The speedway track was known as Longmoor and after the Second World War it became home to California Poppies which raced in the southern area league. Recently parts of the track have been cleared. Since 2007, the Friends of Speedway have a reunion every October when they exchange stories and memorabilia and admire bikes. The speedway machines date from 1928 and the autumn reunion sees them head into California Country Park in their droves, some riding long distances. There is an intoxicating aroma of Castrol R and methanol which recalls many memories.

California-in-England Pleasure Park was founded in 1931 by Alfred Cartlidge on 70 acres of California Country Park woodland. There was an amusement park, zoo, circus, ballroom, swimming pool, boating lake and miniature railway. During the 1950s the site was sold and transformed into a holiday camp. Sadly in 1976 a huge fire destroyed the main building which housed the wonderful glass-floored ballroom and the camp was closed. It is rumoured that the glass was from the old Crystal Palace in London. Today there is an area for mobile homes and log cabins.

The Greenway was opened on 2nd December 2017 to link California Country Park to the new development at Arborfield Green. This is a traffic-free route and the Borough Council intends it to provide a safe route for pedestrians and cyclists. It has a new hardy, permeable all-weather surface made from a mixture of gravel and recycled tyres. There are 26 miles of rights of way in the parish of Finchampstead. The Parish Council and the Ramblers Association work in partnership to improve access and maintain the many footpaths allowing exploration of our area and surrounding glorious countryside. The Bell Barrow, a round burial mound is located off one footpath in Warren Wood. It is believed to be the largest in the county and may date back to the Bronze Age. In 1977 it was listed as an Ancient Monument.

The Finchampstead Baptist Church Centre was opened in April 2010 and is a much-used community centre having a footfall of over 3,000 users each week. It includes a multipurpose sports hall, meeting rooms, a library, children's centre and café. There is an excellent creative, outdoor children's playground in the grounds and a running track and good sports facilities. The café is the local meeting venue and is very popular with all ages. On Sundays the Finchampstead Baptist Church has exclusive use.

The California Ratepayers Hall continues to be active and is managed and improved by the Ratepayers Association – a group of volunteers. Regular users include California Flower Club, Gardener's Club, Knight School of Dance, various exercise classes and California Women's Institute.

California Crossroads continues to have a Post Office plus a couple of shops, two restaurants, a dentist and a garage. Hanging baskets provide colourful flowers to enhance the area. An innovation is the red telephone box which has been transformed into a Book Swap Kiosk. Residents may take books to read and add new titles for others to read. It is the only traditional box in Finchampstead Parish.

Schools within the California area include several nurseries plus Gorse Ride Junior School and Nine Mile Ride Primary School. There are several care homes providing for the needs of elderly residents.

The Gorse Ride Estate has recently begun an extended programme of regeneration. The retirement home Cockaigne Court has been evacuated and is awaiting demolition and the area will be devoted to additional housing.

🍁 CAVERSHAM

Caversham is a suburb in the Borough of Reading, originally a village founded in the Middle Ages. It is situated on the north bank of the River Thames opposite the centre of Reading. Caversham was originally part of Oxfordshire but, in November 1911, the Reading Extension Order was enacted and Caversham became part of Reading.

There are 22 various spellings of the name Caversham from Cavesha, the

1086 Domesday entry, to Cawsome around the 1600-1700s, until the present Caversham.

St Peter's Church, close to Caversham Bridge, dates from 1162. The building is Grade II listed and is the oldest surviving building in Caversham.

The bridges over the Thames have been an essential asset to people living and working in Caversham from early times. During the Civil War, Roundheads and Cavaliers fought to gain the high ground around Caversham in order to dominate and control the river crossing. The village became the centre of travel on to Oxford from London and the meadows and pastures were owned by the Dean and Chapter of Christ Church Cathedral, Oxford in 1546. Hence the name of the fields bought by Reading Borough in 1902 for public recreation.

We have three bridges in Caversham, the oldest one being Caversham Bridge. The original was built at the beginning of the 12th century and was used by pilgrims visiting St Anne's Chapel on the bridge and a well in Caversham, called St Anne's Well, until the Dissolution of the Monasteries. Catherine of Aragon visited the Shrine of Our Lady of Caversham in St Anne's Chapel in 1532, which was later destroyed by Henry VIII. Much later, an iron bridge was built by both Oxfordshire and Reading authorities to meet in the middle of the river. However, this was found to be substandard and the present bridge was built in 1926.

In 1924, the more elegant reinforced concrete Reading bridge was built with a single main span and Brunel-style arches on each bank. It looks splendid at night lit by the original lamps.

The most recent bridge was opened in 2015. Christchurch Bridge is for pedestrians and cyclists and cost £5.9 million. It has a large mast that came from Rotterdam with lighting that is most impressive at night.

While Caversham and Reading bridges could carry traffic, the river was always in danger of regular flooding on the meadows and was a serious problem until the weir and lock were updated and capable of controlling the winter floods. For many centuries the Thames bridges have been a dominant factor in the quality of life for all who live in and around Caversham. Will the problems ever be solved? Perhaps solutions will surprise us all.

Caversham Court Gardens lies on the north bank of the River Thames and has a 950-year history. Around a small dwelling used by priests, a grand old house and gardens grew – long since demolished but the beautiful grounds are open to the public, restored with a £1.2 million Heritage Lottery Fund grant in 2009. It has a Grade II listed gazebo and a number of beautiful unusual trees. There is a tea kiosk in an Arts and Crafts building that began life as a toilet block, built using some rubble from the demolished house. This is where five charities, including the WI, serve teas and cakes throughout the summer.

Caversham House was demolished in 1966 to make way for St Martin's Precinct, built in 1968. The Regal Cinema was built nearby in 1938, but closed as a cinema in 1958. There was also the Glendale Cinema next door to the library, which is now a Gospel Church.

Caversham Library, opposite St Martin's Precinct, was one of many libraries around the world funded by the Carnegie Trust. The library's award-winning design was by the architect William George Hooper Lewton (1865-1914) and was built in 1907. The present clock, with the figure of Old Father Time, was later added at the request of the Caversham Urban District Council. The Grade II listed building is unusual with various sash windows, some of which have a casement window directly above them. This is a very busy library with a variety of activities being carried out, particularly for children.

Baylis the grocers used to occupy the corner of Church Street from 1911 until about 1970; it is currently a restaurant. There have been other great changes in the shops of Prospect Street. Lots of individual little shops have now gone, including Jacksons which was next door to the Post Office. This was very handy for knitters. Across the road there was quite a big Co-op which closed down in the late 1960s, then became Waring & Gillow furniture for some years. Now there are a number of estate agents and cafés which have replaced the wider variety of shops.

Past industries have included, whiting (white chalk that has been ground and washed, used in making whitewash, metal polish, etc) parchment, tanning, boat building and basket making. Currently we have BBC Monitoring, a number of small garage repair centres, and several small printers.

The busy people of Caversham have the opportunity to be involved in a wide variety of activities including Reading Gardeners, British Red Cross, Friends of Caversham Court Gardens, Thames Valley Ancient Egypt Society, Streetdance with Connor, Caversham Bellplate Ringers, Le Cercle Français, Caversham Farmers Market and Vocalese choir, and, of course, the WI!

🍁 CAVERSHAM HEIGHTS

It is said that if you can't afford to live in Henley-on-Thames then Caversham Heights runs it a close second. In fact, as long ago as 1912, *Salters' Guide to the Thames* was calling Caversham 'Reading's Richmond'.

Property prices here are easily as high as any in Reading but, right from the start, Caversham Heights was intended to be select; its name reflecting both its position on high ground to the north of Caversham village and the quality of its houses.

Though it has no defined boundaries, the Heights is the series of long and attractive tree-lined roads which began to grow on the hillside in the Victorian era. From 1898 until 1929, land from the former Toots Farm was sold off, every plot with a covenant attached: a detached house built on the main Woodcote Road, for instance, had to be worth at least £500 and a pair of semis £900.

The aspiring were keen to move here and no wonder. Just across the border in Oxfordshire lies the Mapledurham Estate and the start of the Chiltern Way, where walkers enter an Area of Outstanding Natural Beauty with its chalk streams, rolling hills and spectacular views. To the south lies the River Thames and Reading, with its transport links and employment.

In the early days, however, the Heights remained sparsely populated as Caversham Urban District Council took its time to pave roads and install gaslights. The Heights' first church, a Methodist chapel with a distinctive turret, opened its doors in 1911 before many of the surrounding streets had even been laid out.

During the 1930s new homes appeared gradually. An apple orchard became Woodcote Way, Geoffreyson Road and Shepherds Lane, and a nearby gravel mine became Silverthorne Drive and Carlton Road.

The Heights didn't get its one and only pub until 1935 when the purpose-built Grosvenor House Hotel, complete with its own ballroom, opened on Kidmore Road. Recently revamped and renamed the Caversham Rose, the old Grosvenor became a landmark venue for weddings and parties and was a favourite of commercial travellers.

By the 1950s the Aga Khan owned a house on Richmond Road, handy for visiting the horses he kept in stables just across the Oxfordshire border. The 1960s singer Alma Cogan lived on Geoffreyson Road while a schoolgirl in Reading. A fictionalised Caversham Heights is the central theme of Jasper Fforde's novel *The Well of Lost Plots*.

Caversham Heights' reputation for quality led to years of protest when permission was sought to develop further farmland to the east of Kidmore Road, known locally as Bugs Bottom. Proposals had been going back and forth since 1984 until, in 1989, it was left to Environment Secretary, Nicholas Ridley, to finally grant permission. The area is now a large estate of executive homes.

Today, Reading's go-to suburb has plans in the pipeline for a new primary school, and enjoys a long list of amenities, including two recreation grounds with sports courts, bowls and croquet clubs, two tennis clubs, two churches, two convenience stores, and easy access to two golf clubs – one with a health spa and pool – just across the Oxfordshire border.

🍁 CHADDLEWORTH

Chaddleworth is a sleepy downland village of about 500 inhabitants that has been here for over 1000 years. It is mentioned in the Domesday Book and we have a plaque in St Andrew's church commemorating it. The church itself is very ancient and has been on the present site since at least the year 908. Points of note include that it has some very attractive stained-glass windows. The east facing window behind the altar is of 'splendiferous' proportions and is dedicated to Hugh 'Hugo' Cotesworth, who fought in the Zulu wars. His father, William, and his mother, Adelaide, provided Chaddleworth with its Village Hall in 1873 on land given by Musgrove Lavalin Wroughton. It was referred to by the locals as the 'Iron Room' as it was clad in corrugated iron. The Wroughton family are still in the parish and the current Sir Philip Wroughton was the Lord Lieutenant of Berkshire until quite recently.

The First World War threw up some really interesting facts about this village. It is amazing but true that Chaddleworth sent the second most volunteers (as a proportion of population) in the whole of England to the war effort! We have in the Village Hall a photograph and a tribute to all the brave men of Chaddleworth. The Pearce family, and there are still some relatives living here now, sent 'a band of brothers' who were all killed. But were they? Jack Pearce, known locally as Stocko, actually survived but was recorded as dead on the Chaddleworth War Memorial. He came back after convalescence in France and for the next 74 years he attended the Armistice Day commemoration at the Chaddleworth War Memorial with a wry smile at his supposed demise! He finally died aged 99 in 1992. His wife Ida died at 105 years of age so, as can be seen, Chaddleworth is a place to live a long life!

Chaddleworth has a very active Parish Council and in 1992 became the 2nd Parish Council in the whole of Berkshire to undertake a 'low cost'/affordable housing scheme at The Glebe Field (courtesy of the Diocese of Oxford) built on land leased from them. Ten houses were built expressly for local people. A legal agreement was struck with West Berkshire Housing Association (later to become Sovereign Housing Association). Chaddleworth Parish Council has the final say on who goes into these properties. This agreement has been challenged several times by Sovereign but all to no avail.

In 2007, Chaddleworth Parish Council undertook another low cost/ affordable housing scheme at St Andrew's Close, again with the agreement of the Oxford Diocese on the final piece of available land in the village. This was for 7 affordable houses for local people. Chaddleworth does not have a 'settlement boundary' due to an anomaly in the early 1980s, so no new housing can be undertaken save for section S106 (low cost/affordable) housing.

In 2014, Chaddleworth lost its village pub the Ibex; the only public house of that name in the UK. When opened in 1839, it was named the Star. Later it was renamed the Ibex as a 'snook' to the Wroughton family (local landowners) who frowned upon the local populace partaking of the 'demon drink'. The 'Ibex' was part of the family crest of the Wroughton family and so this was chosen as a coat of arms for the pub.

Mercifully, the Ibex rose again in December 2016 thanks to the Parish Council who convinced West Berkshire Council planning committee that this was a valuable community asset. The Ibex had had four breweries in 50 years (Simonds, Courage, Moreland and finally Greene King). In order to finance its thorough refurbishment the developer Mr John Castle of Letcombe Regis, Oxfordshire needed to build some accommodation. The Parish Council recognised this and went the extra mile to persuade West Berkshire Council to pass the planning application which had been rejected due to the aforesaid settlement boundary issue.

Chaddleworth has several charitable trusts, some dating back to the 18th century. There is the Saunders Wynne and Coventry Educational Trust that still provides funds to support local students. The Fuel Allotment Trust that has developed into a hardship fund to support local people who have fallen upon hard times, and the Village Hall Trust looks after the maintenance of the village hall. This is supported by The 100 Club, made up largely of local parishioners.

Everyone loves a ghost story and Chaddleworth has several. Beneath Jasmine Cottage in Main Street there are some haunted tunnels. I have been told that one of the tunnels eventually leads to St Margaret's Priory which is now inside RAF Welford. That would be more than a mile and I am sceptical. However, I have been in St Margaret's Priory and there is an entrance in the cellar that has been blocked off so who knows! Also, there is a pond long since disused and filled in on Tower Hill in which I was told a young child drowned. Her ghost supposedly haunts Tower Hill. When walking up the hill from Main Street I have witnessed a feeling of very cold air when passing the said pond in warm summer weather. Do I believe it? No.

RAF Welford is in the parish of Chaddleworth and over the years many local residents have worked there and continue to do so. In 1944, United States Army Air Force Waco gliders took off from RAF Welford as part of the D-Day operations. General Eisenhower and Winston Churchill both visited and there are archive photos in the American Air Museum in Welford. Glenn Miller, the famous American band leader, is reputed to have played his very last concert at RAF Welford before he disappeared over the English Channel during the Second World War.

There is a very close relationship with Chaddleworth and our American cousins and this continues right up to today. Many Americans who served at RAF Welford come back to visit and there is an active liaison group.

There is currently an exhibition in the West Berkshire Museum in Newbury, of locally found hoards. As you might have guessed there is a Chaddleworth hoard. The hoard consists of 134 Roman coins dating from AD 268-402. They were found in 2010 by Alistair Cooper who farms at Manor Farm, formerly (in 1840) Butlers Farm. They were all found within a small area and this, plus their dates, suggest they are a single hoard. The coins are copper alloy, of low value, and were probably the savings of a relatively poor man or woman. The earlier coins were worn, showing they had been in circulation for a very long time.

The date of the newest coin, AD 402, coincides exactly with the last issue of bronze coins sent to Britain from Rome. Roman rule in Britain officially ended in AD 410, but even before this date the urban economy was breaking down and money, particularly low value coins such as in this hoard, was ceasing to have any real value. Many hoards date from this unstable period, possibly hidden in the mistaken hope that things would improve and the coins would have value again.

🍁 CHAVEY DOWN

Chavey Down is in the Parish of Winkfield and is one of Berkshire's 'babies'. It lies on the southern edge of the Thames valley between Ascot and Bracknell and was formerly a tract of land in Windsor Forest. Chavey Down was at one time surrounded by an estimated 100,000 acres of wild heathland. By an Act of Parliament dated 21 July 1813, King George III vested in himself all the commonable land within the Forest and disposed of large areas. Chavey Down being common land at that time was enclosed. From that date the old Forest laws ceased to exist. After enclosing land a Deed of Award empowered Commissioners to allocate land to various people for a nominal sum to defray the expenses of Parliament for the Enclosure Act. John David of Bloxham in the County of Oxford was duly appointed last in Winkfield, of which Chavey Down formed part.

The area known as Chavey Down Hill was allotted to the Reverend Samuel Sewell and after various wills and bequests the land finally came in the ownership of Charles Sewell. The area was divided into two roads, North Road and Church Road with building plots on either side. The land in between the two roads, which now consists of the house's gardens, is called Spike Island. These plots were sold to builders who erected cottages which were soon filled with working-class families. The first house to be completed was Rosemount on the corner of Church Road and Priory Road and as the date on this is 1879 it is reasonable to suppose that the village dates from then. The village became known as Chavey Down and the inhabitants formed a close-knit community. Several traders opened small shops in the village which soon boasted a grocer, two bakers and a haberdashery store.

The oldest known building in the area is Chavey Down Farm, parts of which were built in the mid 1600s. This was probably originally a miller's cottage, as old plans and documents refer to 'The Windmill' which was thought to have been on the apex of the road junctions, Longhill Road, Priory Road and Locks Ride. The date the windmill was demolished is not known but Rocque's Map of Berkshire dated 1761 shows the windmill very clearly.

At one time, Chavey Down comprised part of the Manor of Winkfield and Mr C C Ferrand was the last known landowner of that manor. The Manning family owned Chavey Down Farm for many years and provided a very comprehensive service to the new village, not only with farm produce but also by hire of waggons and carriages for local weddings. Mr Manning also allowed the villagers to play cricket and football on one of the farm fields and one of his barns was regularly used as a venue for village entertainment. The property was sold to the last Mr R W Sharples in the mid 1940s and as a compliment to the village he named his racehorse 'Chavey Down'. His only son became Governor of Bermuda and was tragically assassinated in the early 1970s.

The earliest development (prior to the village) was the building of Ascot Priory in Priory Road. Dr Edward Bouverie Pusey purchased a large tract of land in 1861 and was responsible for the first unit of the Priory of Jesus Christ and the Hospital of the Holy Cross and Passion. Priscilla Lydia Sellon was for 30 years its Superior. This was later known as The Society of the Most Holy Trinity Devonport (later Ascot). The sisters founded an orphanage, a ward for sick children and ran a private school known as St Augustine's which was on the corner of North Road and Priory Road. The Sisters also visited the poor and the Priory employed many people from the village.

As the village began to develop, various people in the area contributed to the building known as St Martin's church. In 1900 the new chancel was built

and village funds were raised to pay for this. In 1905 the village received an 'Iron Room' which was delivered by horse and cart. This acted as a village hall, Sunday school and a meeting place for boys' clubs and other functions. In March 1974 St Martin's church was closed for extensive repairs and the 'Iron Room' was demolished as it was found to be unsafe. The church reopened the following year and a new village hall adjoining the church was built.

The area surrounding Chavey Down is still semi-rural, although it is under constant threat of development.

CHEAPSIDE

Cheapside in the parish of Sunninghill, was once the market site for Windsor Forest and derives its name from the old English for marketplace. It lies along the eastern edge of Windsor Great Park. The area of Sunninghill Park which forms the northern boundary to the main triangle of the village had been part of Windsor Forest as a Royal deer park and the first house was built there in 1486. Later it was owned by the Nevilles, one of whom was Gentleman to the Chamber of King Edward VI and an important figure in the reign of Elizabeth I. During the Second World War it was taken over by the American Ninth Air Force as a hospital before it was returned to the Crown in 1947 for the then Princess Elizabeth, but unfortunately the house was burnt down that same year.

The village lies on the route of the Royal Procession to the Royal Ascot races and every year in mid-June the pageantry of the procession makes its way from Windsor Castle, by way of the Great Park, down Watersplash Lane, and on to enter the racecourse near the top of the village by the modern gates built in 1955 for the new 'straight mile'. The old Golden Gates, their cast iron magnificently restored black and gilded, were built, probably in Glasgow, in 1877 when the racecourse was under the patronage of Edward Prince of Wales. Queen Victoria disapproved of this addition to 'the turf' and always spent June in Scotland.

Cheapside was surrounded by large country houses and estates which gave employment to the villagers. Many such as the Georgian Buckhurst Park, advertised in 1798 as 'a modern and excellent family house', still survive as private houses while others are divided into flats. Up to the end of the Second W orld War the village consisted of one straggling row of mostly small cottages with a few others along one side of the other two roads which form the main triangle. Although much infilling of modern houses has taken place, enlarging the village to take its place in the commuter belt, the village still keeps its feeling of community.

At the end of Pump Lane the old pump which was used to water the once unsurfaced road still stands. Few historic buildings survive. Wesleyan Methodist Chapel, built in 1862 was pulled down in 1970, but the one remaining public house still functions. Although called the Thatched Tavern it is slate roofed. The present building dates from 1780 which, in its turn, replaced one of much greater antiquity. But, the true hub of the village is the Village Hall which was built after a true community effort in fund-raising (in which the WI played a very active part) in 1970 to replace a Nissen hut transferred from the American Air Force establishment in Sunninghill Park in 1945.

🍁 CHIEVELEY

Chieveley is a pleasant village in the North Wessex Downs Area of Outstanding Natural Beauty with fine old buildings, some of them listed. Part of the High Street is designated as a Conservation Area containing many ancient cottages and several notably fine large houses of Queen Anne and Georgian period.

Chieveley has a markedly north-south orientation lying west of the A34 and north of the M4. The land on which it sits is relatively flat declining slightly from north to south. Geologically, Chieveley lies on a dipslope and the landscape is characterised by gently undulating landforms, shallow slopes, hedgerows and hedgerow trees, with winding lanes often set in grassy banks. Apart from the church tower, the village is almost totally concealed from travellers on the adjacent trunk roads.

The village settlement is overwhelmingly residential and its proximity to Newbury, Reading and other commuter towns, from which many commercial technology-driven firms operate, makes Chieveley a particularly convenient place to live. The number of working farms in the village is now small. Despite the consequent huge pressures, aided by the traffic-calming scheme, Chieveley remains an attractive village with a strong sense of community.

The Village Design Statement produced by villagers in 2002, aimed to support the West Berkshire Local Plan for Chieveley. The population, which numbered 1,481 in the 2001 census growing to 2,890 in 2011, has been thoughtfully considered in the building of two estates comprising 50 houses, built on former farmland, which successfully join Chieveley to Downend in the north. Chieveley has provided well for a future increase in population by an enlarged and modernised village school incorporating a pre-school that caters for children up to secondary school age. Nearby schools are Prior's

Court, a school for children with autism, and Mary Hare School for the deaf. The village shop and Post Office is located in the heart of the village, performing an important service, particularly for the elderly and for those without transport.

The Medical Practice moved from the High Street in the 1990s to a purpose-built surgery and pharmacy on the site of the ancient Hare and Hounds pub. The village once boasted three public houses but since the Wheatsheaf became a private dwelling only Ye Olde Red Lion remains as a popular meeting place. The Crab and Boar, renamed from the Blue Boar, on the Newbury to Wantage road, dates back to the English Civil War. Cromwell stayed there in 1644 during the second Battle of Newbury whilst his forces spent the night on North Heath.

Our Rector has the care of nine churches in the East Downland Benefice. St Mary the Virgin in Chieveley has eight bells, the oldest dated 1584, and a good team of bell ringers who find refreshment in the Red Lion after the weekly practice. The church has a robed choir who sing on most Sundays in the month.

With an increase in young families in the village the recreation ground has a multi-use games area and skate park, children's play area with climbing frames, swings and slides, bins for use by dog-walkers, and practice nets for the newly established Cricket Club. To mark Queen Elizabeth II's Diamond Jubilee in June 2012 specimen trees were planted around the ground, sponsored by residents and organisations.

The community supports many societies including the Tennis Club with floodlit tennis courts, Floral Group, Garden Club with two annual shows, Short-Mat Bowls Club and Cinema Club. For anyone seeking company there is Cuppa and Cake in the village hall and Tea and Toast in the church once a week. The oldest of the organisations in the village is the Women's Institute, founded here in 1920 with a 4-year break after the Second World War. For the more energetic, the annual Chieveley Chase is a stunningly beautiful 5.7 mile cross-country race with proceeds in aid of Chieveley School PTA. The village is well known locally for its grand Summer Fete held in the garden of The Manor and the splendid Chieveley Fireworks, always held on 5th of November, this event being supported and helped by staff from the nearby MOD establishment. The Village Hall and Recreation Ground are run and managed by a committee made up of representatives of user groups and elected people all of whom are volunteers and give their time freely. The hall facilities are available for hire and are used by many outside organisations.

The Newbury & District Agricultural Society has its showground on the edge of the village, creating an influx of visitors throughout the year to the Royal County of Berkshire Show and other national events. With a fighting spirit, the villagers recently managed to prevent a large waste recycling plant being developed on the adjacent land.

To mark the millennium villagers produced a very comprehensive Hedgerow Survey which incorporated historical records of the area going back to AD 951. This details hedges and their species in the green lanes, fields and footpaths of the area, dating them as far as possible in the hope that they will be preserved and cherished. West Berkshire Council has produced a footpath map of the village showing many beautiful rural walks. The mix of broad-leafed and evergreen trees maintain Chieveley's rural feel even in winter, softening the hard edges of walls and buildings. There are a number of fine species in the village, such as horse chestnut in Downend and cedar in the Manor gardens. The churchyard has sycamore, yew, beech and horse chestnut. The skylarks still sing over Bardown.

The Parish Plan was written in 2011, the result of four years' work by a steering committee of village volunteers. It provides guidance for the Parish Council and West Berkshire Council as to the wishes of the residents for the future of the village, and to influence future policies affecting the community, so that Chieveley keeps its village identity while continuing to embrace change and welcome newcomers to this vibrant community.

🍁 COMPTON

Compton, on the Berkshire Downs, is steeped in English history. Perborough Castle, an Iron Age fort, lies in the south-west of the parish, whilst to the north the Ridgeway, one of the oldest tracks in Britain, defines 1.4 km of the parish boundary and another 1.6 km of it lies within the parish. A lead Roman coffin, a Romano-British cremation/burial ground and a Romano-British pottery kiln have all been excavated in the parish. 281 silver Roman base-metal siliquae coins of late 4th/early 5th century AD were found scattered on a small area of the Ridgeway in the 1980s. The AD 871 Battle of Ashdown between Viking and Wessex forces is thought likely to have been fought on the Downs that lie within the Parish. The Domesday Book records Compton as having two manors, that at East Compton being the greater. Both were given to supporters of William the Conqueror, but later they came into the possession of churchmen, including the Bishop of Bath and Wells. The subsequent manorial history is fragmented, complicated by their being two, or perhaps three, manors in West Compton.

A church almost certainly existed in the early Middle Ages, on the site of the present church of St Mary and St Nicholas. The oldest part was the chantry of St Nicholas, which was torn down in the Reformation, but the lower part of the tower is Norman and the font is mid-12th century. Additions, rebuilding and restoration have been undertaken subsequently. The tower contains a peal of six bells, cast by Pack & Chapman of London, in 1775.

The Berkshire Downs were once extensive sheep-grazing lands, but gradually fell victim to the enclosure movement, as smaller tracts came into private ownership. Much of the farming is arable, though sheep can be observed today. In 1882 a railway line was built, running from Didcot to Newbury (thence towards Southampton). Compton became an important staging post for agriculture and racehorses. The line, which closed in the 1960s, was built on land owned by the family of Lady Wantage, who became a popular benefactress of the village before the Second World War.

The occupational character of the village has changed. Racehorse training has declined. The Harwell Laboratory closed but the site has become an international science and innovation centre. After the Second World War the Institute for Research in Animal Diseases was established and Her Majesty the Queen opened some additional buildings there. The Institute acquired local farms that supported the animals under study. It employed many Compton residents. The evolution of the village into a community of commuters is now well established. The Institute closed in 2015 and the main site is expected to become a residential development that will increase the village population significantly. The Institute's farms were purchased in 2017 by Beeswax Dyson, the farming interest of Sir James Dyson and family that already owned a contiguous estate north of Compton at Churn, and improvements to the land and estate buildings are significantly underway.

In the 19th century a small foundry flourished in the village, owned by T Baker and Sons, famous for its village pumps and water carts. It was a successful company for 120 years, becoming in turn the 'Hoist and Crane' business, and then Jones Cranes. It closed down before the Millennium, to be replaced by a housing development and office/warehouse space for Baxter Healthcare UK, whilst on Old Station Business Park, Carbosynth has become a global supplier of chemicals to scientists in the pharmaceutical and biotech communities.

Compton Primary School and the Downs School thrive together in The Downland Federation. The former has enjoyed outstanding assessments and the Friends of Compton Primary School continues as the PTA to support the school. The Downs School is now a comprehensive secondary school and has approximately 1150 pupils of whom 260 are in the sixth form. It specialises in science and mathematics, the concentration on agriculture and farming when the school was established in the 1960s having diminished.

To mark the Millennium, Compton Parish Council published *The Story of Compton* by Linnet McMahon and David Makin. This is a comprehensive account of the history of the village, illustrated with maps, diagrams and photographs on most of its 100+ pages. It combines information retrieved from archives with recollections of long-standing village residents up to the year 2000. The population of the village continues to grow, with developments of 20-30 houses being added each decade, and its heritage and history is beginning to be more appreciated.

❧ COOKHAM

Cookham village is situated on a particularly attractive part of the River Thames close to the hanging woods of Cliveden, and has been inhabited since Saxon times. It has Viking connections; Odney Common to the north of the village takes its name from the Danish Odin's Eye.

The John Lewis Partnership owns the Odney Club on behalf of their partners. The founder of the John Lewis Partnership – John Spedan Lewis bought the Manor of Cookham as part of the property which formed the Club, but decided not to retain it and the villagers of Cookham subsequently bought the Manor from him and it was eventually given to the National Trust. This means that the National Trust, as owners of the Manor of Cookham, now own all the commons in both Cookham and Cookham Dean.

Cookham has a fine parish church, Holy Trinity, which dates from Norman times and contains many fine monuments including several dedicated to the Young family who have lived at Formosa on the banks of the Thames since the late 18th century. There are also several ancient brasses, together with a copy of Stanley Spencer's painting of *The Last Supper*.

Sir Stanley Spencer (1891-1959) was born and raised in the village and it inspired some of his greatest paintings. He transformed Cookham in his imagination into 'A Village in Heaven.'

A small intimate gallery, beautifully maintained in what was a Methodist Chapel, is situated in Cookham High Street. The Stanley Spencer Gallery has regular exhibitions of Spencer's work and contains the old pram in which he wheeled all his painting gear to local features he wished to paint and there is a full catalogue of all his works including the partially finished *Christ Preaching at Cookham Regatta*, which is on permanent display.

Cookham has always been a centre for art in all its forms and this is perpetuated by the Cookham Festival which is held biennially and which encourages local artists, sculptors, musicians and writers. The village hosts the John Lewis Heritage Centre in the grounds of the Odney Club and includes a small museum dedicated to textiles.

Another well-supported yearly event is Rock the Moor which is a pop concert that is very popular and well attended and raises large amounts of money for good causes.

Most of the recent building development has taken place in Cookham Rise, separated from Cookham village by Cookham Moor. The railway station connecting Cookham and Maidenhead is situated in Cookham Rise, as is another great asset, Elizabeth House. Elizabeth House was opened in 1970 and since then many hundreds of local elderly residents have become members and benefitted from the many facilities offered, not least being the companionship that Elizabeth House provides. The current President of Elizabeth House is Lady Aurelia Young, wife of Lord Young of Cookham, a long-serving MP and Minister, and a statue by her father, the sculptor Oscar Nemon, has been placed in the entrance of Elizabeth House.

Cookham has a special link to the ceremony of 'Swan Upping', which takes place along the Thames every July, as the Queen's swan keeper is a resident of Cookham. Since medieval days the swan has been considered a royal bird and no one can own a swan without royal permission. Many of the London Guilds used to share this privilege, but now only the Dyers and Vintners claim this honour. The Swan uppers used to nick the beaks of the cygnets, the unmarked birds remaining the property of the Crown. Nowadays the birds are ringed. This ancient ceremony stems from the time when the Guilds undertook to raise and maintain companies of bowmen for the King's defence.

Cookham has an active Women's Institute among its very many other organisations.

🍁 COOKHAM DEAN

It is hard to imagine now but in the early 1800s Cookham Dean was a wild and godless place, and a favourite resort of the gypsy fraternity. It was an ideal place for poaching with its closeness to Bisham Woods which meant that those evading capture by the Cookham Constable had only to escape into the woods to do so.

There were residents in the Dean living in cottages of wattle and daub, with thatched roofs and earthen or clay floors. They were almost as lawless as their gypsy neighbours with cockfighting, dog fighting and occasional badger-baiting taking place and with the settling of personal quarrels by fist fights.

In 1840 the vicars of Cookham and Bisham were determined to bring civilisation to Cookham Dean. They prevailed upon the Rev George Hodson, newly ordained at Cambridge, to accept the challenge. In September that year the Bishop of Oxford licensed a small cottage for worship. Hodson moved in and his ministry began on 5th November 1843.

The foundation stone for the church was laid by the Vicar of Cookham on 15th July 1844 and the church was completed and consecrated by the Bishop of Oxford on 15th May 1845.

Formal education came to Cookham Dean when Rev Hodson first held classes in the cottage he bought in 1843. A new school was formally opened by the Bishop of Reading on 9th November 1899. It has been enlarged and extended but is still a place of pride and joy for today's residents of Cookham Dean.

From 1800 the woods in Cookham Dean began to be replaced with fruit orchards, a speciality being the black Circassian cherry imported from Russia. This is widely believed to be how the term "Kaffirs" came to be used for the local people. There is now a rebirth of the Kaffirs which is a group of residents who arrange charity events in the Dean every year for many good causes including the Air Ambulance.

Cookham Dean is a thriving village with pubs and restaurants and a well-used village hall, which is administered by the Village Club. All kinds of events are organised by the Club, which is a well valued village amenity.

Cookham Dean has a thriving Women's Institute which started in November 1920. The WI has its own hall which is a useful addition to the amenities of the village. There is also a highly successful sister WI, Dean Rise Women's Institute, formed in 1992, which also uses Cookham Dean's hall for its meetings.

Situated on the village green opposite both the WI and village hall there is a war memorial. This memorial was dedicated on Sunday 23rd November 1919. It was recently refurbished and rededicated on 11th November 2016. The two minutes' silence and planting of crosses, bearing the names of those who died, by the village children was witnessed by some descendants of those who gave their lives, together with members of the Parish Council and the Prime Minister, Theresa May. It was a most moving ceremony closely following the original service of 1919.

Perhaps the most famous resident of Cookham Dean was the author, Kenneth Grahame, who came to live with his maternal grandmother, Granny Ingles, and his siblings at The Mount, following his mother's death and his father's descent into alcoholism. Grahame spent the happiest two years of his childhood in Cookham Dean. Playing in the fields and woodlands close to the Thames inspired his most enduring work, *The Wind in the Willows*. He returned to Cookham Dean with his wife and young son in 1906, living at Mayfield, which was later converted to Herries School and is still a flourishing prep school. Bisham Woods close by, now known as Quarry Woods, is widely accepted as Kenneth Grahame's 'Wild Wood'.

With its close proximity to London, Cookham Dean is a delightfully rural and beautiful village.

🍁 CRANBOURNE

The parish of Cranbourne has been formed comparatively recently, cut out of the parishes of Winkfield, Old Windsor and Sunninghill. The Victorian Gothic church, built by Benjamin Ferrey in 1850, is of flint and stone. It was dedicated by Bishop Wilberforce, who argued fiercely against Darwin over *The Origin of Species*, and was known unkindly as Soapy Sam. Some of the stained-glass windows are designed by William Morris. The Alexander Chapel is in memory of Field-Marshal Earl Alexander of Tunis, who died in 1969. His house was not far from the church where he worshipped.

One of the oldest schools in Berkshire was founded at Cranbourne in 1709 by Richard, 1st Earl of Ranelagh for 'twenty poor Protestant boys and twenty poor Protestant girls'. It became known as the 'Green School' as a uniform rather like the more famous Blue Coat School was provided for the children. Every Whit Monday they paraded outside Winkfield Church to receive a new set of clothes. The number of admissions increased over the years and in 1880 a larger school was opened in Lovel Road called Winkfield Cranbourne Ranelagh C.E. School. The original school building is now called Cranbourne Hall.

When the grammar school in Bracknell was opened in 1908 it was named Ranelagh School. Cranbourne School then dropped the name Ranelagh but retained part of Lord Ranelagh's coat of arms on its badge. Today it is known as Cranbourne Primary School and caters for children of infant and junior age.

Lovel Road takes its name from the family who were important land owners in Norman times. Plaistow Green Farm, built in 1569, said to be originally a hunting lodge, has associations with the Jacobite Trust. An inscription on one of the walls includes the Jacobite emblem of a six-point star.

🍁 CRAZIES HILL & COCKPOLE GREEN

Crazies Hill is an outlying hamlet in the north ward of Wargrave, and leads on to Cockpole Green in Hurley Parish. It is thought that both their curious names can be accounted for thus: Crazies Hill was almost certainly named because 'crazies' is an old country name for buttercups, whilst on Cockpole Green there was once a cockpit, where cockfighting took place.

The hamlets formerly had a large number of inns for the small population, but now only the Horns (which stood on the edge of the old Windsor Great Park) remains. Springlands for many years housed a hand laundry, and there were many wells in the village. Rebecca's Well remains as a local landmark.

During the Second World War, land at Upper Culham farm was used as an RAF airfield, and the factory at Warren Works started in disused hangars.

Thistle House, on the top of Crazies Hill, was built in 1930-31 as a convalescent home for children by Sir Campbell Rhodes in memory of his wife Eleanor Wemyss, after whom it was originally named. It closed in the 1960s, and was then bought by David Greig, the butcher, whose emblem is the thistle, and who used it as a training college for a time; but it is now a private house.

In Victorian times there was also a brick kiln, and the old claypit is now a haven for foxes and badgers. Three ash trees in the meadow at Kiln House are said to mark the site of the kiln.

It is well-known that 'The Crazies', which stands opposite the Mission Hall, has the Georgian front of the old Henley Town Hall as a facade.

🍁 CROWTHORNE

The village of Crowthorne owes its existence to the proximity of Wellington College and Broadmoor Hospital, around which the village has grown. Wellington College, built about 1859, is a national memorial to the Duke of Wellington, whose name and those of his generals find echoes in the titles of roads and inns of the neighbourhood, e.g. Duke's Ride and the Iron Duke.

Broadmoor Hospital was built about the same time on a high spur of the ground near Caesar's Camp. According to an old resident, the former inhabitants of the district were known as Broom Squires or Broom Dashers, whom he described as 'good-living people, having a semi-underground life, all of whom had an altar of sods with bits of glass stuck in the top'. Such were the 'Aborigines' of Crowthorne.

The Devil's Highway, a Roman road, crosses the village and two Roman milestones are in existence still. Although most buildings are modern, one Tudor cottage remains in the woods towards Owlsmoor. Crowthorne would appear to have wider boundaries than is expected, being bounded on one side by Owlsmoor, formerly called Newfoundland after an original squatter called New with numerous progeny; and on the other by California.

Crowthorne, once part of the Parish of Sandhurst, acquired its name because the postal authorities wished to give it a name to facilitate deliveries from Wokingham, instead of York Town, Surrey (which with Cambridge Town became known as Camberley). 'Albertonville' had been suggested in honour of the Prince Consort, but luckily the suggestion of 'Crowthorne', after some thorn trees at Brookers Corner, at the top of the village, was adopted. In the Domesday Book, Crowthorne Farm appears as a separate holding in the Royal Forest of Windsor, although the present farm holdings do not date back to the days of William the Conqueror.

There are memorials to three men who died in the Crimean War at the famous charge of the Light Brigade in the old churchyard.

Since 1950, the population of Crowthorne has greatly increased, due partly to the setting up of the Road Research Laboratory nearby and also to the building of quite a number of very attractive housing estates, and, as part of the evolution, some of the smaller shops in the high street have disappeared, to be replaced by supermarkets. The village also has an excellent community hall, the Morgan Centre, with good parking facilities, which houses many of the events and activities run by local organizations.

🍁 CURRIDGE

Curridge is a pleasant place to live and ideally situated near the M4 and A34 whilst being a quiet wooded area resplendent in spring with flowers and beautiful walks.

Its history can be traced back to AD 953 when King Eadred granted Cusa's Ridge to his minister Aelfric. The settlement was visited by King John, and Oliver Cromwell is said to have stayed at the thatched farmhouse Lanolee Farm in 1644. More recent history is reflected in names. The small chapel on Chapel Lane is now a private house. Kiln Terrace is a reminder of the brick making that carried on until the Second World War. Church Lane is where services were held in one end of the school building until 1965 when the church closed and moved to Hermitage.

The school was built as a private school for Mary Wasey and her sister Jane Stackpole (sisters of Thomas Wasey of Prior's Court). In 1886, after their deaths, the land was given to the Chieveley Primary School Board with a proviso that it could be used as a church on Sundays and Holy days.

The WI Hall was built on land for which they paid a peppercorn rent to the Church Commissioners until members and local residents raised enough money to buy the land. The WI Hall is still used today by the WI, Horticultural Society, Residents' Association and other village affairs.

Curridge covers a wide area with scattered development which has grown up over recent years, the largest being Curridge Park with about 43 houses. There is no shop but there is a thriving garage which sells almost everything and a pub known as the Bunk, so named because it was frequented by local workers who had bunked off work for a prolonged lunch break!

There is a village playground run by trustees and used by the school. There is a thriving riding school and the local woods provide excellent riding facilities. Altogether Curridge is a popular village.

🍁 DATCHET

Datchet, or Daceta as it is named in the Domesday Book, still preserves its character as a village. To the south it is bounded by the River Thames and to the north by the M4 motorway, whilst the Queen Mother Reservoir lies to the east and the playing fields of Eton to the west. From early days the traffic from London came through Datchet via the London Road past the church, then across The Green to the Manor Hotel, down the High Street and over the old river bridge to Windsor. The South West Trains line from Waterloo which cuts through the village originally had its terminus at Datchet until 1849 when the extension to Windsor across Home Park was agreed to by Queen Victoria. In 1851 the two bridges, Victoria leading to Windsor, and Albert to Old Windsor, were built and the old bridge at the end of the High Street was taken down.

The noble spire of the church of St Mary the Virgin dominates the village. Part of the present building dates from the 13th century, but in 1857 it was largely rebuilt, and extended in 1864. Inside are various memorials to benefactors of the village and the churchyard is the resting place of Robert Barker, printer to Elizabeth I. He bequeathed the revenue from five acres of land and his house to the village in 1644. The wall alongside the churchyard is of Elizabethan structure. The charming interior contains old beams and antique furnishings.

On the other side of The Green stands St Mary's C of E Primary Academy which was founded in 1844 for the education of the poor. Between the shops and the post office there is an arched approach to the WI hall built in the 1950s by George Scott, a local builder. He gave the building to the WI as he was impressed by the work of his wife and her friends who belonged to Datchet's WI, founded in 1948, but with no permanent meeting place. On this side of The Green are also the Manor cottages and the Manor Hotel, parts of which date from the 15th century. In 1742 the Datchet Manor was sold to the 2nd Duke of Montagu who also acquired the estate of Ditton Park (now owned by CA Technologies).

The High Street leading over the railway crossing to the Thames contains several Georgian houses terminating in the Post House, a charming Regency building. The river front is very pleasant with grassy slopes shaded by chestnut trees and presenting delightful views towards Windsor and downstream. Returning to the village green via Queen's Road and "May's" crossing there is a former 17th-century inn which is now a Costa Coffee.

On The Green opposite there is an oak tree planted by Lord Montagu of Beaulieu to commemorate the award to Datchet of the best kept village in Buckinghamshire in 1966. Datchet moved into Berkshire in 1974. The market

Datchet

cross was erected by Mrs Crake, a great benefactor to the village, for the Diamond Jubilee of 1897. On the main green, is a memorial inscribed with the names of the Datchet men who fell in the First and Second World War.

Before 1900 much of the centre of the village was occupied by a large pool which overflowed when the river rose. In 1894 severe flooding was recorded and again in 1947 when the water level was over the top of the white posts which surround The Green and residents were supplied with food and a doctor by a boat. A further flood occurred in 2014, but steps continue to be taken to prevent such a reoccurrence.

Datchet is fortunate in possessing a fine recreation ground in Horton Road comprising playing fields, tennis courts, football pitches and children's play area. It was opened in 1951 by HRH Princess Margaret and was obtained largely due to the efforts of Charles King, Chairman of the Parish Council at the time. Datchet Village Hall was built in the 1960s following a bequest from the owner of Wilkinson Sword, Denys Randolph, after he sold the razor blade section of his business to Gillette.

Among the famous people who have resided in Datchet are Sir William Herschel, the astronomer, William Corden, RA, painter of scenes of the village, Watson Watt, the inventor of radar, Billy Cotton, Donald Pleasence, Evelyn Ellis who drove the first motor car in the country to his home in the village, and Thomas Sopwith who landed his light aircraft in Datchet. Dame Vera Lynn sang at the Pavilion Club on the Thames Riverside, where Edward VIII secretly met Mrs Wallis Simpson.

Datchet WI Hall is regularly hired for a wide variety of functions, and is home of a lively group of dancers, called Datchet Border Morris, who traditionally perform every Boxing Day morning on The Green.

🍁 EARLEY

The name derives from Anglo-Saxon, *Earn* – eagle, and *leah* – a wood – Eagle wood. Domesday mentions two main manors – Erlegh St Bartholomew, later known as Erlegh Court, and Erlegh St Nicholas, later Erlegh White Knights – so named because of chapels dedicated to these two saints on the two manors. Neither had a font nor bell, but a wooden cross was erected in an enclosed space on which palms were hung on Palm Sunday.

The de Erleghs held the manors for some centuries; one John de Erlegh in 1292 was known as The White Knight – hence the re-naming of the manor. The leper hospital of Reading Abbey owned lands at Earley White

Knights, the revenue of which was devoted to lepers.

Earley nowadays is not a village in the true sense of the word. It is an extended area of Reading, with its boundary only two miles from the town centre. It covers an area of approximately 2000 acres and has lost all traces of its ancient history. The size and population does not include that of the rapidly expanding area of Lower Earley which extends to the M4.

The old Dreadnought public house, once the only one in Earley, is used as a Sailing Club House by the University of Reading, who have also built a large Hall of Residence in Earley.

The Parish church of St Peter was completed in 1844. At this time, looking towards Wokingham, Hungerford Lodge could be seen and one or two cottages where Earley station now stands, but for the rest it was open country.

The Manor of Maiden Erleigh was formed in the 14th century, and after many changes of ownership through the years, it was purchased in 1903 by the millionaire Solomon Joel, well known in horse racing circles, who in fact had a racecourse on the Estate. He donated a piece of his land to the village to be used for sporting purposes, and this is well used to this day. It was opened in 1927 by the Duke of York (later King George VI) and is known as the Sol Joel Playing Field.

The ancient Estate of Bulmershe Court once belonged to the Abbey Danding. In the 18th century it became the home of Henry Addington, first Viscount Sidmouth, Statesman and Prime Minister. The house has now been pulled down and Bulmershe Teacher Training College occupied the site until it merged with Reading University in 1989, creating the Bulmershe Court campus.

🍁 EASTBURY

Eastbury lies between Great Shefford and Lambourn, in the green and winding Lambourn valley. The stream runs between parallel roads, on either side of which are timber-framed, thatched and tiled roofed cottages and barns, plus larger houses of brick and flint, while footpaths lead up to and over the Berkshire Downs to the ancient Ridgeway on one side and to the Roman road, Ermin Street, on the other.

Eastbury is a fairly compact village, with most of the houses built along the river banks which in many places are planted with flowering shrubs and bulbs. The river rises in Lambourn and has the unusual feature of flowing in the summer and being dry for three miles or so for three or four months in autumn and winter. The stream is crossed by two road bridges and three footbridges joining the two roads which traverse the village: Gumbletons, then Top Arch by Eastbury Manor, Church Bridge, somewhat wider than the other footbridges to accommodate the hand-cart hearse used in earlier days, leads from the Old Vicarage to the church of St James the Greater, then Pigs Bridge, and lastly the stalwart road bridge, Bottom Arch. Nearby is Pigeon House, early 17th-century, used in medieval times as a retreat for the Black Monks of Wallingford, where they hunted and fished, as portrayed on a fine carved arch in Lambourn church. Close to Pigeon House is a fine octagonal dovecote, dated 1620, where beautifully fitted chalk blocks form nesting spaces for 999 pairs, and a self-propelled spiral stairway made egg-collecting easier. Unfortunately, after several changes of ownership and the dividing up of the Pigeon House fields and buildings, the dovecote is not so well cared for nowadays.

At the Lambourn end of the village is the splendid Manor, dating from before 1429, and added to over the centuries to form the gracious mellowed brick and stone building with gables and interesting clustered chimney stacks which we see today, backed by its cornfields and woodlands. A manor has stood there from the date of the Norman Conquest in 1066 (the date that everyone knows!).

The Church of St James the Greater was designed by G. E. Street and built in

Eastbury

1851 at the instigation of Robert Millman, Rector of Lambourn. It is a flint and stone structure consisting of chancel and nave, with a very steeply pitched tiled roof and a small bellcote for two bells at the east end. Opposite the north door is the window Laurence Whistler engraved to celebrate the lives of the poet Edward Thomas, killed in action at Arras in 1917, and of his wife Helen, who lived in Eastbury for the last twelve years of her long life. The design shows chalk downland and woods, with the village of Steep in Hampshire, where the Thomas family lived for some years, and a thatched gamekeeper's cottage in Hodson Bottom, near Swindon, where the couple spent a short honeymoon. Across the landscape lines from several poems are engraved. Since his death the works of Edward Thomas have become more and more widely known and Helen's books, *As it Was* and *World Without End*, tell the poignant but triumphant story of their life together. The window, an idea of their younger daughter Myfanwy, who taught at Lambourn School for 21 years, retiring in 1975, was made possible by the generosity of nearly 700 people from all over the world and from all walks of life. It was dedicated in 1971, when Lord David Cecil and Professor R. George Thomas spoke of the poet and his wife and read from their works.

In the small square opposite the church stands the Prayer Cross of St Antoline where, up to as late as the 19th century, itinerant preachers, trade union agents and others stood upon the steps to harangue and be heckled by those who came to listen. As far back as the 16th century processions took place to and from this Prayer Cross to the Cross standing before the church at Lambourn and to Wodebury Cross at Shefford Woodlands.

In 1791 John Sarjent gave his garden and orchards to provide education for 25 poor children. As the average age of the population grew greater, the need for a school became less, and the village school was eventually closed, and the children in the village attended schools at Great Shefford, Lambourn and later Hungerford or Newbury.

One of the chief industries of the neighbourhood is the training of racehorses, and many famous trainers have their establishments at Lambourn and nearby.

Chalk-loving wild flowers abound in the woods and downland and some rare species have been found here. There are many beautiful walks, where the keen country-lover need hardly see a main road.

Like a number of villages these days, with the nearness of the M4 many of the cottages are bought and modernised by weekenders and commuters, and the quality of village life is very different from what it was even 25 years ago. But there are still several villagers who can recall with nostalgia the 'old days'.

🍁 EAST GARSTON

East Garston nestles in the chalk downs of the Lambourn Valley. Its name is thought to be a corruption of Asgar's Tun. Asgar (or Esgar) the Staller, owned over 300 hides of land in nine shires but, having supported the defeated King Harold, forfeited his holdings to the invading Normans after 1066.

Despite its lack of a shop and school and its limited Post Office and bus facilities, the village is situated in beautiful countryside with easy access to major routes, and is an attractive place in which to live. Its demography has changed significantly over recent years but there are still families that can claim a long association with its history. The village is blessed with several attractive cottages, some of them thatched. "Cornbaggers" located at the middle bridge, provided the interior location for the film *Quiet Weekend*.

The church, All Saints, was built c. AD 1100, and evolved over subsequent years, to include the addition of a south aisle and porch in the 14th century. The greatest alterations, enforced by general deterioration, took place in the late 19th century when the Seymour Chapel and Chancel were restored and the southern arcade was rebuilt. In 1880 the much acclaimed stained-glass window was installed on the east wall.

Non-conformity was widespread in the area during the 19th century. A Wesleyan Methodist chapel, constructed in 1820, in Rogers Lane, was replaced on the same site in 1869 only for it to pass into private ownership in 1936. A similar fate befell the Primitive Methodist chapel, built in 1860 on Front Street (then Big Street). It survived as a place of worship until 1977. Quakers still worship in the Friends' Meeting House, constructed on the site of a previous building in 1979.

Around 1862 a farm cottage, the home of the Ferrebee family, became a pub, the Queen's Arms. Greatly extended since, the inn, popular with the racing fraternity, is a thriving entity attracting custom from a wide area.

In 1859 peaceful East Garston became the focus of national attention when its vicar, the Reverend Randolph, refused to bury the 5-week-old son of a respected farmer, Elijah Bew, because the child had not been baptised. When this was disproved, the vicar resorted to claiming that the child was not a parishioner. Most newspapers, particularly the London dailies, were extremely scathing in their comments, not only with the Reverend Randolph but also with the Bishop of Oxford, Samuel Wilberforce, (the son of William Wilberforce) who backed him. The vicar, later, in a private letter to Elijah Bew, admitted that he refused to bury the child to punish the father for being "schismatic" i.e. worshipping in a Non-conformist chapel.

The village received more national attention with the advent of what was called the Windsor Tragedy. Charles Wooldridge, born in East Garston in 1865, became a trooper in the Royal Horse Guards based at Windsor where he met and married Laura Ellen Glendall. In a fit of jealous rage he killed her in 1896 and was executed at Reading Gaol in July of the same year. He was the inspiration for Oscar Wilde's famous poem *The Ballad of Reading Gaol*.

The Manor of East Garston, part of the Ramsbury Manor estate, was bequeathed to Francis, the 5th Baronet Burdett, on the death of his aunt, Lady Elizabeth Jones in 1800. Despite his privileged background, he held extremely radical views and was twice imprisoned when an MP. The parish of East Garston remained part of the Burdett estate until 1919 when Robert, the 8th Baronet Burdett, facing rapidly changing social and economic conditions, was obliged to sell it, together with the manor of Eastbury.

🍁 EASTHAMPSTEAD

Although much of it has been enveloped by Bracknell New Town, and therefore it is no longer strictly a village, Easthampstead is an ancient parish. In the Domesday Book it is referred to as 'Lachinstede' which is of Saxon origin. By the beginning of the 13th century it had become Easthampstead. Roman remains have been found, to the south of the area, but Caesar's Camp, within that part – a fine place for dog-walking! – is misnamed, for this was the site of an Iron Age fort.

The Manor House in Easthampstead Park, on the Wokingham side of the parish, began life as a hunting lodge in Windsor Forest. This was incorporated in the old mansion, which was pulled down in about 1860. The present Victorian mansion, built shortly afterwards by the Marquis of Downshire, remained with that family until 1954, when it was sold to Berkshire County Council and became first a teacher training college, and later a centre for further education. There is also now a secondary school in the grounds.

The Downshire family were great benefactors to the village. Lady Downshire was responsible for the complete rebuilding of the parish Church of St Michael and St Mary Magdalene, whose windows were designed by Sir Edward Burne-Jones and executed by William Morris. The church stands on a small hill, and its high tower can be seen from quite a distance.

The parish originally extended further to the north, joining Warfield and Winkfield, but the creation of the new parish of Bracknell in the 19th century separated and reduced all three.

The second Marquis of Downshire rebuilt eight cottages opposite the church for the poor of the village, parts of which were incorporated in the infirmary which later became the Union Workhouse. Today this is Church Hill House, providing mental health services. Another interesting mansion is at South Hill Park, on the opposite side of the parish. The present Edwardian house, built by Lord Haversham, stands on the side of one built in 1760 by William Watts. During the Second World War it was taken over by the Royal Sea Bathing Hospital of Margate. After their departure it fell into neglect, and was rescued by the Ferranti Company, who rented it for their administrative department, from the New Town Development Corporation. Now it is the Arts Centre, and home of the ambitiously designed Wilde Theatre.

Although Easthampstead has many housing estates in its midst, some green areas remain, and it is still possible to find peace in the woods and fields on the outskirts.

 EAST ILSLEY

Ilsley is mentioned in the Domesday Book, though there are signs of earlier Roman and Saxon settlements in the area. Evidence of strip fields and lynchets can be seen on the surrounding downs.

East Ilsley stands in a fold of the Downs, midway between Abingdon and Newbury, on a crossroads of two important roads. From east to west is the ancient and tranquil Ridgeway which passes just north of the village, and from north to south is the busy A34. Until 1966 it ran through the centre of the village since it was a meeting of two major trade routes. This made the village an ideal place for a market and it was originally called Market Ilsley or Chipping Ilsley as a result. One reading of the origin of the name Ilsley is 'Hildeslei', meaning a woodland clearing associated with a man called 'Hild'. A charter from Henry III saw the creation of a Great Corn Market in the Middle Ages. Later, because of the growing wool trade, it turned into the famous sheep market to which James I gave approval.

The sheep market was held every alternate Wednesday, between April and October, averaging no fewer than 25,000 sheep sold in one day, with as many as 80,000 sold on occasions. It was second only in size and importance to Smithfield. It was said that on market days the children could get from one side of the village to the other on the backs of the sheep without touching the ground. The market brought graziers from the home counties, Herefordshire and Buckinghamshire, who took the sheep and fed them for the London market. Sales dwindled in the early 20th century and the last market was held in 1934.

Because the markets brought in lots of people to the village on a regular basis, it was inevitable that services sprang up to cater for their needs. So it was that Ilsley became famous for its many pubs. There is a well-known rhyme:

> Ilsley remote among the Berkshire downs
> Has this distinction o'er her sister towns
> Far famed for wool, though not for spinners
> For sportsmen, doctors, publicans and sinners

This makes the place sound rather unsavoury, but visitors needed shelter and sustenance. Many of these so-called pubs were little more than residents opening up a spare room once a fortnight and making a little extra money. The often quoted figure of 21 pubs is an exaggeration, a misunderstanding, caused by the fact that often a pub would change its name for a while and then revert back again. This has led people to believe that there were more pubs than there actually were.

There are now just two places of worship, St Patrick's Catholic church and St Mary's Anglican church. The Baptist chapel, built in 1864 has now closed. The Church of St Mary stands at the top of the hill overlooking the village. Parts of it date from the 13th century, with the North Aisle added in 1845. Another rhyme, this time not peculiar to East Ilsley goes:

> Sleepy Ilsley, drunken people,
> Got a church without a steeple
> And what is more to their disgrace,
> They've got a clock without a face.

It was not at all unusual for clocks to be without a face at this time. East Ilsley's original clock mechanism was made by the local blacksmith at the end of the 17th century and ran perfectly for over 200 years until it was replaced by the present clock in 1885. This shows the time on a five-foot convex copper dial, originally painted black and gold. There is a strong tradition of bell ringing, the tower boasting a peal of eight bells. An inventory of 1547 records 'Thre grete belles and a lytell bell', and even earlier in 1504 a bequest in a will suggests that the church had a steeple.

Notable buildings include the Hall, which is early Georgian, and Kennett House which is a little earlier, about 1700. They stand facing each other across Broad Street, and are probably not the first buildings on their respective sites. Both were used as private schools in the 19th century, the Hall for boys, and Kennett House for girls. The Ilsleys Primary School, which has been on its present site next to the churchyard for 110 years, caters for 60 children mainly from East and West Ilsley. Rated 'good' by Ofsted, it is federated with Hampstead Norreys.

The Millennium Green to the south of the village was created as one of 256 such spaces all over England to mark the Millennium. It is a green space for informal recreation, secured for 999 years, and will remain an open space never to be built on.

East Ilsley is also famous for racehorses. It was the Duke of Cumberland, brother of George II, who discovered that the downs surrounding this area were ideal for training horses and he set up his famous stables at Kates Gore, just the other side of Gore Hill. At one time there was even a race track on the downs above the village, close to the Ridgeway. Until recent times there were several racing establishments in the village. Today there remains just one, Summerdown Stables, built in 1993.

East Ilsley used to be an important centre for the administration of law and order with a police station, complete with resident sergeant, cells and a courtroom where local sessions were held. There is no longer a resident police presence today.

Like many villages today East Ilsley has lost its shops and Post Office, but there is a daily bus service to Newbury, via neighbouring villages.

🍁 EMMBROOK

Emmbrook is to the west of Wokingham, and is, in fact, a part of the town, yet still retaining its community spirit. Until about 1964, it was only a small hamlet, but a great deal of development took place, a large comprehensive school was built and two primary schools.

The Emmbrook School opened a new £2 million English block in 2015 and a new Maths building was opened in 2017.

Other local amenities in Emmbrook include three pubs the Dog and Duck, The Rifle Volunteer and The Emmbrook Inn (formerly the Thatched Cottage), shops, a village hall and a social centre.

The village's name is derived from the Emm Brook, which flows through the centre of the area to join the River Loddon.

Emmbrook WI was started in 1936 in a building which was erected in 1867, and was affectionately known as the 'Tin Hut'. The WI had a 25-year lease on the hall but, in 1976, with the help of the local council a management committee was formed and, with a considerable amount of voluntary help, a new hall was built around the old one, complete with new kitchens and cloakrooms. Emmbrook WI, sadly, is now disbanded but the hall is still very much a focal point of the village.

🍁 EMMER GREEN

The name of the village is believed to derive from an old Saxon word Eamere meaning 'a lake beside a stream'. The once sizeable lake is now but a pond. The stream could be 'the swillies', which runs from the west side of the pond down to the River Thames.

Before piped water came to Emmer Green at the turn of the 20th century, villagers relied upon the springs for their drinking water. One of these, Chalybete Spring in Surley Row, was reputed to have healing powers, especially for the eyes, and the water was regularly bottled and sold. Villagers drew water from the pump opposite the pond, and carried it home with the aid of a yoke.

The stone dragon over Emmer Green Post Office was originally over the blacksmith's shop on that site, and was made at Emmer Green Brick Works. The blacksmith's shop, in an ideal position for travellers to and from Reading, probably dated back to the 16th century, and undoubtedly was one of the busiest spots in the area before the advent of the motor car.

The early 16th-century White Horse inn has Elizabethan oak beams and floorboards. Until the 1920s groceries were sold over the counter and beer drawn from the barrel; skittles and quoits were the regular pastimes of the locals there of an evening, right up to the end of the First World War. In the late 1800s and early 1900s, firemen had their headquarters in the yard of the early 19th-century Black Horse inn opposite. Several residents still remember the firecart being pulled out by hand and, with much shouting and encouragement from the onlookers, charging off down the road.

Within living memory, it was the custom at a funeral for six pall-bearers to carry the coffin on their shoulders from Emmer Green all the way to St Peter's Church, Caversham, with a change of pall-bearers halfway. Old survey maps show a right of way from the pond, across the fields to Bottle Cottage in Surley Row, then down Rotherfield Way. Fortunately for the pall-bearers the foundation stone of St Barnabas Church was laid in 1924 and the finished church was consecrated five years later.

Though largely an agricultural area, a brick-kiln was built in about 1654 on land known as Homer's Field, then under Sonning Manor. The Brickwall cottages were originally offices and stables for the horses used on the brickfield.

During the Second World War, the Reading archives were stored in underground caves in the area, as were the cardboard coffins ready for possible gas victims — praise be, they never needed to be used! The caves are very large, extending from the old brick-kiln, under Kiln Road, and the woods on the other side. They came into being when chalk was quarried for agricultural purposes.

Rosehill House, standing in 14 acres of ground, was once part of Caversham Manor, the first building being erected in 1791. Martin John Sutton, of Suttons Seeds, lived there, the house then being called Kidmore Grange. In 1923 it was bought for the Oratory Preparatory School; then from the outbreak of the Second World War until 1958 it served as the Salvation Army Headquarters. The house has since been converted into flats and a housing estate has been built on the grounds.

St Benet's Home, which was built and maintained by Dr Powell of Derby Road in 1902, was a Church of England home for young boys. They attended the local village school. This building has now been demolished and is the site of another sheltered housing complex.

There are a number of springs, now underground, in the area, and over the years swallow holes have appeared. In 1955 people noticed an unpleasant smell at a pond in Camp Wood. There was a sudden loud noise and the pond soaked away! But that was not all, for three hours later, with an explosive roar, four fully grown trees disappeared into the ground in a matter of seconds, sending up a great water spout. Sixty five years before, near Brickwall House, locals had been enjoying themselves at one of the regular dances that were held in the small hall. They made their way home unaware how near they had been to tragedy. By the next morning the hall had disappeared into the ground!

Surley Row is a very ancient, narrow, winding road, along which are a number of interesting houses, including Caversham Hill, c.1810, the Tudor Old Grove House, and No. 46 Surley Row, which used to be the 18th-century Gardeners' Arms. The garden of 164 Kidmore End Road appears to be a virtual treasure trove, having yielded, amongst other things, a 150-million-year-old Coxcomb Oyster, prehistoric hand axes, Roman and 16th-century coins and medieval pottery.

Nowadays, only by a stretch of the imagination can Emmer Green be called a village, so linked up with Caversham and Reading has it become, though it is still only a few minutes' walk out into the countryside.

🍁 ENBORNE

The ancient parish of Enborne lies immediately west of Newbury. Indeed, the boundary shifted a few hundred yards westward in the 20th century in favour of expanding Newbury, but the parish remains very roughly square in shape, bounded north by the River Kennet, and south by the River Enborne (known as the River Aleburn until a century ago, so not the origin of the parish name). Like its western neighbour Hamstead Marshall, Enborne's settlement is scattered across farmland, and there is no village focal point.

Historically Enborne comprised two manors, but no manor houses have survived. It's been suggested that Cope Hall, a medieval mansion near Skinner's Green, demolished in the 1960s, may have had that status. Enborne Lodge was another substantial residence, known as Larcorns until rebuilt by Robert Valpy in the 19th century. It became a school in the late 20th century, but is now part of a gated residential development.

Biggs' Cottage, in the south of the parish, was the overnight stop of the Earl of Essex before the First Battle of Newbury (1643), and it subsequently enjoyed the reputation of being haunted, although Essex lived and left to fight elsewhere for another three years. Wheatland's Farm, on the eastern border, also featured in the battle, taking in so many of the casualties that it became known as the Hospital.

On the western side of Enborne the 12th-century church of St Michael and All Angels stands on a hilltop next to Hamstead Park (part of which lies in Enborne parish). Often combined with Hamstead Marshall in the past, the Enborne rectory now also serves Inkpen, West Woodhay, Combe and Kintbury. Enborne's elegant Georgian rectory passed into private hands in the 1960s.

A cottage beside the church occasionally housed boys' boarding schools run for the gentry by rectors, but education for village children was provided further down the hill, thanks to a grant of land and money from Lord Craven and the Rev Charles Johnson in the 1820s. The school still thrives today as a Church of England primary school with around 70 pupils.

Enborne's main economic activity continues to be farming and rural enterprise such as a kennels, a plant nursery, a circus headquarters, a green burial ground and a riding school. There are two pubs: the historic Craven Arms stands on the border with Hamstead Marshall, and the 20th-century Bowler's Arms on the eastern side. (The Woodpecker, often thought to be an Enborne pub, actually falls within Newbury.)

Enborne has survived a succession of disruptive planning projects. The Kennet and Avon Canal linking Reading to Bath opened in 1810, and the

London to Penzance railway line first appeared in 1843, but both of these merely skirted the northern edge of the Enborne. The Didcot to Southampton railway bisected the parish north-south in 1882. It closed in the 1960s, but the route was brought back into service for the controversial Newbury bypass in 1997.

Southern Enborne was once considered a possible route for the M4 around Newbury, but the idea was discarded in favour of a northerly alternative. The so-called Enborne Valley Reservoir Project, first mooted in 1892 and revived at regular intervals thereafter, would not have impinged upon the parish itself, but in 1987 Thames Water built the Enborne Grange reservoir on land at the top of Bell Hill. This £3.5million project stores 30,000 cubic metres of water for thirsty Wash Commoners.

In 1958 a Royal Observer Corps post was discreetly built in Cope Hall Lane. One of 14 in Berkshire, this hidden, underground facility was designed for monitoring aircraft, nuclear explosions and radioactive fall-out in the event of the Cold War becoming hot. It was dismantled above ground in 1991, but the sealed underground chamber may yet baffle future archaeologists.

In 2000 a proposal was aired for 1,700 new houses on Sutton estate fields between the Newbury boundary and the A34 (the 1643 battlefield site). Enborne Hedges, as this development was called, was rejected, but infill between Newbury and the bypass is considered an ever-present threat.

In 2001 a philanthropic bequest of land at Wash Water to Newbury hospital prompted another keen local controversy when it translated into a planning application for housing. By 2009 this development was completed on two sites, the westerly one, Knoll Gardens, being in Enborne.

Enborne's sporting heritage includes a robust series of horseracing meetings in Georgian times, but today it is the home of well-known Wash Common Cricket Club which, in addition to cricket matches, stages a popular Bonfire Night party and other social functions for families. The club founded the Bowler's Arms.

Enborne still achieves fame in compilations of English folklore for an ancient manorial custom, whereby widows found guilty of sexual incontinence were required to parade their shame by riding backwards upon a black ram, reciting:

Here I am
Riding upon a black ram
Like a whore as I am
And for my crincum crancum

> *Have lost my bincum bancum*
> *And for my tail's game*
> *Have done this worldly shame;*
> *Therefore I pray you Mr Steward, let me have my land again*

Thereby, so the story goes, they might regain the copyhold of their late husband's farm. (Copyholds were contingent upon legitimate descent.)

The ceremony was admitted to being something of a rarity when first written up in 1684, but the story gained currency from *The Spectator* in the 18th century, embellished with such entertaining detail as to strain credibility. Nonetheless the story continues to be repeated.

🍁 ENGLEFIELD

Englefield lies six miles west of Reading. The name is first attested in the Anglo-Saxon Chronicle for AD 871, when a battle was fought on the hill above the village, marking an important victory by King Alfred over the Danes. The original meaning isn't certain but Anglefield, indicating settlement by the Angles, or Engla feld meaning English Field became Englefield over time.

The single road through the village is known as The Street. The outlying farms and cottages make up a very small part of the 14,000-acre Englefield Estate, the hub of which is the Elizabethan mansion, the residence of Conservative MP Richard Benyon and his family. Previous occupants of Englefield House include the original owner, Sir Francis Englefield, the Earl of Essex, Sir Francis Walsingham and Sir Henry Benyon, Lord Lieutenant of Berkshire. Each played an important part in the history of Englefield.

The house overlooks the deer park. On summer weekends cricket matches are played in the park, which is also the scene of other activities such as concerts, flower shows and equestrian events. The pleasure gardens, with a wonderful display of rhododendrons and azaleas in the spring, are open to the public. The house has been the film location for a number of movies, including *X-Men: First Class*, *The King's Speech*, and *Great Expectations*.

St Mark's church rests in a well-kept churchyard. The memorial on the left before entering the church is dedicated to the large number of children who died, and for 'merciful deliverances' during two measles epidemics in 1890 and 1893. The church contains some interesting relics. A stone figure of a knight and a wooden effigy of a lady are both 13th century, whilst the canopied memorial to Thomas Englefield is now used as a communion table. In May

2017 the sister of the Duchess of Cambridge, Pippa Middleton, married financier James Matthews at the church and a reception was held at Englefield House.

The Church of England primary school of 1865 was saved from closure in the early 1970s by merging with children from Sulham and Tidmarsh schools. At one time, the numbers were as few as 17, but in the early part of the century 126 pupils were taught in the original small school. A scholar of that day tells of pupils being sent to look at the date inscribed on the wall of the cottage opposite the shop to see how many yards there are in a mile, namely 1760, the date the cottage was built.

There is no public house in the village but a thriving social club exists to satisfy the thirsts of the local population and those from outside the area, and serves the club's very own Englefield Village Ale. The club, built in 1880 was originally a reading room for men only but despite its Victorian exterior it has been completely modernised inside and women are now welcome.

Englefield Garden Centre and the village's Five a Day Market Garden can also be found in the centre of the village. The latter was founded in 2009 and is a community initiative selling seasonal produce and working closely with schools and groups to educate people on growing produce, healthy eating and sustainability. The Stores and Tea Room are another popular attraction for the village and are well-known for the delicious cakes.

✿ ETON WICK & BOVENEY

Eton Wick lies on the north bank of the Thames immediately west of that most famous of English public schools, Eton College. To the north-west can be seen the cooling towers of Slough Trading Estate and to the south-east the facade of historic Windsor Castle. The exact beginning the village is not known, though by the early 13th century it was an established community known simply as The Wick. Archaeologists excavating in a field opposite the church in 1984 discovered Bronze Age pottery, bones and flints and pinpointed a burial mound and long barrow, indicating occupation in the late Stone Age.

For at least seven centuries Eton Wick, in the County of Buckinghamshire, was part of the parish of Eton. With the 1894 Civil Parishs Act Eton Town became an Urban District and the remainder became the civil parish of Eton Wick. Already, however, the village has spread beyond the parish boundary into Boveney, giving rise to a new community known as Boveney New Town though it was more than a mile from the tiny riverside village of Boveney. When

Eton Wick & Boveney Women's Institute was formed in 1933 Eton Wick and Boveney New Town were still separate parishes though they shared the same churches, school and village hall. In 1934 both were taken into the Urban District of Eton and, except for ecclesiastical purposes, the remainder of Boveney was merged with Dorney Parish. It continues so today in Buckinghamshire while in 1974 Eton Wick and Eton Town were incorporated into the Royal Borough of Windsor and Maidenhead and transferred into Berkshire.

From its founding in 1440 the influence of Eton College in the village has been considerable. The Provost was Rector and College Chapel, the parish church. The College was an important landowner and employer and, within living memory, boot and shoe making, tailoring and laundering were undertaken in many village homes. Today many village people work in the boys' houses, laboratories, playing fields and offices. In the past, wives of College masters played a major role in running village welfare and social activities, but this link now seems largely to have been severed.

The oldest building in the village is Bell Farm House, built about 1360 and still with most of its original timber-frame walls. Four more timber-framed houses survive – Saddocks Farm, Crown Farm, Little Common Farm and Long Close.

The foundation stone of the Church of St John the Baptist was laid in August 1866 by Provost Goodford. Prior to this a room of the village school was licensed to hold services. The site for the new church, plus £100, was donated by Queen Victoria. The Methodist Chapel was built in Boveney New Town in 1886, with money raised from subscriptions, under the inspiration of Mrs Tough, a formidable lady who had great influence in the village. In 1964 the Roman Catholic Church of St Gilbert was built opposite the old recreation ground.

The first school was built in 1840 on a site now occupied by the Post Office shop, but by 1880 the schoolroom was so overcrowded as to be 'unwholesome' and the present school was built in 1888 on land given by the Crown, on which Lammas rights were relinquished. The school was enlarged in 1958 and again in 1965.

The Village Hall was given to the inhabitants of Eton Wick and Boveney in 1906 by former Eton College housemaster Edward Littleton Vaughan – a great benefactor to the village who died in 1940. His widow, on her death in 1951, bequeathed a stained-glass window in the village church in memory of her husband.

An important feature of Eton Wick is its Commons and Lammas Lands, the rights of which have been jealously guarded over the years. The term 'lammas' usually applied to meadows used as common pasture after the hay was cut, but here it also embraced the open fields over which the village hayward grazed the horses and cattle after Lammas Day or as soon as harvest had been gathered. In so many parishes these common lands were lost through enclosure, but in the 19th century Eton College as tithe owners, and the Crown, supported the villagers and commoners of Eton Wick in their opposition to the Inclosure Bill which John Penn, Lord of the Manor of Eton and of Stoke Poges, tried to push through Parliament. The defeat of the Bill in 1826, celebrated by the town and village with bonfires and feasting, has enabled farming to survive in Eton Wick.

It is interesting to note that when some Lammas Land was sold in the 19th century to the GWR for the Slough-Windsor branch line, the money paid as compensation for loss of lammas rights was used to buy the old Recreation Ground for the villagers. However, confirmation of the rules and regulations of the Commons and Lammas Lands at the Manor Court held in Eton College Hall in 1948 made it impossible to take such land for building. Lammas rights could not be extinguished, but could be transferred from land needed for development to other land in the village.

In 1965 the Commons and Lammas lands were registered under the Commons Registration Act and this should mean that only by another Act of Parliament can the land be released for building. Further large scale building developments should now be impossible in Eton Wick and the village should be able to retain its rural atmosphere and privacy combining the pleasures of village life with the convenience of its proximity to London and Heathrow Airport, and to the employment and shopping facilities of the large towns surrounding it.

🍁 FIFIELD

Fifield is a small village or hamlet about a mile south of the A308. It is built around a triangle (known to locals as 'the circle') of three roads; Fifield Road, Forest Green Road and Coningsby Lane, with a short 'leg' in each direction before the junction of the roads. Although small, Fifield is an old village being recorded in 1608 as consisting of 12 acres.

Opposite Coningsby Lane is the Old Cottage which dates back to the 17th century, and next to the cottage is Fifield Chapel, a wooden building. The visitor should take a good look at the chapel before turning into Coningsby Lane. This is a narrow lane, much favoured by walkers and their dogs, and horse riders.

Grove Farm House is where, in 1867, the Fifield Village Mission was founded by Thomas Reynolds, the owner of Grove Farm. At first the mission was held in a barn, but later a wooden chapel was built. A later owner of Grove Farm preferred its room to its company so in 1897 the chapel was moved on rollers to its present site. Naturally, everyone turned out to watch this extraordinary feat. Mr Nathanial Micklem of Fifield House paid for the removal.

All the farmland on the right of Coningsby Lane belongs to Coningsby Farm – the farmhouse being opposite Yew Tree Cottage. The farm land on the left belongs either to Grove Farm or, further on, to Ledgers Farm, the farm house of which is in Forest Green Road.

On the corner of the Fifield and Forest Green Roads stands the Braywood Memorial Hall built in memory of those killed in the First World War. Captain Brittain at that time lived opposite at Fifield House and he played a large part in the building of the Hall. There has been a Fifield House since before 1591 when 'William Norreys, Black Rod of the Order of the Garter and Comptroller of Works at Windsor castle, died, aged 68, at his home, the House of Fifield'. It is believed that the present Fifield House, opposite the Fifield Inn, is not built on the site of the original house.

On the left of Fifield Road, after passing the entrance to Deep Meadows, there is a modern estate with a village shop (there were no shops in Fifield until 1955) and then the row of pre-war council houses. Fairview cottage, once two cottages, belonging to the New Lodge Estate, carried the Van De Weyer crest. Back in the early 1950s Diana Dors and her husband, Dennis Hamilton, were frequent visitors here. A few more yards and the visitor is back at the start of Coningsby Lane and has walked (or driven), as do many of the villagers on a fine Sunday afternoon, 'round the circle'.

🍁 FRILSHAM

Frilsham is an unspoilt, secluded village lying alongside Yattendon but now separated by the M4 motorway which cuts through the delightful countryside and beech woods. The little church of St Frideswide, originally Saxon with Norman and later additions, has a rare round churchyard, which indicates pagan origin.

Children from Yattendon CofE Primary School make an annual walk, carrying banners, to the St Frideswide Well where legend has it that the water from the holy well cures the blind. On a beautiful site among the beech woods is the Frilsham Clubroom and sports ground. Close by is a small, popular pub called the Pot Kiln.

Between the villages of Yattendon and Frilsham are some curious and interesting chalk caves, although today they are sadly overgrown.

A camera is a must when visiting this attractive village as there is much to delight the eye.

FINCHAMPSTEAD

The village is blessed with distinct traces of its early history – part of the Roman road from London to Bath, via Silchester, runs right through the parish, marked on the map as the Devil's Highway.

Some walls and the very fine font of St James' Church are the original, possibly Saxon. An oak tree facing the churchyard entrance was planted in 1887, commemorating Queen Victoria's Golden Jubilee.

During 1967 the Warren Lodge Barrows were excavated in Warren Woods. It is estimated that they date between 2000 and 1300 BC. There are two barrows, one is a large Bronze Age bowl and the other possibly the remains of a bell barrow. In recent years, to preserve the barrows, trees have been removed to prevent further root damage and fencing has been placed around the barrows so you can still walk through the grounds to view them, but hopefully it will help to preserve them for the future.

Finchampstead

Located in St James' Church tower is the beacon that is lit on special occasions. It was lit for the Millennium, for the Queen's 90th birthday in 2016 and on 11th November 2018 to commemorate the end of the First World War.

The Queen's birthday celebrations in Finchampstead village included over 300 parishioners who toasted her health whilst eating birthday cake and watching Berkshire Bedlam Morris Men dancing. On this day the Queen lit a beacon in Windsor to launch a chain of more than 1,000 beacons throughout the country to mark her birthday. The Finchampstead beacon was en-route.

The Ridges, National Trust property since 1913, commands a view over the Blackwater Valley to Hindhead, south-west to Cottingham Clump, and west to Inkpen Beacon, now obscured by tree growth. Finchamstead Ridges was owned by the Walter family, then owners of *The Times* newspaper but, following financial difficulties, the estate was broken up. Thanks to a group of local people, who raised the money by local subscription, it was then gifted to the National Trust. To these Ridges Henry VII is said to have ridden with his son Prince Arthur, to meet Catherine of Aragon after her arrival in England, as the Prince's bride. Spanish custom forbade a bride to be seen by the groom until after the marriage ceremony, but Catherine lifted her veil to face Arthur. Little did that young Spanish girl know what lay ahead of her during her eventful and tragic life in England.

Finchampstead WI holds monthly meetings in the Memorial Hall in the village. During 2018 Finchampstead WI celebrated the centenary of their first meeting. One of the members of the WI created a wonderful new banner to mark the occasion and many celebrations were held to mark this special event. The ladies of the WI planted a copper beech tree as a living and lasting memory of this occasion in the Memorial Park.

The Memorial Hall in Finchampstead is well used for birthday celebrations, weddings and other large gatherings. Quiz nights, sports activities, the Finches Pre-School, the Friendly Finches Group and the RSPB meetings are also held in the hall as it has excellent facilities and a stage that can accommodate productions and demonstrations. The social club is alongside the main hall with bar facilities and outside seating to enable spectators to view the cricket matches.

🍁 GRAZELEY

Grazeley village was part of the Kingdom of Wessex in the time of King Arthur. In 1086 William the Conqueror held Hartley Dummer, and early history from then centres on three Manors in Hartley, Diddenham and Grazeley, which was variously spelt Greyshull and Griesley, and formed part of the Manor of Sulhamstead Abbots. In the 13th century, the Manor of Grazeley came into the possession of Reading Abbey and a Luke de Grazeley also held land. The rent in 1539 was £9.15s.10d. per annum and in 1541 when the land was granted to Sir John Williams, the rent due to the Crown was £19.11s.2d.

In 1525, during the reign of Henry VIII, a Samuel Woodcock lived at Moor Place Hartley, and Woodcock Lane exists to this day. Samuel Woodcock's daughter, Mary Spiers, left money to enable local children to be taught to read the Holy Bible and the school still benefits from the bequest. In 1834 a Charity School was built beyond Gravelly Bridge, as a result of a sermon preached by the Reverend G. Hume, to carry out the terms of Mary Spiers' will. The present Parochial Church School was built by Mr Merry of Highlands in 1860 to replace the original, and he also endowed 20 boys with boots and 20 girls with cloaks, the buttons being marked 'G.S.'. Money was also provided by Mr Merry for a Nursing Trust.

The New Parish of Grazeley was established in 1860, due to the efforts again of the Reverend G. Hume of Shinfield who was concerned at the long distances his parishioners had to travel to his church in Shinfield. With local help, particularly that of Mr Merry, he raised the necessary funds to build Holy Trinity Church. Mr B. Ferry, a famous church architect, was engaged in 1849 and the completed flintstone church was consecrated by Samuel Wilberforce, Bishop of Oxford, on 18 September 1850. The east window, by the firm of O'Connor, showing the crucifixion and the four evangelists, was dedicated to the memory of the Reverend Hume, who died in 1845. This window is mentioned in the late John Betjeman's *Murray's Berkshire Architectural Guide*.

Edward VII acquired Hartley Court sometime during the late 1890s or early 1900s and it is remembered that one of his favourites, to whom he granted the title of Lady de Bath, better known as Lillie Langtry or the Jersey Lily, the actress, lived in Hartley Court for some years before her death.

Mary Mitford, author of *Our Village* whose father bought Grazeley Court, after winning £20,000 in the Irish Sweepstake, wrote 'wandered down a winding lane amidst green meadows, all alive with cattle, sheep and beautiful lambs in the spring'. Grazeley Court was rebuilt by Dr Mitford, renamed Bertram House and is now sadly demolished, but Mary Mitford could still take her long walks today and see and write about these features, even perhaps, come across the brown snakes which startled her.

Basildon Park

Caversham Court Gardens

Cookham Dean War Memorial

Hampstead Norreys well

Datchet

Hamstead Marshall church and gate piers

Hungerford

Littlewick Green

The Kennet and Avon Canal, Newbury

Haymaking, Pinkneys Green

Abbey Gateway, Reading

Chapel of Christ the Redeemer at Culham Court, Remenham

Shinfield Infant School

Sonning

St Denys' church, Stanford Dingley

View across Streatley Warren

Old Abbey buildings (previously Douai School), Upper Woolhampton

The Wargrave and Shiplake Regatta, Wargrave

West Ilsley

🍁 GREAT SHEFFORD

Great Shefford village lies in the Lambourn Valley in the North Wessex Downs AONB. Its name comes from the Old English for sheep ford. Half a mile downstream is the hamlet of East Shefford, while on a ridge two miles to the south is the hamlet of Shefford Woodlands. The parishes of Great and East Shefford, also known as West and Little Shefford, were united ecclesiastically in 1926 and civilly in 1972.

A Saxon graveyard from the 5th and 6th centuries was discovered in East Shefford in 1890 during construction of the Lambourn Valley Railway. Excavations at the time and in 1912 revealed that the site had about 95 graves of men, women and children aged from 0 to 70. Saxon and Roman objects buried with them included a sword, spear-heads, knives, buckles, brooches, beads and glass vessels, indicating a relatively prosperous community.

The tiny, redundant church in East Shefford may be late Saxon. A small round-headed window cut into medieval paintings is evidence of its early origins. East Shefford manor was once owned by the Fettiplace family and in the church there is a beautiful 15th-century alabaster tomb of Sir Thomas Fettiplace in his armour, with his Portuguese wife Beatrice beside him.

St Mary's, the parish church, has a picturesque setting overlooking the river and downs. At least 800 years old, it has flint walls and one of only two round towers in Berkshire. The south doorway dates from about 1200 and has a pointed arch with zig-zag ornamentation, while several small, lancet windows

Great Shefford

are from the 13th century. Other, larger windows were inserted in the 14th and 15th centuries when Great Shefford manor was owned by the Kentwood family. It was also during this time that an octagonal top was added to the tower. The church has remained essentially unchanged since then. Restoration in 1870 added aptly-chosen inscriptions to all the internal walls; one above the organ reads, 'I will praise Thee and Tby faithfulness O God Playing upon An Instrument of musick'. In 1883 the artist and designer, NHJ Westlake, designed paintings and stained-glass for the east end.

Glimpses of parish life in the 18th century come from published writings. One particular rector, the Rev Richard Forster, kept the parish registers meticulously, unusually recording the age and cause of death of those he buried. This revealed that although many inhabitants succumbed to consumption and fever, others lived into their eighties. When he had ten years of records, Forster wrote a letter to the Royal Society that was printed in their Philosophical Transactions. He demonstrated that the number of people in Shefford was increasing, as it was in the country as a whole. Another letter of Forster's assured readers that, contrary to popular belief, the bite of slow-worms was harmless, as he had seen a Shefford thatcher and his wife both suffer no ill effects from being bitten. Later in the century the case of Richard Langford of Great Shefford was cited in medical journals. He had the rare and very unfortunate distinction of catching smallpox twice, once when he was a month old and again in his fifties.

1830 was a momentous year in Great Shefford. On a snowy February afternoon in the harshest winter for nearly a century, a crowd of two hundred gathered outdoors to listen to Thomas Russell, a ranter, or travelling Primitive Methodist preacher. His preaching so impressed one couple that they built Berkshire's first Primitive Methodist meeting-house. Alarmingly, the lord of the manor, the Marquis of Downshire, briefly threatened cottagers with eviction if they attended meetings. The third wet summer in a row followed the harsh winter; harvests failed, bread was expensive and farming work was scarce. Simmering discontent culminated with rioting in November, when mobs of men went from farm to farm seeking higher wages, breaking threshing machines and demanding money. Afterwards three Shefford men were sentenced to transportation. Despite petitions organised by local farmers, parish officials and tradesmen the men were deported to Australia.

Support for the Primitive Methodists remained strong and in 1833 when Russell left Berkshire for Birmingham, the newly-formed Shefford Circuit had a membership of 1,300 and supported fifteen missionaries. The Primitive Methodists were soon joined by Wesleyan Methodists who built chapels in both Great Shefford and Shefford Woodlands. By 1911 the chapel in Shefford Woodlands was redundant and it was converted into St Stephen's church to save churchgoers the walk down the hill to St Mary's. The interior is notable today for its extensive wood carvings, especially for memorials to men who died fighting in the Great War.

The village's chapels have now gone, as have the mill and railway. A few thatched cottages remain, but in Church Street two were lost to a fire in 1879 and another six in 1908. On the second occasion a fire that started in the thatch of a barn on the north side of the road spread rapidly to two adjoining cottages, and then a brisk breeze blew the flames across the road to four more. Fortunately there was plenty of water in the river and villagers formed a chain for passing along buckets of water. However, despite the best efforts of the Lambourn and Hungerford fire brigades the cottages were destroyed and the cottagers lost most of their possessions. Today, two timber-framed Tudor houses remain in Church Street: Gable House and Hillside. Gable House was formerly the Greyhound, a traditional inn traceable back to Elizabethan times.

For centuries arable agriculture was the mainstay of life in Shefford. Whilst the land is still farmed, a number of the farm buildings have been converted into business units. Many of today's 1,000 or so inhabitants commute a considerable distance to work, while an increasing number work from home. Facilities include a primary school, pre-school, shop, post office, petrol station, car repair garage and The Swan public house.

🍁 GREENHAM

The ancient parish of Greenham on the south-east of Newbury has changed over the last thirty years. This is partly from necessity, partly due to government policy for building due to national housing shortages and lastly due to change of circumstance. The avenue of poplar trees leading towards Newbury racecourse was deemed dangerous after one fell during high winds in 2014 and was found to be hollow. To date, eight trees have had to be felled. New trees have been planted to take the place of all the trees. They have yet to reach maturity but will, hopefully, look as splendid as the originals in time.

The old bridges over the canal from Greenham Mill to Hambridge Road have been replaced by more substantial structures giving easier access for prams and cycles with the use of ramps rather than steps, thus allowing more people to enjoy the peaceful surroundings along the canal bank. At Hambridge Road, turning towards the racecourse, a new steep road bridge over the railway leads to a large housing development spreading towards Thatcham on one side and enveloping the racecourse on the other. Blocks of flats replace the golf course and original car park. This is to comply with government legislation that each council should be responsible for building a certain number of houses needed because of an acute shortage of housing nationwide. The racecourse is still a focal point for visitors and there is improved parking for coaches and cars. However, many events have to end earlier in the evening to avoid disrupting residents in the new housing.

Greenham church, once isolated, is now part of a community of more development with an estate built along Water Lane as far as Pyle Hill. The green space opposite the church awaits more development with planning permission for 72 further houses to be built in the near future.

With the advent of so much new housing it would seem that Greenham is slowly disappearing but there is the former American Air Base. This was the scene of much activity during and after the Second World War, notably as home to cruise missiles from 1981. This attracted the Peace Camp protestors, mostly women, who camped outside the base, making their cause national news and dividing the local people between those in favour of action and those against the disruption caused by continuous protests. It was 1991 before the last missile was removed and a battle continued between the Ministry of Defence who wished to retain control of the Base and the local council who wanted the land returned to the people. It was not until 1997 that the land was bought back for £7 million by the newly formed Greenham Trust and two further years before the fences were fully removed and the runways broken up, thereby allowing cattle to graze on the common and wildlife to become re-established. The missile bunkers remain a closed area. A memorial has been made for the Greenham Peace Women and there is an area of commercial units near the former main gate that includes the Old Chapel Textile Centre which houses the National Needlework Archive and the "Country Wife" mural. This piece of textile art was commissioned for the 1951 Festival of Britain and the various crafts being carried out by ladies in the centre of the piece were made by members of the WI. Prior to coming to Greenham this mural hung at the WI's Denman College until late 2009. It can be viewed on days when the Centre is open. Finally, the Control Tower has opened as a café, encouraging people to use the Common and study the wildlife on the many walks available – a welcome escape from all the housing development. In 2015 the Common, including the area around the missile bunkers, was used in the making of a *Star Wars* film. It has also been used for a *Top Gear* programme. The main event held in 2017 was the community production entitled "Greenham – One Hundred Years of War and Peace," a free open air event staged for two evenings portraying both one hundred years of the history of the Common and the 20th anniversary of the Greenham Trust.

The Common is now managed by the Berks, Bucks and Oxon Wildlife Trust (BBOWT) on behalf of the Greenham Trust, ensuring the preservation of the habitat and wildlife. BBOWT also manage Bowdown Woods, just a short distance along Burys Bank Road, where well-marked walks provide year-round interest through the nature reserve.

Although large areas of Greenham have been lost to development and more is planned for the future, there is still plenty of opportunity to enjoy the beauty of nature following the return of the common land to the people.

☘ HAMPSTEAD NORREYS

There has been a settlement for more than 2000 years in the wooded valley on the upper reaches of the River Pang that is now known as Hampstead Norreys.

The village and outlying hamlets were recorded in the Domesday Book in 1086, when it was known as Hanstede, meaning farm settlement in early English. As the village grew it prospered and flourished and in the Middle Ages was renamed Hampstead Sifrewast.

The village nestles on the banks of the River Pang, which is a winterbourne chalk stream, and the fast running water, together with the local woodlands and good grazing, have attracted people for thousands of years. There are Bronze Age burial mounds in Park Wood, an Iron Age hillfort close to the village, as well as sites of Roman villas and settlements on the slopes above the river.

St Mary's Church is situated in the very centre of the village and has, over the centuries, played a central and pivotal role in village life. The church has stood on the same site since the 12th century and has witnessed many changes during its long 900-year history. The building is substantially 12th century but additions and alterations were made in the 15th and 19th centuries.

The opening of the railway to Didcot, in 1882, had a huge impact on village life. Previously, the movement of goods and people had been restricted to the pace of the horse and cart. Now, for the first time, people were able to visit nearby towns and villages in a fraction of the time and a large array of goods could be delivered by the freight trains using the line as they travelled between Southampton, Newbury and Didcot. Sadly, the line closed in 1965.

The Second World War airfield, which was built in 1940 on a plateau above the village, also brought great changes. Originally built as an RAF Bomber Command Operational Training Unit, it was used from the mid 1940s until hostilities ceased in 1945. It was home to several squadrons of Wellington bombers as well as Tiger Moths, Whitleys and Horsa Gliders. Many pilots were trained here in preparation for the D-Day landings.

Things seem to happen in 'threes' in Hampstead Norreys for there have been three schools (1848, 1955 and 1987), and three village halls. The first opened in 1918 after the end of the First World War and was named the Memorial Hall, in memory of those who went from the village and never returned. The second opened in 1970 and was a pre-fab construction. The present hall opened in the mid 1980s. There have also been three pubs, the White Hart, New Inn and the Railway Hotel.

Today the village has a population of about 800 and is a vibrant and pleasant place to live. Situated in an Area of Outstanding Natural Beauty there are lots of beautiful walks across the fields and woods surrounding the village. The school is thriving and the White Hart is a great place to visit for a drink or meal. There is also a wonderful community shop and café which is manned mainly by volunteers and is an excellent place for people to meet and greet over a cup of coffee.

There was great excitement in 2017 when the village was chosen as a finalist for the national competition of Village of the Year. Over 400 villages nationwide took part, so to get down to the last four villages was considered very creditable. The judges commented that it was the thriving community spirit which was considered outstanding and the prime reason that the village did so well.

❦ HAMSTEAD MARSHALL

Hamstead Marshall lies four miles west of Newbury, on the Berkshire-Hampshire border. The railway marks its northern edge, and the River Enborne forms the southern boundary. The eastern and western boundaries used to follow no discernible topographical logic, suggesting ancient origin, but in 1991 these were realigned to suit modern bureaucracy. In total the parish covers 750 hectares (1,850 acres).

Most of the village lies within the North Wessex Downs Area of Outstanding Natural Beauty. Farmland and woodland predominate, but the jewel of the parish landscape is Hamstead Park, spreading over several hundred acres, with copses, Saxon fish ponds, a medieval park pale, the site of the former manor house and its Regency successor. The park is privately owned, but a public footpath running through is popular with walkers.

The River Kennet flows across the top of the parish, as does the Kennet and Avon Canal. Hamstead has a lock and a (former) mill on the waterway and, with Hamstead Park close by, the area attracts visitors in good weather. Holiday barges and a horse-drawn excursion boat pass through regularly.

Although a Saxon village once clustered near the church, this disappeared as settlement spread south. Houses are now scattered between five separate hamlets: in the north, around the church, mill and lock; in the far south around Holtwood; to the west at Chapel Corner; centrally at Ash Tree Corner (the largest); and lastly, two or three houses still stand on Irish Hill, a remote, windy site which until the 1920s had its own cottage community and a small whiting factory. In all Hamstead has around 120 homes, most owner-occupied.

There's been almost no development in the village since the 1970s; new-build applications are usually turned down on the grounds that they would constitute forbidden infill. Around 16 of the houses and barns are Grade II listed. Some council houses were built around Ash Tree Corner, but sales in the late 20th century have brought Hamstead's social housing stock down to 17.

The village name dates from the 12th century, when it was the homestead of William, Earl of Pembroke and Earl Marshal to four successive kings: Henry II, Richard the Lionheart, John and Henry III. The office and its royal connections continued to be associated with the village, and Edward III is known to have visited his Earl Marshal here more than once. All that remains of the Earl Marshal's castle is an earthwork within a private garden, but it is a scheduled historic monument.

In 1620 the manor of Hamstead Marshall was acquired by the Craven family, with successive barons and earls owning the entire village. In the 1660s the first earl built a magnificent palace on the edge of the park. It burnt down in 1718 and all that remains today of its grandeur are eight pairs of Grade I listed gatepiers and some walling that encloses the old mansion grounds. Some pairs are still attached to the wall; others stand adrift in fields.

Recently some building work uncovered several yards of a mysterious tunnel running northwards from the mansion site. Brick-lined, and wide enough for a man to stand, it was dated by archaeologists as 17th century, but its purpose is unknown. Older villagers say that it's one of several, all now closed up for safety.

Hamstead was the seat of the Craven earldom, although the family owned several other estates. However, a series of misfortunes forced a progressive selling-up from the 1930s onwards. The last and biggest sale – 540 hectares (1,336 acres) of the village including the family seat in Hamstead Park – took place in 1984 following the death of the 7th Earl of Craven. The family is now in Sussex, although the 9th earl continues to own Morewood, a house and sporting estate of around 300 acres in the village.

St Mary's Church began as a chapel of Kintbury, but acquired its own first rector in 1241. It's small, and relatively unspoilt. From the early 19th century the living was often combined with that of Enborne, and today both parishes are grouped with Inkpen, Kintbury, West Woodhay and Combe in a joint benefice. From the 1830s to the 1930s there was also a Congregational chapel, which gave Chapel Corner its name.

Hamstead also had a school until the 1930s. When it closed the building became the village hall, and it still serves this purpose. In addition to private hire it is used for a pre-school, for village socials, assorted classes (oil painting, yoga, dancing, keep fit, dog-training), garden society meetings, band practice, the bonfire night party and as the local polling station. A regular feature of recent years has been the monthly community market, which attracts custom from well beyond the village for artisan bread, cheese, home-made cakes and preserves.

The White Hart Inn served the village for well over three centuries before closing in 2015. A casualty of economic and legal changes, it now looks set to be turned into housing. The loss of the White Hart has reduced Hamstead's stock of jobs, but some employment is provided by the Organic Research Centre (ORC), which since 1980 has been run from Elm Farm, the foremost farm in the village since Victorian times. The ORC is an active participant in village life, hosting many events, projects and meetings. Next door, the Dogs Trust at Plumb's Farm takes in and re-homes unwanted dogs.

Scattered geography is challenging for social cohesion, but the parish council, St Mary's church council, the village hall committee, the website and village newsletter all contribute to a flourishing, connected community in Hamstead Marshall.

🍁 HAWLEY

In the centre of the bridge, over the River Blackwater, the boundaries of three counties meet; Berkshire, Surrey and to the south Hampshire, in which lies the parish of Hawley, (in the old records spelt Halle). Formerly an outer tything of Yateley, it was just a collection of small farms and cottages reached by gravel tracks and surrounded by vast open desolate stretches of heather-covered common land, or great wooded areas – part of the Forest of Windsor.

Sir Francis Dashwood, notorious politician and statesman of the 1740s and founder member of the Hell Fire Club, stabled his many racehorses at Hawley House and used the house as a resting place when he was on one of his wild racing sprees. The clock on the stable block is dated 1743. At the turn of the 19th century, Field Marshal Sir Linthorn Simmonds resided in this house. He had had a brilliant military career and was 'a real Christian gentleman'. He helped with the arrangements to bring the ex-Empress Eugenie of France to come and live nearby. They were great friends and the Empress kindly allowed the villagers to hold their Horticultural Shows in the grounds of Farnborough Hill. Few people know that in 1922 Princess Mary and her husband Viscount Lascelles spent a fortnight of their honeymoon in Hawley, at the home of Lord Revelstoke.

Another resident was Admiral Sir Charles Denniston Burney, who invented the paravane (a device for protecting ships against mines) which brought him a great fortune. He also helped design the airships R100 and R101.

By far the oldest part of Hawley parish is the village of Blackwater. At one time it was called Duddas brook, the explanation being that 'dhu' means black, 'dwr' is water. The Saxons would no doubt have spoken these words phonetically and they would have become Dudda – Blackwater.

For centuries the famous Blackwater Cattle Fair was held annually in November on the wide open spaces of commonland around the great cross-roads. It was listed in Old Moore's Almanac as the largest cattle fair in the south of England. Horses would be brought up from the New Forest, with them came the blacksmiths with their bags of shoes and anvils. Some of the cattle were driven hundreds of miles from Wales and the West Country, moving about ten miles a day. At the fair travelling musicians supplied the entertainment, while cheap-jacks and gypsies sold their wares. After two days of buying and selling came riotous jollification at the Pleasure Fair, the stalls and booths being set out along the roadside.

It seems that Blackwater has always been well provided with drinking places, being situated on the highroad from London to Exeter. It boasted two ale-houses and three large coaching inns in days gone by, welcome havens where passengers could rest while the horses were changed. Travelling was a perilous experience and there was need of the formidable blunderbuss carried by the guard, as highwaymen and robbers roaming the wild desolate heathland often relieved the passengers of their money and jewellery. In 1746 a reward of £200 was offered for the capture of a highwayman who held up and robbed a mail-coach at Blackwater.

The coming of the railway in 1849 opened up a whole new way of life and before the First World War there was a staff of fourteen men and a boy at Blackwater, so it must have been a very busy station.

Over 100 years ago Hawley contained many elegant houses set in beautiful grounds. The pine-filled healthy air attracted people to settle in the area and the village folk were employed in the stables, gardens and in domestic service; the church was well supported and in the local school a very high standard was always found when HM Inspector made his annual visit to examine the children in all subjects – indeed in 1895 Hawley was the first school in the locality not to be inspected, yet full grants were given. The following words penned in 1894 are as appropriate today as they have been throughout the years, 'the popularity of Hawley School continues to grow in favour, not only with parents in this parish but with our neighbours also.'

Inevitably the village grew in size as the years passed by, and since the Second World War the London overspill has greatly increased the population and diminished the fields and open spaces. Due to many residents having connections with the military establishments nearby we now have a 'moving population' – people come and people go, but Hawley goes on for ever.

🍁 HERMITAGE AND OARE

Hermitage lies in a wooded area a few miles north of Newbury on the B4009. It now has a population of 2000, with 800 houses. In comparison, the recorded numbers in 1870 were a population of 434 with 95 houses.

The village is served by one shop/post office in the High Street. Sadly the butcher's closed in 2017. The Fox and the White Horse public houses are still in business. In addition there is a garage. The garden centre has been refurbished to include a café, and the buildings on the same site comprise a garden machinery sales and repairs shop, clothing outlets and various smaller businesses.

Approaching Hermitage from the west are Denison Barracks. Formerly the base of the Royal School of Military Survey, it is now home to the headquarters of the army's 77th Brigade.

The Church of Holy Trinity was built in 1835, and the attractive lychgate was the gift of Colonel West in 1947 as a memorial to his wife.

The primary school has been considerably enlarged to cope with the growing population and now has 190 pupils.

Within the last twelve years two new housing estates have been built – Forest Edge at the north end on the site of the old brick works/industrial site, and Hermitage Green to the south near what was the old railway station. Both estates are well off the B4009. Along the main road through the village, bungalows have been demolished and replaced by large houses, and many more houses have been extended, leaving very few smaller properties.

Hermitage House has recently been demolished and in its place three large dwellings have been built.

The village hall served the community from 1962 until it was demolished in 2015 and the gap filled by four detached houses. A new village hall was constructed on land to the north of the village beside the Forest Edge housing development. The attractive architect-designed building has two halls and opened for hire in 2015. Behind the hall are a recreation field, a wildflower and nature meadow, and woods which are popular with walkers.

Hermitage still has a bus service to Newbury, and school buses transport pupils to secondary schools. Some older residents can recall catching the train at the station or Pinewood Halt with their families to shop at Newbury before the line was closed in 1967. However, most people now have cars and the traffic has increased considerably, both through the village and on the M4 motorway. Thankfully, Hermitage still has its attractive lanes.

Chapel Lane, named after the long-gone Methodist Chapel is remembered by the name of a dwelling built on the site of the Chapel called 'Cappella' (Italian for chapel). Also in this area is the cottage which D H Lawrence rented when he lived in the village between 1917 and 1918. Joggers take their exercise on the pavements, and there is good walking through the surrounding footpaths and woods.

In contrast to Hermitage, Oare still remains a quiet hamlet. The pretty little church of St Bartholomew is infrequently used, and the redundant farm buildings are now used for commercial purposes.

🍁 HOLYPORT

Situated between Maidenhead and Windsor, Holyport is an attractive hamlet whose principle features are its extensive village green and pond, the surrounding houses of various periods, and the two public houses, the George and the Belgian Arms. The name Holyport refers to its probable status as a market centre controlled by the Church in the early medieval period.

It is believed that there has been a settlement in the area since Roman times, with Roman artefacts found during the building of the M4. There is also evidence of Roman roads in Moneyrow Green and Stud or Sturt Green that are part of Holyport.

The main settlements date from William the Conqueror. In 1208 the ruling manor was Philiberts, owned by Hugh de St Philibert who died in 1248 after which time the estate belonged to the de Cresswell family. During the following centuries the estate changed hands regularly and the house was rebuilt several times. Its most famous visitor was Charles II who called upon Nell Gwynne, whose residence it was for some time. The manor house of Philiberts no longer exists as it was demolished after the First World War. Other important properties still in existence include Chuffs owned by William Chuff in 1426 and Gays owned by John Gay in 1455.

Three more recent properties of note are Bourne Bridge Lodge, The Lodge, and Linden Manor. Bourne Bridge Lodge was the country seat of Sir Robert Sidney during the 19th century. Sir Robert was a descendant of Sir Henry Sidney, Lord Deputy of Ireland during the reign of Queen Elizabeth I.

The Lodge was a family home but it was used in the Second World War to provide rest and recuperation for wounded US service personnel. Following the end of the war it was returned to the family until the estate was sold and the house became a residential nursing home. In the grounds of The Lodge a real tennis court was built in 1889 and is one of the few remaining in the country. It is now a privately owned club with membership by subscription. Linden Manor was once the home of the Marquess of Milford Haven whom Prince Philip visited regularly during his youth.

The name Foxley occurs in some form on several properties in Holyport. The Manor of Foxley was owned by Sir John de Foxley in the 14th century. It left the de Foxley family in the late 15th century. In 1925 the late Col. A. E. Marnham MC, JP bought part of the original de Foxley estate and it stayed in his family until 1976 when the greater part of the estate was split up and sold. The house is now a privately owned residential nursing home.

It was at Cadogan Riding Stables, now Cadogan Close, that Princess Elizabeth and Princess Margaret when children, received riding instruction from the owner, Mr Horace Dayer-Smith. The manager of the stables for some time was the father of Dick Francis, champion rider and thriller writer.

The oldest property on the green is possibly 'Rails' and the derivation of the name may be connected with falcons. It has always been understood that falcons were kept in the house during the 16th century for use by hunting parties from Windsor Castle. The property has been a home since then and has been sympathetically restored and extended in recent years.

A Wesleyan Chapel was built in 1835 on the west side of the green. Before 1835 the congregation had met in an upper room of the Belgian Arms. The congregation vacated the Chapel many years ago and it fell into dereliction until its demolition some years later.

The Belgian Arms has an interesting history. There has been a beer house on the site for over 200 years. The Henley Brewery took it over in 1896 when it was called the Eagle. During the First World War there was a prisoner of war camp in the grounds of Philiberts and the German soldiers marching past the pub on their daily exercise would stop to salute the eagle, a depiction of the Prussian Eagle. The residents objected to this and the name was changed to that of the area where the fiercest fighting was taking place at the time, namely Belgium.

The George has been a public house since the 16th century and an interesting feature of the licence was that the licensee had to be a master butcher. This prevailed until approximately 1970 when the then tenant moved the butchery business to a shop.

The Village Fair has been held on the green on the first Saturday in June of each year since 1946 when fundraising was started to build the Hall. Organised by the War Memorial Hall Fair Committee it raises funds for the Hall and local organisations. The Hall, nearby in Moneyrow Green, was built in 1954 as a tribute to those from Holyport who fell during the Second World War. The War Memorial to the fallen of both wars, built in 1918, is near the pond.

Development has taken place beyond the green with several housing estates and various infilling. The population has more than trebled since the 1960s but the heart of the village has retained its charm, due largely to its status as a conservation area enshrined in 1969.

The Parish Council commissioned a sundial to be built on the green commemorating the start of the third millennium. It reflects the long association of cricket played on the green until traffic conditions made it unviable and Holyport Cricket Club moved to a site behind the Village Hall. The statue shows a cricketer of 1846, his bat representing the 'gnomon' (the part of a sundial that shows the time by casting its shadow). The sundial has been set to tell local sun time for British Summer Time. Built into the plinth is a time capsule containing items selected by children who attended schools within the parish and which suggest how the children wished the Millennium year to be remembered.

⚜ HUNGERFORD

The ancient market town of Hungerford is situated on the western edge of Berkshire a mile or so from both the borders of Hampshire and Wiltshire. It nestles between the North Hampshire Downs and the North Wessex Downs, between the confluence of the Rivers Dun and Kennet.

The town was not mentioned in the Domesday Book of 1086 but is recorded as a settlement in 1109. Inhabitants of the hamlets and villages situated north of the River Kennet were disgruntled at the high taxes imposed on them by the priory of St Frideswide, Oxford, so they crossed the river and built a new settlement from the Bath Road southwards up the valley, known now as the High Street.

In medieval years the inhabitants were clearly ambitious as they made full use of their freedoms granted to them by King Henry III and delivered by Simon de Montfort, the goodly Earl of Leicester and Lord of the Manor.

Soon after, markets and fairs were granted by charters of King Edward I and his son. At this time arable farming was established successfully and even today the 'lynchets' can be seen east of Down Gate. These are 6-acre strips, which was the amount two oxen and a man could plough in a day.

Later, in 1365, the fishing rights were granted to the inhabitants by John O' Gaunt, fourth son of King Edward III. Rightly or wrongly he is still regarded as the town's benefactor and was the action man representing his father in defence of English territories. There is no doubt that these charters were conveyed to the townsfolk but they were lost in the 16th century, which is a whole tale in itself.

The town became legally organised on the appointment of the first Constable John Tuckhill and officers. Richard Lange was the first bailiff in 1458.

There is little evidence of the Hocktide Court until the mid-16th century when the Steward organised jurymen in a formal court to run the civil affairs for the inhabitants for the protection of their valuable privileges and rights. The court was presided over by the Constable of the day to see fair play. This still remains today and the regulations of the court are much the same as they were in 1583.

The commoners are summoned to attend the Hocktide Court in the Town Hall at 8 o'clock on the morning of the second Tuesday after Easter.

First the regulations of the court proceedings are read over by the Steward, then names are called over and a jury is appointed and sworn. Those who fail to attend the court are

Hungerford town badge

fined. The accounts for the year are presented by the Constable, new officers are appointed and the rules are read and approved. The court is dismissed by the Steward 'upon another summons'. The Constable invites the court to join the traditional luncheon, these days held in the Corn Exchange.

At 9 o'clock, before the court assembles, the constable presents to the 'Tuttimen' (tythingmen) their staves of office decked with spring flowers, and sends them on their way with the words 'god speed and do your duty well'. They are to visit all commoners' houses to collect head pennies or a tip for keeping the peace during their year in office. Where there is no money in the household the Tuttimen have to make do with a kiss. In recognition of the inhabitant's loyalty to King William III, Prince of Orange, oranges are given out to all by the Orangeman, who accompanies the Tuttimen during the day that finishes at 9 o'clock in the evening.

We return to the Constable's luncheon where a traditional five-course lunch is served with ale and watercress to 180 commoners and guests. The Steward runs the lunch, first inviting the vicar to say grace, and when all are seated the Ale Tasters are invited to pronounce on the ale. In reply they taste the ale and say 'we declare a goodly brew'. After the lunch and plates are cleared away the punch makers bring in large bowls of steaming Plantagenet Punch made from a secret recipe. The Constable is invited to propose the traditional toasts 'to the Queen, Duke of Lancaster' and with all remaining on their feet a second toast 'to the immortal memory of John O 'Gaunt'. Three further speeches and toasts follow. Finally the Steward closes lunch by asking for the tables to be removed and the Blacksmith to prepare for 'Shoeing the Colts'. This requires all new guests to the luncheon to be caught, usually up ended, and a nail driven into the shoe until the unhappy incumbent shouts 'punch.' The blacksmith then withdraws the nail and presents this and the horseshoe to the guest in exchange for £5.

All then are invited to attend the Three Swans Hotel for anchovies on toast to be washed down by more drinks. The day is complete when the Tuttimen return having completed their duties to the Three Swans.

There is Court Leet the following Friday and the new Constable and Steward lead the officers and the commoners, along with the organisations of the town, to church accompanied by the Town Band. The Constable dismisses the parade on its return to the Town Hall and invites all to slake their thirst in the Three Swans.

During the many centuries there have been many threats to rights and privileges enjoyed by the commoners. Each has been fought off by wise and determined officers and commoners of the Hocktide Court.

At the same time the canal builders and the representatives of Isambard Kingdom Brunel in 17th and 18th centuries found more than their match when planning to build first the canal and then the railway through the town. Each in turn was built and opened for business at their expense but on the terms of Hungerford.

In November 1688 it was the Constable John Butler who welcomed William, Prince of Orange to Hungerford. He was married to King James II's eldest daughter Mary, both Protestants. Her Catholic father had fled to France, ousted from the throne, and it was in Hungerford where the commissioners of James II met with the Prince of Orange to negotiate terms with him to ascend the throne. This was achieved at meetings in the Bear Hotel. It was settled that he should share the crown equally with Mary and that he should forego the king's prerogative, which made way for the world's first parliamentary democracy.

In the late 19th century, Parliament formed a local parish and district council to speak for the inhabitants and Hungerford elected its first parish and district council to represent local government. Soon after, the Town & Manor of Hungerford Charity was pressed into the Charity Commission, much to the distress of the Constable and Feoffees (old trustees) now subject to a triennial election. Nevertheless, the charity remained for the benefit of the inhabitants of the town.

During the First and Second World War Hungerford was a centre of much military activity. Encampments were set up as a good central assembly area for troops for deployment to continental Europe. In the Second World War 55,000 British, US and Canadian parachute assault regiments were assembled for deployment by RAF Transport Command aircraft and gliders to Normandy for D-Day and later to Arnhem. On 10th August 1944 General Eisenhower, Commander of Allied Forces in Europe, visited Common Port Down to meet and decorate returning men of the US 101st paras.

After the Second World War, and during the years of rationing and austerity, little happened as there was no money. Later in the fifties however, there was significant house building, mainly by the council but also private housing and industrial development.

All went well until 1986 when all four of the main employers in the town were moved or closed down. However, after a major effort to find new business accommodation Charnham Park was proposed to the district council for planning consent. This worked and the business park now returns sales of £100 million annually.

The traditional trade in antiques and the supporting services still is a major feature of Hungerford, together with a thriving retail high street which provides most services required. For public transport there are fast services by rail to London and the West Country and local bus services give an adequate service around town and to the outlying villages.

Hungerford retains over 60 diverse sporting clubs and other organisations to meet everyone's requirements, including a public library.

Hungerford has a privately owned and managed Town Hall, a Parish Council known as Town Council. The Parish should have a chairman but there is a Mayor of the Parish Council. How about that to be different?

🍁 HURLEY

The ancient village of Hurley is halfway between London and Oxford, being 55 miles from both by river. It has been occupied since the Bronze Age. The Domesday Book (1086) records a church at Hurley, a manor with 25 villeins, 12 cottagers, 10 serfs, 19 ploughs, a mill, 2 fisheries, 20 acres of meadow, a wood for swine and about 120 acres of arable land. William the Conqueror removed the Saxon owner Asgar and conferred the property upon the Norman Baron Geoffrey de Mandeville. In 1976, the villagers bought this ancient lordship of the manor for £2,500. A wall plaque and a hand-inscribed book record the story and names of subscribers. The plaque can be seen on the wall by the graveyard entrance.

The Hurley Priory was founded by de Mandeville for a cell of monks from the Benedictine Abbey at Westminster in 1086 and was endowed with the advowsons (patronage) of many of the surrounding churches. The remains of the Priory, dissolved by Henry VIII in 1536, centre round the church, much reduced in size and known today as St Mary the Virgin. The original cloisters and monks' dormitories can be identified by the stone stringing and blocked up windows and doors. The enormous Tithe Barn, converted into a private residence in 1950, and unusually well preserved dovecote date from the mid-13th century.

One of Hurley's noteworthy mansions no longer exists. After the Dissolution of the Monasteries, Hurley's monastic estate was purchased by John Lovelace in 1545 and his family became Lords of the Manor. They built Ladye Place mansion on the site of the ruined Priory and in its crypt, the 1688 Glorious Revolution was plotted. The 3rd Lord John Lovelace was a staunch supporter of the cause to place on the throne of England the protestant Prince of Orange and his Stuart consort, William III and Mary. Fellow aristocratic conspirators

St Mary the Virgin church, Hurley

to the plot are said to have entered the crypt by way of underground tunnels
that led from the river to avoid detection. This Elizabethan mansion became
derelict and was pulled down in 1838. Much later, a smaller house also named
Ladye Place was erected near the church. All that remains today of the original
Ladye Place mansion is the crypt, which is located on the old monastic estate
grounds, now split into private plots within the ancient monastic walls.

Another historic house is Hurley House located on the High Street. It is 17th
century and was probably built as the dower house to the original Ladye Place
mansion. The current Manor House, opposite Hurley House and now divided into
separate freeholds, is early 20th century and was built for Dame Irene Vanbrugh,
reputedly in the style of the famous British architect, Edwin Lutyens. Dame Irene
was a leading name in British theatre for more than 50 years. She and her husband,
Dion Boucicault Jr, an actor and stage director, are buried in Hurley's churchyard
of St Mary the Virgin. During the Second World War, American troops were
stationed at Hurley and the Manor House was a base for OSS operations. The
village inhabitants have long known of a connection with America during this
time, but more details emerged in 2013 when classified CIA documents were

released. Hurley's Manor House estate, code name VICTOR, was requisitioned in July 1943 and was a centre of communication and intelligence activity. More than 160 personnel were accommodated in temporary buildings on Manor House grounds, resulting in compensation for local farmers and improved roads. Also, on the High Street adjacent to Hurley House, are three 17th-century almshouses. These are still in the trusteeship of the Hurley Church Estate and were completely restored in 1969.

Some two miles from the village is the old mansion house of Hall Place and the history of Hall Place, originally known as La Halle, is associated with that of the village of Hurley. The earliest records show that La Halle was in existence in 1234 as Hurley's manor house. It was owned by John de Hurley and his descendants until 1372 when it was acquired by the Hurley Priory. It was then surrendered, with the Priory, to the Crown during the Dissolution of the Monasteries. After various owners it was purchased in 1728 by a London lawyer, William East. East had the existing early Georgian mansion built and it is now part of the grounds belonging to the Berkshire College of Agriculture, previously the Institute of Grassland and Environmental Research until disbanded in 1992. Just across Henley Road from the College is the Temple Golf Club through which, allegedly, a private driveway was created for exclusive use by King Edward VII's famous mistress, Lillie Langtry, to discreetly reach the nearby now demolished Temple House at Bisham, for their assignations.

Much of the land between the River Thames and the main Henley-Maidenhead road is part of Hurley Farms Ltd, owned and farmed by the Burfitt family, of whom three generations live in the village. The Hurley Lock area is also home to the Freebody boatyard established in Hurley since 1933 and run by the Freebody family who have lived and worked on the Middle Thames since the 13th century. They build and restore a variety of classic timber river and lake craft, moored right on the river, and are one of the few remaining boat builders doing so. Of Hurley's various pubs, two are most interesting. The Dewdrop on Ashley Hill was founded for the use of the Windsor Forest foresters and is now a popular walking pub and The Old Bell on the High Street was built in 1135 as the guest house of Hurley Priory. In 1545, the inn along with the Hurley Priory was passed to the Lovelace owners and it is believed there still exists, concealed by panelling near a fireplace in the lounge bar, the entrance to a secret passage running from the inn to that of the now demolished Ladye Place mansion. The Old Bell is reputedly the oldest working inn in Britain. Its current incarnation is hotel-restaurant and popular wedding venue. Its past excellence drew such well-known figures as Churchill, Eisenhower, Elizabeth Taylor, Errol Flynn and Princess Margaret.

Hurley is a magnet for visitors at all times of the year, not only for its ancient history but also for its proximity to the River Thames. The weir at Hurley Lock is considered a premier UK site for freestyle kayaking and the riverside is popular for moorings, camping (open air and caravan) and rambling walks to Marlow or Henley, with the Hurley Lock Café and Church summer cream teas (June to August) as convenient pit stops. These activities draw many in the summer months and the council car park and High Street restricted parking spaces fill quickly at weekends. So be warned! Summer also brings two very popular traditional events, the Hurley Fete on the last Saturday of July and the Hurley Regatta on the third Saturday of August. Further testament to Hurley's history and charm is the repeated use of its various locations and buildings for the TV programme *Midsomer Murders*.

🍁 HURST

When the Vikings had an encampment at Reading, over 1,000 years ago, the land surrounding the village we now call Hurst was part of the great forest of Windsor. The Saxon king Ethelred and his brother Alfred tried to attack the Viking stronghold but were driven back through the forest; they retreated to the marshy meadows on the eastern banks of the River Loddon. The Saxons called those meadows Whistley. The name Hurst came into use much later.

Abingdon Abbey, which had been founded before the Vikings established themselves at Reading, needed supplies of food and materials to maintain the community. The Saxon kings endowed it and other religious houses with lands that were to form manors. One of those manors was at Whistley which King Edgar granted to Abingdon Abbey in the year AD 968.

When the Normans compiled the Domesday Book in 1086, they duly recorded that the manor at Whistley belonged to Abingdon. It was shown to have a mill, a fishery, some land that was used for crops, and some woodland for pigs. Over the years oak trees were felled and sent down the River Loddon and Thames, some to make choir stalls for the Abbey. And fish, mainly eels, were transported in large numbers to the Abbot's kitchens.

The people at Whistley had established their own church by the year 1084. First it was a simple wooden structure, but later stout Norman pillars of limestone were erected to support a more substantial building, and they are still to be seen in the church. It was the Dean of Salisbury's scribe who first used the word Hurst. He recorded the Dean's visits here in the 13th century and wrote down 'the chapel at Herst, dedicated to St Nicholas'. The word 'hurst' means a wooded hill and he used it to identify the church which served Whistley. Over the centuries, Hurst has become the name of the area.

During the Civil War, the Harrisons of Hurst House lost most of their wealth supporting Charles I. The unfortunate king is said to have played on Hurst Bowling Green in more peaceful times. In those days the parish of Hurst was much larger than it is now. Then it encompassed Twyford, Winnersh, Sindlesham, Bearwood and Newland. Twyford was formed into a separate parish in the last century, as were parts of Winnersh, Sindlesham and Bearwood. Another boundary which disappeared then was an old county boundary. For centuries, part of Berkshire was regarded as being in Wiltshire. This curious situation came about because the Earls of Salisbury regarded the land they owned here as part of their holdings in Amesbury. So, for legal reasons, part of Twyford, Hurst and Wokingham were atttached to Wiltshire.

In the 19th century Hurst was primarily an agricultural village. Osiers were grown on the banks of the River Loddon and either made into baskets locally or sent to the markets in London. The river abounded with eels, pike, roach, dace, gudgeon, tench and carp, and it supplied water for the mills at Sandford and Whistley. Whistley mill was used to manufacture paper. There were blacksmiths at Wards Cross, Davis Street and Dunt Lane, and a wheelwright's shop in Davis Street.

A brewery once existed in School Road and there were numerous pubs, beer sellers and drinking houses. Two of the oldest inns are the Castle and the Green Man. The Castle was once called the Church House and the rents from it helped to support the church. Later it became known as the Bunch of Grapes. Three other notable inns which are now just a memory were the Crown, the Barley Corn and the Half Way House.

Since the days when the heaths, moors and commons were enclosed, the railways and motorways have arrived, and the land which was cleared of forest to make way for agriculture, is now providing sites for building, gravel workings and a country park. It might be that Hurst's role in the future is to provide recreation, and a patch of green, in the middle of what seems to be the inevitable urbanisation of this part of Berkshire.

INKPEN

The parish is located in the North Wessex Downs, 7 miles west of Newbury and designated as an Area of Outstanding Natural Beauty; its designation helps protect the area from over-development and major changes to its character.

Inkpen and its neighbouring villages have a very irregular and tight pattern of country lanes winding through dappled woodlands, which are very attractive and sometimes sunken with steep enclosing banks that result in a strong intimate character. Its landscape has a wide woodland framework, with an important area of heathland and spectacular views to Walbury Hill, otherwise known as Inkpen Beacon, the highest chalk hill in Britain from where you can sometimes see several counties. Inkpen contains remnants of classic England, the red phone boxes and pillar boxes, the duck pond, the church, two pubs, farms and barns and half-timbered cottages. Inkpen's unique layout leads directly to its most prized assets, the peace and seclusion that its residents enjoy. The night sky is becoming an increasingly rare site in built-up, urban areas and so the lack of street lighting is a prized asset in Inkpen.

We have three Sites of Special Scientific Interest. Inkpen Common and the Crocus Field are both managed as nature reserves by the Berkshire, Buckinghamshire and Oxfordshire Wildlife Trust (BBOWT). The oldest known building in the village is St Michael's Church, which dates from the 13th century. It would seem that as the oldest part of the village grew over the centuries, its settlements and livelihoods spread eastwards through the woods, clay-pits and streams out as far as Inkpen Common.

St Michael's Church (Anglican) continues to play an important part of village life and keeps the village informed about events by regularly compiling and delivering an issue of the *Inkpen & Combe Bulletin* to every household.

Inkpen

Inkpen is a centre for recreation; cycling, horse riding and paragliding are popular. It is abundant with wildlife, flora and fauna. Inkpen possesses an extensive network of well maintained footpaths and bridleways with 51 Rights of Way, and considerable effort is made to ensure these are maintained in a state that as far as possible enables them to be used throughout the year.

The Inkpen Memorial Playing Field, known as the 'Rec' (1946), is situated in middle Inkpen and the ground covers an area of 3.14 hectares. It contains two football pitches, a cricket pitch, two all-weather tennis courts with overhead floodlighting, a children's play area, a sports pavilion which can be used for meetings, and changing rooms with modern showers and plenty of car parking spaces. The playing field is well used throughout the year by local sports clubs and the primary school and for village events. It is home to the Inkpen 92 Group (it used to be the WI but in recent years has changed its membership to include men).

The Village Hall (1924) is well maintained and used for various club meetings, entertainment and social gatherings and is located at Upper Green. Inkpen Market is held monthly and sells locally grown produce and has a variety of stalls from local suppliers. Inkpen Primary School educates the children from the parish and surrounding areas from the age of 5 – 11 years. When weather conditions are appropriate, considerable numbers of people are attracted to Inkpen Hill for hang gliding and parascending. There are two public houses. The Crown & Garter and the Swan are located on the east and west sides of the parish; both serve restaurant meals and offer overnight guest accommodation.

The Inkpen of today has become part of a much more mobile Britain and the village in recent years has a commitment to broadband which helps sustain village life. Villagers are able to work from home and form a vibrant living and working environment for the next generation. The village's unusual geographical situation and layout are an advantage and the unspoilt character and isolated peacefulness are seen as benefits rather than drawbacks.

🍁 KINTBURY

Kintbury is one of the largest parishes within West Berkshire and is situated between Hungerford and Newbury with around 2,600 inhabitants. The village is located to the south of the River Kennet, the Kennet and Avon Canal and the Great Western Railway.

Its historical roots are documented as a Saxon settlement known as the 'Holy Place' and the name Kintbury derives from 'Cheneteberie' which relates to the chalk escarpment on which the main part of the village is built. There is further evidence that indicates Mesolithic occupation and a Roman bath house alongside the river which would have been on an east to west valley route over 10,000 years ago when England was joined to the continent. The centre of the village has the benefit of St Mary's Church, a Grade I listed building that dates from the 11th century with many interesting architectural and memorial features.

The village and its constituent manors and estates are mentioned several times in the Domesday Book and it is thought that the population at that time would have been about 100. The people of Kintbury, through the ages, have been predominately engaged in agriculture and the area is still mainly rural although the number of agricultural workers declined substantially during both the 19th and 20th century with the advent of larger and more modern machinery. Such changes in the 19th century provoked a nationally known riot in 1830, with many workers complaining bitterly about their declining wages because of the introduction of machinery. The rioters visited many farms, destroying machinery, burning hayricks and demanding money. When the law caught up with the rioters many were imprisoned or transported to Australia. One unfortunate, William Winterbourne, was hanged at Reading Gaol. There was such a strong feeling that the rioters had a justified cause that

Kintbury

St Mary's church, Kintbury

the vicar ensured he was buried in St Mary's churchyard. A ceremony takes place each year on 11 January to recognise this sad event.

Kintbury has seen many changes over the years, such as the decline of the whiting trade when chalk was mined all over the village and sent off to London on barges, and later via the railway when that came in 1847. The canal came close to closure in the 1950s but was rescued by strength of opinion locally and the Kennet and Avon Canal Trust was formed. The railway still provides a regular service to Newbury, Reading and Paddington and this facility, along with relatively easy access to the M4, has encouraged development of the village through recent decades. Despite the growing population the number of pubs has declined from eight to three in the last 100 years. The number of shops has also declined but those that are still with us provide a vital service to villagers.

Kintbury continues to be an attractive place to live with its primary school, station, doctors' surgery, three village halls, a sports hall, a well-used recreation ground and plenty of protected open space at its centre. It has a number of vibrant organisations including two amateur drama groups, the Kintbury Volunteer Group, three active sports clubs and many others.

🍁 KNOWL HILL

Knowl Hill now has a population of approximately 1000 people split by the A4 trunk road. It has a thriving school for children up to the age of 11, currently with 150 pupils which will soon increase to 210. It has become an academy school linked with White Waltham and Bisham schools and serves a wide area with many of the children travelling in from Maidenhead.

St Peter's Church is now part of the Parish of Wargrave with St Mary's. St Paul's Mission Church in Warren Row is the third in the parish. It is a tin tabernacle building, bought in kit form for just over £100 is 1894 and made of galvanised iron sheeting. St Peter's is supported by a small but enthusiastic and hardworking congregation. Fundraising has been taking place over the past five years to make improvements, including installing toilets and a new kitchen. It has an interesting connection with Jane Austen whose nephew, James Austen-Leigh, was the first vicar.

The final Knowl Hill Steam Rally took place in 2004 and the Littlewick Show has moved from Braywick in Maidenhead to the old steam rally field with great success. The Knowl Hill Village Association started life as the Knowl Hill Community Forum in 2001 to bring together and represent the interests of residents. It organises a wide range of community events including a biennial music festival. Knowl Hill Village Hall was built with funds raised by the first few steam rallies and is now well used by a wide variety of clubs and organisations. These include several dog training clubs, the WI, Girl Guides, CAMEO (Come And Meet Each Other), badminton and bowling and is the hub for village gatherings. The doctors from Wargrave still provide a twice weekly service in the property adjacent to the village hall. Hurley Parish Council meets in the village hall on a rotation basis with Littlewick Green and Hurley village. The two playgrounds in Choseley Road (one for younger children and a kick-about area for older children) have both benefitted from grant funding in recent years and are well equipped.

Agriculture no longer plays such a large part in the life of the village but the surrounding countryside is unspoilt with virtually no development owing to its green belt status. Most new building is infill or on small brownfield land. Star Works which was the old brickworks, was taken over by Grundon about twenty years ago as a landfill site. It will reach capacity in the next few years and be landscaped over. The hydroclave built to deal with hospital waste will remain.

The oldest pub, the Seven Stars and its coach house, has been converted to housing and the barn behind has been developed into a handsome dwelling. The New Inn and the newly renovated Bird in Hand continue as restaurants and the Royal Oak on the common is the meeting place for locals.

The village has a variety of shops and businesses including a tool shop, a café, a local store, a kitchen supplier, a garage and a plant nursery. Arthur Nutt retired from his dairy business about twenty years ago (his delicious green top milk was legendary) and the farm is now a wonderful organic garden.

🍁 LAMBOURN

Lambourn 'is 9 miles from anywhere, (on) the road to nowhere'. This description of Lambourn was written in 1881 to explain the need for a railway. More than a century later, Lambourn can still seem remote, despite its proximity to the M4. The village is situated in a downland valley on the northwest edge of Berkshire, bordering Wiltshire and Oxfordshire, in the heart of the North Wessex Downs Area of Outstanding Natural Beauty. With a population of roughly 3,000, Lambourn is a robust, rural community and a major centre of racehorse training.

The village takes its name from the Lambourn, the bourne (or stream) where sheep, raised on the Downs, were washed. The upper reaches of the River Lambourn are seasonal, fed by springs which depend on rain water percolating through the chalk and raising the water table. When the water table is low, the river runs dry, often from late summer until February.

There is archeological evidence of human activity in the vicinity of Lambourn going back to late pre-historic times, with the remains of ancient field systems, burial mounds, pottery and the Bronze Age Crow Down Hoard, discovered in 2004. The Lambourn Downs were intensively cultivated from as far back as the Romano-British period.

In AD 899 King Alfred the Great left the royal estate at Lambourn to his widow Ealhswith and the distinctive oval pattern of the Saxon settlement still dictates the street pattern around the Minster church of St Michael and All Angels. The church, with its Norman nave, Father Willis organ and ring of eight bells, is one of several notable buildings in the village.

Beside the church, in Three Post Lane, stands the impressive entrance to the Isbury Almshouses. Founded in 1502 by John Isbury (or Estbury) the current buildings were erected in 1852 by Henry Hippisley of nearby Lambourn Place. Even older, Hardrett's Almshouses, in Chapel Lane were already established by 1469 and are probably some of the oldest buildings in the village.

Lambourn was known as Chipping Lambourn, 'Chipping' indicating a market, but the Post Office reduced the name to Lambourn (no 'e') in the early 20th century. Lambourn had charters for a market and two sheep fairs by 1446. The sheep fairs were held on Edward's Hill, near the present school, and show the importance of sheep farming from medieval times. Spiced 'Clementy' cakes were baked for the autumn fair, held on the feast day of St Clement. In recent years the sheep fairs have dwindled away and houses cover the site, but a market takes place in the Square around the ancient Market Cross every Friday, and a variety of goods can be bought, from fresh fruit and vegetables to shoes.

Although the number of shops has declined, Lambourn has two supermarkets, one of which houses the Post Office, a hardware store, a newsagent, a chemist, an estate agent, a butcher, a hairdresser, a saddler and a betting shop. There is also a café, an Indian restaurant, a Chinese takeaway, a fish and chip shop and a bar. There are fewer pubs than in the past, with the imposing Red Lion on the Square having been converted into apartments, but the George and the Wheelwright's Arms continue. The local unitary authority, West Berkshire Council, supported by Lambourn Parish Council, runs the library and the Lambourn Centre, which provides a gym and leisure facilities. The library, under threat of closure in 2016, was saved by a vociferous local campaign and staff are now supported by volunteers.

Other services include the doctors' surgery, a dentist, a fire station (manned by local volunteers), and Lambourn Primary School, which has an uplifting view across rolling downland.

Many clubs and societies operate in Lambourn. These include toddler groups, Brownies, the WI, sports clubs, a camera club and a horticultural society. Although villagers do complain of a lack of activities for young people, it has proved difficult to gain enough support to maintain a Youth Club. The annual Carnival is held on the Sunday of the August Bank Holiday weekend and the Carnival Committee also organises the Guy Fawkes fireworks display.

The surrounding Downs offer many opportunities for walkers. The Lambourn Valley Way, which forms part of the link between the Ridgeway and the Thames Path, passes through the village before joining the course of the Lambourn Valley Branch Railway. The railway was completed in 1898 but was closed to passengers in 1960.

There are daily bus services to Newbury and Swindon. Once a week, the 'Wednesday Bus', which is as much a social gathering as a means of transport, runs along the Lambourn Valley and over the Downs to Wantage for a morning's shopping.

In the last 30 years Lambourn has seen a good deal of housing development, but there is a shortage of affordable housing, especially for those involved in racing.

For many people, Lambourn is synonymous with racehorses. The deep, unploughed downland turf, ideally suited for gallops, attracted public trainers from the mid-19th century. Today there are over 1,400 horses in training, most in Upper Lambourn, and strings of horses, ridden by stable lads and lasses from all over the world, are a familiar sight in the mornings. Some of the country's best-known Flat and National Hunt trainers are based around Lambourn. Famous

Lambourn

names connected with Lambourn are legion: Fred Winter, Fulke Walwyn, Nicky Henderson, Peter Walwyn, John Francome and A.P. McCoy to name but a few. Champion horses abound: Felstead, Grundy, Party Politics, Many Clouds, Buveur d'Air – the list goes on. Visitors to the annual Good Friday Open Day enjoy touring stable yards and watching the special events. Since 2009 Lambourn has been home to Oaksey House, which provides specialist rehabilitation for injured jockeys. Racing Welfare Lambourn supports those involved in racing and their families. The livelihoods of many villagers are connected with horse racing, working in the stables or providing allied services.

Nestled in the Valley of the Racehorse, Lambourn is a busy, working village, with a surprising number of services and activities, and a great community spirit.

LAMBOURN CLEMENTY CAKE
This recipe was recreated by WI member Doris Penfold and her husband John.

Ingredients
200g plain flour
1 x 5ml spoon bicarbonate of soda
¼ teaspoon salt
2 x 5ml spoons ground cinnamon
2 x 5ml spoons ground ginger
75g soft dark brown sugar

100g black treacle
100g golden syrup
150g butter or margarine
2 eggs
30ml milk
Optional: 50g sultanas or seedless raisins

Method
Grease and line a 28cm by 18cm cake tin
Sift together the flour, bicarbonate of soda, salt, cinnamon and ginger
Add the sugar
Heat the treacle, syrup and fat gently in a saucepan until the fat has melted
Beat the eggs and milk together
Beat the melted mixture into the dry ingredients, then beat in the eggs and
    milk
Pour into the tin and bake in a moderate oven 180C for 20 minutes
Reduce the heat to warm 160C and bake for a further 25-30 minutes until
    firm to the touch

🍁 LANGLEY

With the change in the county boundaries in the early 1970s Langley, already
brought into the borough of Slough in 1931, was moved into Berkshire.

Before the war the village was almost wholly agricultural, consisting of
a number of farms stretching over a large area from the railway in the north
to the Bath Road in the south. These were worked by well-known farming
families: Seymour, Major, Emmett and Lobjoit to name some, and employed
many men. Others worked in the brickfields adjacent to the Grand Union
Canal, where London Stock bricks were made, and some were in the service
of the last Squire of Langley, the late Sir Robert Harvey, who lived at Langley
Park and owned the beautiful parkland surrounding it and the fine tract of
woodlands to the north known as Black Park. After Sir Robert's death in 1931
the estate became the property of the Buckinghamshire County Council, and
now both Langley Park and Black Park are open to the public.

Though the population of the village at that time was quite small, all the
essential shops were to hand – butchers, a bakery, a post office with sweetshop
and newsagents' business, a Co-operative grocery and drapery store, a cobbler,
a chemist, hardware store and a printer, and a blacksmith who, of course, was

a vital craftsman in an agricultural community. At the centre of the village was Langley Hall, at that time the home of the Actors' Orphanage, and every year the children put on a superb Christmas pantomime in their own Bijou Theatre, which delighted everybody, and people came from miles around to see it. The local Flower Show, an important annual event in the village, was held in the beautiful grounds of the Hall, also cricket matches between the boys' team and a team of famous actors used to be played. Sadly for Langley, the children of the orphanage moved further out into the country just before the outbreak of war, but fortunately the Hall, a listed building, has been beautifully restored and is now a school, Langley Hall Primary Academy.

The 12th-century parish church of St Mary the Virgin remains in its old-world setting, with beautifully restored almshouses, the Kedermisters to the south and the Seymours to the north. The old Red Lion Inn stands opposite the church gate. St Mary's church contains the famous Kedermister Pew and Library – the latter unique as an example of an early 17th-century church library.

During the war industry had encroached upon the village, notably the Hawker Aircraft company, and when hostilities ended in 1945, it was not long before Langley was chosen to be one of the places to develop for re-housing Londoners who had been made homeless by the war. This happened in the early 1950s and many old houses and cottages were demolished, and farmland done away with to make way for new housing estates which included housing, shops, schools and churches. Later on a very good library and a medical centre were built.

With the many changes which have taken place over the years, Langley has lost most of its old identity, but because of its modern development and the availability of work in the area, it supports a thriving community.

☘ LECKHAMPSTEAD

Leckhampstead stands on high ground halfway between Wantage and Newbury, close to the Ridgeway, in West Berkshire. The village houses are a mix of old and new, with some 20 being listed as 'buildings of architectural or historic interest'. St James' church is one of these buildings, being an S.S.Teulon designed church with a Grade II listing. The church was completed in 1859 but includes artefacts from the original Saxon church dedicated to St Edmund which was situated in Hill Green (part of the parish of Leckhampstead) and demolished in 1860. The Jacobean pulpit, 13th-century font and altar rails

Leckhampstead

from this church have been preserved and are in use in the present church, which is itself an example of the gothic style of architecture with a flint and brick exterior and polychromatic patterned interior created with terracotta, cream and black bricks. In the past the village also supported Methodist and Wesleyan chapels, but both of these have closed and the buildings are now private houses.

An Ordnance Survey benchmark can be seen in the wall outside the church. These benchmarks were originally used when producing maps to calculate the height of land above ODN (Ordnance Data Newlyn i.e. sea level determined at Newlyn in Cornwall). These marks are no longer used by the OS who now use GNSS (Global Navigation Satellite System) data to provide this information.

An unusual war memorial, which includes a clock with hands made of bayonets, stands on the green in the middle of the village. The minutes are marked by machine-gun ammunition and the Roman numerals by rifle ammunition. Shell cases rest on the staddle stones surrounding the memorial, and the chain linking the stones belonged to a battleship which fought in the Battle of Jutland. There is also a Commonwealth War Graves Commission headstone in the graveyard erected in 2017 to mark the grave of a soldier from the village who lost his life in the First World War.

The village was fortunate enough to be given land many years ago for a recreation ground which is used as a football pitch and children's play area. There is also a Village Hall, where the WI meet each month. Leckhampstead WI was one of the vanguard of WIs set up in England and is still meeting each month despite the demise of a number of local village groups. The present group, although relatively small, is active both within the monthly meeting and through membership of the Book Club, Craft Group and organised outings. Leckhampstead is part of the Lambourn Group which meets annually for a joint meeting with Lambourn and Hungerford WIs.

🍁 LITTLEWICK GREEN

It is not surprising that television film-makers have frequently chosen Littlewick Green as a location. The place has all the attributes of a typical English country village: a village hall, a pub and a church, all spaced around a well-kept, statutorily recognised village green on which cricket is played throughout the summer and which is the site for many village festive events.

Many villagers delighted in watching filming in the village – many slayings have been committed for *Midsomer Murders* and *Mr Bean* had a chaotic episode with sheep and dogs all over the green – and have lent their homes and even appeared as voluntary 'extras'. We are proud to have had as former residents Ursula Vaughan Williams, Peter Bromley the popular sports commentator and perhaps the best known of Littlewick folk, Ivor Novello, who bought a house here in 1927, renamed it Redroofs and spent many weekends in Littlewick throughout the Second World War. He often gave performances, sometimes with showbiz colleagues, in the Village Hall for local societies. His popular song 'We'll gather lilacs' was inspired by the lane running past Redroofs and the village school. His former home is now a flourishing theatre school, counting Kate Winslet among its distinguished alumni. He is commemorated by a bust in our church, St John the Evangelist.

A form of our name appeared in print in the 10th century but we can trace our existence much further back to Roman times, since aerial photography shows the outline of a villa just to the south of the green, conveniently placed for the main route down to the important Roman cities at Winchester and Salisbury. Still occupied are houses around the green dating back to Tudor and Georgian days.

Recent times have seen many changes: our Church of England village school closed in 1985, reopening a little later as a Montessori primary school, whose new owners were intrigued with its large array of junior lavatories.

At a time when declining congregations and increasing costs are a serious concern for parish churches, our own, dating to the late 19th century, with its enthusiastic management, appears to have bucked the trend. Grants and donations have been achieved to secure much-needed refurbishments; family-services are very popular and overall congregations are growing. Many visitors are drawn to its well-known feature: over the altar there is a large nativity painting in oils gifted locally from a large house in the mid-20th century but shrouded in mystery as to its actual age. Is it from the Middle Ages or merely a copy or pastiche? Investigations and consultations continue as to its provenance and its artist.

Littlewick's Cricket Club, founded in 1810 (by a very few years the second oldest in Berkshire) sports two elevens in local leagues and a thriving well-coached junior team. The 1st XI has had notable successes over the years in the Julian Cup, an early knock-out competition long pre-dating but similar in format to today's T20 matches. Despite varying fortunes over the years, it swept all before it in the Premier Chilterns League in 2016.

The Village Hall, built and given in trust to the village at the end of the 19th century, languished for many years and became dilapidated from lack of use, but with a village appeal, some grants and donations it has become an attractive and welcoming centre for many local activities. Not least of these are the monthly meetings of the century-old afternoon WI branch and the recently formed evening branch, the Littlewick Belles. It also has a Beaver Group, midweek Art Classes and an Exercise Group, as well as serving as the headquarters and pavilion of LGCC. With excellent kitchen facilities, new toilets, showers and changing room, it forms a popular centre for meetings, parties and a wide range of village activities.

However, it could be argued that our attractive pub on the edge of the green, aptly called the Cricketers is a leading focal point for our social scene, although the village now also has a small hotel, the Riders, on the A4, on the site of a previous pub and the long defunct village store. A bridge club and a book club also meet regularly in each other's homes.

In modern times, increasing traffic and demands for property accessible to London, airports and motorways have thrown a girdle around the village. A mushroom farm, founded locally and giving employment to villagers has been supplanted by executive houses, many more similar homes have been built in the surrounds of the Green, but sadly few of them have lain within the means of young families in the area. Nevertheless the village core still survives and flourishes, as has been regularly witnessed by the great success of local events and celebrations for young and old alike organised by the locally elected Littlewick Society.

The village has evolved over many centuries and, more or less in its present form, over many modern decades. It consistently faces up to threats and challenges and still looks to the future with determination and optimism.

❦ MAIDENHEAD

Since Edwardian days Maidenhead has been a place for fun. Once it was champagne parties, punts and Guards Club occasions, culminating in the season's most fashionable event 'Ascot Sunday'; a day of finery on the river. A now-demolished riverfront hotel called Skindles was the haunt of royalty, politicians, actors, and writers — and a place for illicit liaisons. During this era Maidenhead was known as the Jewel of the Thames.

Much of the town's history revolves around the river. The first wooden bridge was built in 1250, near Boulters Lock. The present Grade I listed stone bridge was built in 1777. The town was an important stopping place for coaches on the road from London to Bath as travellers were afraid to cross Maidenhead Thicket in the dark because of highwaymen, which meant the inn and tavern trade grew.

With the advent of the trains Brunel's 'Sounding Arch' railway bridge was built in 1839 and the coaching era came to an end. This bridge featured on a commemorative stamp celebrating Brunel's bicentenary in 2006. It is the widest brick arch bridge in the world! The best place to find out more on the early history of the town is Maidenhead's excellent Heritage Centre.

Maidenhead town has suffered from flooding and in 1894 there was the greatest flood on record. The worst flood of the 20th century was in 1947 but the completion of the Maidenhead Windsor and Eton Flood Alleviation Scheme (known as the Jubilee River) in 2002 provided protection against floods of 1947 proportions.

There are many notable buildings and statues. These include The Boy and the Boat which can be found at the top of King Street. The Companions on Ray Mill Island and a bronze hippo which stands at the entrance to North Maidenhead Cricket Club were both stolen but fortunately have been replaced. The Clock Tower situated outside the station commemorates Queen Victoria's Diamond Jubilee and a statue of Sir Nicholas Winton stands on Platform 2/3 of Maidenhead Station. Maidenhead's Football Stadium in York Road is the oldest FA stadium in continuous use in the country.

The town is proud of its Olympic athletes, understandably often in sports connected with the river. Rowers Bert Bushnell and Katherine Grainger have won Gold medals and Cath Bishop with Katherine Grainger won Silver medals. Paralympic athletes are even better represented. Tom Aggar has won a Gold and a Bronze, Jeanette Chippington came home with 12 Olympic medals in swimming then another at paracanoeing; she is the daughter of one of our former WI members. Rider Sophie Christiansen won three Gold and a postbox in Maidenhead High Street was painted gold in her honour. Sophie is patron of SportsAble, a facility here for sports and activities for the disabled. After the 2016 Rio Olympic Games, Maidenhead athletes brought home a huge medal haul in rowing, kayaking and hockey.

Ivor Novello bought Redroofs at Littlewick Green as his country house; this is now an independent theatre training school. Richard Dimbleby lived on Boulters Island and other residents included Vesta Tilley, author Hugh Lofting, actress Geraldine James (*Calendar Girls*), Wallace Waite, co-founder of Waitrose, and Diana Dors. Gerry Anderson made his famous puppet films here and the Spice Girls lived together in a 3-bed semi before their rise to fame.

One of the town's most famous residents was Sir Nicholas Winton (the 'British Schindler') who organised the rescue on special trains of 669 children, mostly Jewish, from Czechoslovakia on the eve of the Second World War.

Maidenhead has appeared in at least 20 films and 15 TV programmes. Among them: the Town Hall doubled as the hospital in no fewer than three *Carry On* films and local places featured in Benny Hill's *Ernie* plus episodes of *Mr Bean* and *Count Arthur Strong*. The former Guards Club was Cruikshanks Hotel in *Kind Hearts and Coronets*. Artists JMW Turner, James Tissot and Edward Gregory have all immortalised the town in paint.

The Borough of Maidenhead was joined with Windsor in 1974. This was followed by the formation of the new parliament constituency of Maidenhead in 1997. The town is twinned with towns in Germany, France and Italy.

In the past, Maidenhead was known mostly for its three breweries (and a thriving temperance movement!) as well as radio and car industries but is now home to the UK headquarters of Johnson & Johnson, GlaxoSmithKline, Three UK, Volvo, Adobe and The Commonwealth War Graves Commission. Bovilles art shop is one of the last independent art shops in the county and there is a flourishing Arts Centre at Norden Farm. Carters Steam Fair is based in the town and is a regular visitor. Local newspaper the *Maidenhead Advertiser* is run by Baylis Media Ltd which established the Louis Baylis Trust. The Trust donates generously to local charities and good causes. Diverse faiths are represented in the town and there are branches of well-known organisations such as the WI, Lions, Rotary, Townswomen's Guild and the Talking Newspaper for the Blind as well as many others.

Much of the investment coming into Maidenhead results from there being a station on the Crossrail line. Maidenhead is already superbly connected but from December 2019 four Elizabeth Line trains an hour will allow passengers to travel through central London without having to change, improving its linkages with the City. The present regeneration of the area heralds 'Roux at Skindles' restaurant, new homes, leisure facilities and the waterways are being opened up so that one day Maidenhead may once again be the Jewel of the Thames.

🍁 MORTIMER

Stratfield Mortimer is a rural village, situated between Reading, Basingstoke and Newbury. We have easy access to the M4 and M3, and the coast. Historically, the village dates back to the Romans. Stratfield is a Saxon word meaning 'open land'. The village of Stratfield was given by William the Conqueror to one of his supporters, Ralph of Mortimer, hence the name Stratfield Mortimer.

In recent times, the population has increased to 4500 residents and by 1400 houses. It has two churches, one of which dates back to Anglo-Saxon times but was rebuilt in the 1860s by a local benefactor. Mortimer has changed considerably in the last 35 years but still retains its character, surrounded by green fields and woods. Mortimer's listed Brunel railway station, carries commuters to London, Basingstoke and Reading, and is an important transport asset to the village. Residents can also drive to the 'Park and Ride' at Three Mile Cross to catch a bus into Reading. There is a regular bus service in the village that goes to Tadley or Reading. St Mary's Junior School stands in the old part of the village and St John's Infant School is next to the church in the main part of Mortimer.

So what has changed in Mortimer in recent years? At the bottom of Mortimer the Post Office closed, together with the garage which sold petrol and serviced vehicles. These buildings became private houses. The Fox and Horn, originally called the Railway Inn, has now become an Indian restaurant. At the rear of its car park, the Bowling Club and its clubhouse closed in the 1990s. The farm building by St Mary's church has been converted into houses. We are lucky enough to retain the Fire Service, which is in the middle of the village, and is run by local part-time firemen. Sadly, we lost the Working Men's Club. It was demolished in early 2000, making way for a group of houses now called Blewburton Close. Mortimer Hall was a satellite of Padworth Sixth Form College but has been converted into residential houses and flats.

We also lost the Pick Your Own farm where the village picked fruit. The area now called Strawberry Fields has 100 plus houses and, with excellent planning, it nestles into the background.

We do still have an impressive War Memorial in the centre of the village where the British Legion and other local groups pay their respects each November. Mortimer has a public open space called the Fairground, with a dog walking area. It is managed by the Parish Council and has a new play area for older children, a table tennis table, and a football and keep-fit area. A new Community Hall was built for the residents to use and is managed by a Trust. It is hired out to clubs and for parties. Mortimer 2012 WI meets there.

Mortimer is surrounded by woodlands and footpaths; beautiful places for residents to walk and explore. Horse riders can buy permits to ride the woods. The village has a newsagent, café, garage, estate agents, several hairdressers, Travel Agent, and Chinese takeaway. We are also home to an exceptional builders' merchant and dog grooming parlour. Mortimer has an excellent doctors' surgery (defibrillator outside!) and dentist, supported by the chemist. A Volunteer Bureau organised by Mortimer and Burghfield is a useful service for those who need to travel to hospital and doctors' appointments etc. The Library is now run by volunteers aided by a librarian from West Berkshire Council. The last bank is now closing, due to modern technology, and the Post Office has recently become a gift shop and café, but Budgens – who took over Sewards – have opened a post office within their supermarket.

In early 2000 a group of residents formed an organisation called Mortimer Village Partnership which was inspirational in establishing new organisations in the village. They set up a social media page so residents, if they wished, could be informed of events going on, pass on information and seek recommendations. MVP organise annual events like The Scarecrow Trail and The Fun Day, both of which bring in thousands of visitors, as well as Clean up Days, lunch clubs, theatre trips and family events. The village has many clubs, societies and amenities ranging from tennis, cricket, football, drama, film, book clubs, art, walking, bell ringing, and of course Cubs, Scouts and Brownies. There are thriving small businesses, artisan producers of chocolate, sausages and home-made bread. There are also gardening and dog walking services, builders and carpenters, together with architects and technology companies. Superfast broadband and new builds have taken us into the 21st century. Mortimer is a thriving village.

The village is about to have 130 new houses built in its centre. Village residents, through a Neighbourhood Development Plan, decided how they wanted the village to develop – they chose the preferred land location and planning ideas, which was accepted by West Berkshire Council as a planning document via a referendum.

With regards to well-known residents, who knows who might pass you by? Perhaps an actor, a TV personality, a judge or two, war veterans, Bletchley Park code breakers? In bygone days you would have seen Queen Wilhelmina of Holland or Haile Selassie from Ethiopia walking through the village. The village is a safe haven.

Mortimer has changed. The population has increased by about 25% but new developments have sprung up to house them. The transport system has made the village an attractive place for families to live. Businesses have come to the village bringing further employment opportunities. Although there has been closure of financial institutions, probably due to the internet, others have sprung up in their place. Mortimer has access to leisure facilities nearby and gravel extraction lakes provide water sports. All kinds of people live in Mortimer – many have lived here all their lives and new people have come in, but the mix of people makes it a pleasant place to live. Of course Mortimer 2012 WI is a thriving club and welcomes all the ladies of any age to their monthly meetings.

MORTIMER WEST END

Mortimer West End is just within Hampshire but it has been linked to its larger neighbour, the Berkshire village of (Stratfield) Mortimer, for centuries.

Not many villages in Britain can boast of having a Roman amphitheatre within their boundaries. The amphitheatre was built circa AD 60 on the outskirts of the Roman town of Calleva Atrebatum (now known as Silchester). The amphitheatre however lies within the boundaries of Mortimer West End. It was originally built of timber and although there is no evidence of exactly what it was built for, it is thought that it was probably for gladiatorial contests, animal fighting, public executions and equestrian displays (as horse bones were found there). It could hold 7,250 standing and 3,600 seated.

In the 3th century the amphitheatre was rebuilt in stone (as it is seen today). In the 12th century it was fortified and occupied when a timber hall was built in the arena. From the early 15th century until the 1970s the arena was used as a farmyard for The Mount farmhouse.

What we see today are the earth banks which would have housed the timber seating, with a low stone and flint wall around the edge in evidence. This wall would originally have been three metres high as it was the wall of the arena.

In more recent times, the Church of the Holy Saviour, more commonly known as St Saviour's, was built and endowed by local landowners, the Benyon family, in 1856. The north window of this pretty church is a stained-glass reproduction of part of Albrecht Durer's *Crucifixion*. Other windows have changed over the years but the beautiful west window is especially notable; it is a Benedicite (or blessing) window which depicts birds, animals and plants of the area. The west window was unveiled in 1953 as a memorial to the Reverend Rogers (1915–1945); it was designed by Christopher Webb in consultation with the Rev Rogers before his death.

During the Second World War, Queen Wilhelmina of the Netherlands stayed at a house called Laneswood. At that time, Laneswood was within Mortimer West End, although its site is now part of Mortimer. After the war, Laneswood became a children's home; the building is no longer in existence.

The Turners Arms pub reflects one of the principal occupations of villagers in the past, when Mortimer West End was part of one of the largest wood-working areas in the country. Traditional crafts and trades of the time included besom making, bowl turning, charcoal burning, bark stripping and hurdle making. Another local pub, the Red Lion, dates back to the 17th century.

Queen Elizabeth II visited Mortimer West End in 1974 to see Sanbal, one of her stallions, who was standing at Simms Stud Farm. The facilities at this site were used as livery stables after they ceased to be a stud farm; at the time of writing there are no horses present, but it is hoped that renovation work will be carried out, allowing the stables to be used for horses again.

🍁 NEWBURY

Newbury was built at a natural crossroads; a gap in the downs from Southampton and Winchester leading through Newbury to a ford or bridge over the River Kennet thence north to Oxford. This point is the narrowest in southern England between London and Bristol. Today this crossroads is more marked than ever. The main A34 bypasses the town to the west and the old A34, now the A339 passes just east of the town centre buildings. These two roads cross the east/west running River Kennet, the Kennet and Avon Canal, the London Paddington railway line to Plymouth and finally the A4 London to Bath Road and also the M4 from London to Carmarthenshire. So perhaps you first heard of Newbury in connection with its notorious traffic jams and then the fight to build the Newbury Bypass. Despite and because of this, Newbury is a market

Bridge across the Kennet and Avon Canal, Newbury

town with its own special history of innovations and battles.

Two English Civil War battles were fought here. The Parliamentarians had the upper hand on both occasions. The first was at Wash Common in 1643. It was a head-on clash between the two armies and resulted in some 2,500 dead on the battlefield. The King's army withdrew during the night and this allowed the Parliamentary army under the command of the Earl of Essex to return to London intact. It is said that for the first time Parliament realised that the King could be beaten. The second battle was to the north of the town in 1644 and left Donnington Castle in ruins and Shaw House, the home of Lord Dolman, with musket shot holes in its walls.

If you approach Newbury from the north on the A339 you will pass Vodafone's HQ, a tent-like building on your left. Travel on and the sculpture you will see on the Robin Hood Roundabout is called *Couple in Conversation* by Johannes von Stumm. It was commissioned by the Town Council in 2007 for a theme of Communication.

The town centre has a mixture of buildings. If you park near the Canal Wharf you will see the modern library with its pavement mosaic. The mosaic tells Newbury's story from early times to the Greenham Common Airbase and was created by Paul Forsey. Nearby there is a series of timber-framed buildings which were the Cloth Hall and are now used as the West Berkshire Museum and so on to the Market Square in front of the Town Hall. The Victorian Corn Exchange and the Granary and Cloth Hall reflect the town's past prosperity from farming and wool.

Walk out of the market place and follow the canal westwards to the town lock. On the north side is another sculpture commissioned by the Town Council called *Ebb and Flow*, a huge granite bowl which fills and empties as the narrowboats pass up and down the Kennet and Avon Canal using the Town Lock. Its sculptor was Peter Randall-Page and it is carved from Dartmoor granite. The Kennet and Avon canal proceeds westward to Bristol through glorious countryside via Hungerford and Pewsey.

Newbury sits in the centre of good farmland and is surrounded by downlands. It has been prosperous over many centuries. The people of Newbury have been generous to their fellows and to the town itself. In 2003 Newbury people raised £1million to equip its new West Berkshire Community Hospital.

Founded in 1393 by Sir Richard Abberbury, the Donnington Hospital Trust now manages 67 almshouses and provides pensions to retired people in need. Queen Elizabeth I came to Newbury 1568 to re-open these almshouses. She came again in 1596 to grant Newbury its Charter. There are more almshouses to the south, Upper and Lower Raymond Almshouses. The Tudor buildings in Argyll Road were refurbished in the 1920s by Dr Essex Wynter, originally for the use of retired nurses from the Middlesex Hospital. Twelve new almshouse flats have just been completed by The Charity of Mrs Mabel Luke.

The first Mayor was Bartholomew Yate in 1596. The names of all the Mayors from Bartholomew Yate to the present incumbent are on the walls of the Town Hall Council Chamber. The Town Hall is often open on a Saturday morning so you may be able to pop in and see them. In 1997 a new tradition began and two Town Councillors stand on the Town Hall steps from 10am until noon each Saturday ready to help their fellow citizens and visitors.

John Winchcombe, aka Jack O' Newbury, has been credited with being the originator of factory-style wool production, certainly he had a workshop of 30 to 50 looms. He endowed much of the 16th-century building in St Nicolas Church.

If you are spending a weekend in Newbury there is horse racing at the racecourse. The chalk Berkshire Downs are famous for training racehorses. The Corn Exchange and St Nicolas Church are used for concerts and Newbury has a multiplex cinema once more.

The Watermill at Bagnor just outside the town was converted in 1968 to become a theatre. It is a professional theatre with an extremely good reputation and is set in the beautiful river valley. Watermill productions have won several national Olivier Awards.

Newbury and West Berkshire has beautiful countryside. There is much to discover in the area; old houses, historical sites, good shopping and cafés, and above all, friendly people.

❧ OAKLEY GREEN

Oakley Green starts a few hundred yards from the Braywood Memorial Hall down Oakley Green Road, placing Braywood Cricket Club in Fifield. It stretches the whole length of Oakley Green Road (B3024) until it joins the A308. Although limited to this stretch of road, there are many houses set back along unmade roads, so that Oakley Green has a greater depth than at first appears.

The first part of Oakley Green (coming from Fifield) is considered by the inhabitants not really to be in Oakley Green but in Braywood and many of the properties have Braywood in their name. Although the powers-that-be have given the people of Braywood addresses in Oakley Green, Windsor, they have Maidenhead telephone numbers.

The houses on Oakley Green Road are a mixture of old and new, but it is often difficult to decide which are the genuinely old houses as many new ones are built in a traditional style. One house, Clairvaux, which appears to be very old and looks as though it should have church associations, is in fact fairly modern.

Many houses in Oakley Green stand well back from the road and are reached by long drives or are down unmade roads which are hard on a car's suspension. One of the former is Willow Farm, once the home of Michael Sadleir, the author of *Fanny by Gaslight*. One of the latter was Nightingale Cottage, up Tarbay Lane. Here lived for many years Dr Esther Rickards, a noted lady doctor and in later life, a breeder of spaniels and a widely acclaimed Dog Show Judge. After her death, the villagers of Oakley Green and Fifield raised money for a memorial to her, and placed a seat outside Braywood School with a memorial plate. Unfortunately, the seat was stolen. The seat now outside Braywood School was provided from the Council Lottery Fund, but a new memorial plate has been added.

Oakley Green now ends at Fairacre Farm, and the Army houses built on Broom Farm look for their leisure and shopping towards Dedworth and Windsor, although the school, Alexander First Primary, built in 1972 mainly for the Army children, retains a 'village school' atmosphere and is located in Oakley Green.

❧ OLD WINDSOR

In Saxon times, Old Windsor was the largest 'town' in Berkshire. However the Normans undermined its importance by building their great fortress on the outcrop of rock above the River Thames two miles north west.

The Thames was a convenient highway and the richness of the alluvial plain meant that a thriving town grew up. Further south along the river is the flat meadow of Runnymede, made famous by the signing of the Magna Carta in 1215, although historians believe that it probably took place across the bank at Ankerwyke. In June 2015 a ceremony took place at the Magna Carta Memorial to celebrate 800 years of the signing of the Charter, 'Freedom under the law'. A new memorial set of 12 bronze chairs called 'The Jurors', sculpted by Hew Locke, now stand in the meadow representing concepts of law and key moments in the struggle for freedom, rule of law and equal rights.

At Coopers' Hill, there is the beautiful Air Force Memorial dedicated to the memory of airmen who have no marked grave. It was opened by the Queen in 1952 and the view is magnificent.

The Church of Saint Peter and Saint Andrew down by the river was originally Saxon but was destroyed and rebuilt in 1216. A restoration took place in 1863.

Although there is no Women's Institute in Old Windsor there is in Windsor Great Park, which lies within the parish. The parish includes the Long Walk with its two and a half mile avenue from the Castle to the Copper Horse statue of George III. Much of the Park is open for the public to enjoy. Before 1930 there were no gardens, but today the Savill Garden, the Punchbowl and the Valley Gardens are beautiful places to visit.

There are many famous houses in Old Windsor. The De Vere Beaumont Estate, formerly Beaumont House, was once a Roman Catholic Boys' Public School and then became a training school for International Computers (ICL). The old hospital in Crimps Hill is now a complex of houses called Bear Rails and Battersea Dogs & Cats Home has a large establishment in Priests Hill.

Today Old Windsor is a large thriving community but is still known as 'The Village'.

🍁 OWLSMOOR

Owlsmoor is part of the parish of Sandhurst, located in the south-west corner of Berkshire on the borders of Surrey and Hampshire. Owlsmoor was a part of the Windsor forest and consisted until the 19th century of heath and woods with no major settlement.

In 1860-1862 a lunatic asylum was opened in Crowthorne, which at the time was part of Sandhurst. It was known as the Broadmoor Criminal Lunatic Asylum, now known as Broadmoor Hospital. One of its prime access roads was Owlsmoor Road and this led to the creation of a small settlement in Owlsmoor where there had previously been an area occupied by gypsy travellers.

The area to the north of Yeovil Road was used to fell timber, which was used for pit props in the mines and in the trenches for the First World War. This work was carried out by Canadian lumberjacks who lived in black timber barrack huts, some of which survived until recent years near the top of College Road. A railway line was constructed in the felling area to take the timber to a station where it was loaded onto horse-drawn carts. This is the reason why the road between Cambridge Road and Owlsmoor Road was originally called Station Road.

The first church was erected in Owlsmoor in 1880. It was a small mission church named St George's, known locally as 'The Tin Church'. Then in 1959 a larger Canadian Cedar construction took its place. These churches were under the parish of Crowthorne but in the early 1970s, with massive development imminent, Owlsmoor Road and its access to Broadmoor was closed, causing the church of St George to be transferred to the parish of Sandhurst. Before the community centre was built the church was used for church services, community events such as dances, fun evenings, Guides, Scouts, etc. since it was the only meeting facility in Owlsmoor. After 33 years' service, in 1993 the wooden church was demolished. It was replaced by the current brick-built church and was consecrated by the Bishop of Oxford.

In 1967 Owlsmoor consisted of about 54 houses, located in Owlsmoor Road, Oak Avenue, Yeovil Road, and with clusters in Victoria Road and Cambridge Road. This soon altered in the 1970s when the government required land to be released for housing and Berkshire County Council identified Sandhurst/Owlsmoor as one of its preferred sites. After much planning discussion the infrastructure was laid out comprising a main feeder road from Yorktown Road up to the roundabout at Magdalene Road, an extension to the sewage treatment works in Sandhurst, and a development of a new surface water drainage system down to the Blackwater River, which allowed for the development of approximately an additional 2000 houses. Further development in the Sandhurst area and an increase in traffic led to the extension of a feeder road up to Nine Mile Ride in Crowthorne which is now the Sandhurst/Crowthorne Bypass.

Owlsmoor Women's Institute held its first meeting in the wooden church on the evening of Monday January 4th 1974. It was founded by Mrs Elsie Morley with the help of Mrs Polly Tabor. They collected a nucleus of 25 members. Mrs Elsie Morley became the first President of the branch. With the village developing so quickly it gave newcomers the opportunity to make new friends and participate in village life. The meetings today are held in the Community Centre at 2 pm on the third Tuesday of the month with speakers, demonstrations and competitions.

The village is now a thriving community with many clubs and activities for everyone.

 # PADWORTH

Padworth is known to have been settled as far back as the Saxons and there are a number of banks and ditches known as 'Grim's Ditch' which date to this era. They are believed to have been built to protect the older northern routes into Roman Calleva (now Silchester). It is believed that the Saxons who settled were possibly called Padda hence the place became Padworth or Paddas Farm. Padworth is recorded in documents such as the *assize rolls* and the national *feet of fines* and the Domesday survey.

There have been a number of large Manor houses with influential families in the area over the years including Padworth House, Ufton Court, Husseis and Aldermaston House. Many rivalries and disputes existed between inhabitants, some of which ended up in local court proceedings. In addition to the grand mansions of the rich there were also a number of single-room common cottages, particularly in the area of Donkey Lane on Padworth Common; these residents also appeared with regularity in local courts. Most misdemeanours resulted in fines for minor infringements of commoners' rights, but two Padworth men were hanged at Mortimer for the murder of an old labourer on Padworth Common!

The area was affected by the Black Death in 1348 with estimates of a 40% death rate over a four year period in the area. The area also saw action during the Civil War and it is estimated that approximately 300 men were killed in Padworth Gully during a surprise attack by Prince Rupert's cavalry. These unfortunate souls were buried in pits in Padworth churchyard and a memorial in the church wall tells the story.

Padworth church is a lovely, very small Norman building constructed in 1130 which houses medieval wall paintings, decorated doorways, and monuments to both the Brightwell and Darby Griffin families who owned Padworth House for many generations. The enclosure of the common land at Padworth was via a private Act of Parliament of 1811 and resulted in limited compensation for those affected. There are a number of fine timber-framed and thatched buildings as well as buildings of other ages and styles. Padworth Common still has a pillory (out of use) near Old Tom on the Reading Road.

Padworth is now a peaceful community with a relatively low population for Berkshire. The majority of Padworth's inhabitants live down the hill and nearer to Aldermaston station. The common land is now managed by the Berks, Bucks and Oxon Wildlife Trust due to the populations of rare species including the nightjar.

The village is now seeing many more houses being built but it does not have a village shop, post office or school. However, despite this it does have a thriving pub and the recently renovated village hall is well used by the community.

🍁 PANGBOURNE

Pangbourne means 'Paega's People's Stream', showing that it was the home of an early Saxon chief and his retinue. The place is first recorded in a grant of land here from the Bishop of Leicester to Beorhtwulf, the King of Mercia (the Midlands) in AD 844. This monarch is prominently depicted on the village sign. It shows Beorhtwulf, with the Charter and a Saxon ship over the name of the village. Kenneth Grahame's book, and the symbolic willows, add a modern touch to the design. The Pangbourne village sign, which is an attraction to visitors, was originally erected in 1961 and has undergone recent restoration.

St James the Less Church, which dates back to AD 843, was rebuilt in 1868 leaving an existing brick tower built in 1718. Church Cottage west of the churchyard, once the old smithy, was the home of Kenneth Grahame, author of *The Wind in the Willows*, who found inspiration by the ever-changing riverside. He died here in 1932. The Swan public house also has a literary connection, for it was immortalized in Jerome K. Jerome's *Three Men in a Boat*.

Pangbourne College stands on a hill south-west of the village on the site of an old Folly Tower. It was founded by Sir Thomas Lane Devitt and his son Philip in 1917 to educate and train boys for the Royal or Merchant Navy. It is now a co-educational day and boarding school with 400 pupils, although some naval traditions are maintained. In the grounds of the college is the Falkland Islands War Memorial Chapel. It was built to commemorate the lives and sacrifice of all those who died in the South Atlantic in 1982. It was officially opened in March 2000 by HM Queen Elizabeth II. It houses an extensive library of every book written about the Falklands War as well as the RAF Cottesmore *Diary of Memorabilia* and many other precious documents.

Pangbourne Village Hall was first built as a church hall in 1950 and was used by Pangbourne village school as overflow classrooms. The building became the Village Hall in the 1970s and in 2008 was substantially extended and refurbished. It is now in use every day including weekends for various activities, clubs and craft/art exhibitions.

Pangbourne is ideally situated alongside a beautiful stretch of the Thames on the junction of the Rivers Thames, Pang and Bourne and is classified as an Area of Outstanding Natural Beauty. The south branch of the Ridgeway, (thought to be the oldest road in Britain) via Upper Basildon, drops down into the valley at Pangbourne, where the Thames could originally be crossed by ferry and later by bridge since very early times. The Thames Path can also be joined at Pangbourne where you may walk from the source of the river in Kemble, Gloucestershire to the Thames Barrier at Charlton in south-east London.

Pangbourne has excellent rail and bus links to Reading, London and Oxford. The village is easily accessible by car with a good range of shops, cafés and restaurants including a family-run butcher, Green's of Pangbourne, established in 1950. It has won thousands of accolades and was crowned Britain's Best Butcher Shop in 2011. In recent years Pangbourne has also become recognised as a centre for high-end sports cars. The demographic of the village has also changed with a younger commuter population, particularly with the commencement of the Crossrail and the electrification

Pangbourne

of the railway line. It is interesting to note that Roman finds were made on Shooter's Hill, when the railway line was first cut in 1839, namely 40 gold, silver and brass coins dating from AD 69 to AD 383, along with many skeletons.

A beautiful stretch of river known as Pangbourne Meadow, which lies to the east of Whitchurch Bridge, is owned by the parish and has been since the 1930s. The adjoining portion of the meadow was purchased by the National Trust and the whole meadow is controlled by the Parish Council. There is an annual Village Fete on this site every June which includes the very popular Dragon Boat race event. Nearby is The Dolphin Centre which offers a wide range of water and land-based courses throughout the year for children (over eight) and adults. The building was rebuilt in 2010, but the original building dates back to the 1940s when it was bequeathed to them by a Mr Dolphin! Also crossing the Thames Meadow at Pangbourne is the Whitchurch Toll Bridge which is an outstanding feature of the meadow. This bridge connects Whitchurch on the Oxfordshire side to Pangbourne on the Berkshire side. It was first built in 1792 and was made of wood and cost 2d. to cross. It was rebuilt again in 1852 and then in 1901/2, as an iron bridge. It was then reconstructed in 2013 and reopened in 2014. Both the Toll House and the Bridge are Grade II listed structures. The volume of traffic has increased considerably over time and it is in frequent use. The toll is currently 60p each way for vehicles under 3.5 tonnes. Other tariffs apply.

Berkshire County Council has designated the centre of the village as a conservation area, under the Civic Amenities Act. The area includes the High Street, The Square, and the area around the church. Today the village has greatly expanded with a huge volume of traffic passing through it. At one time there were several banks in the High Street, but these have now all gone. The library remains open but for only a few days each week. On the positive side there are very good social amenities and transport links and it still remains a very desirable place to live.

🍁 PEASEMORE

Peasemore lies to the north-west of Chieveley and has the ancient sheep drove road, the Green Lane to the Ridgeway, as its eastern boundary. A Stone Age axe head found in the orchard of Princes Farm makes it conceivable that the village could have been inhabited since the Stone Age. Its original name was Praximer but there have been many variations over the centuries.

St Barnabas church, Peasmore

It appeared in the Domesday Book with three Manor Houses, though one of these moved to the ownership of Beedon upon the marriage of the owner's daughter. The remaining two Manors came into the hands of Henry VIII, who ran them both as one. The first of these still bears the name of Peasemore Manor and was once owned by Thomas Chaucer. The second was Gidley and this was owned by the Hatt family. Hatt is one of the first names on the church register and is of Saxon origin; only one member of this great family remains in Peasemore.

In the 13th century two pieces of land were given to the Priory of Poughley, the first to Peasemore House, which was an annexe to the Priory and formerly known as Priorside; the second piece was Priors Wood, which then covered about 100 acres of land. Dutch elm disease caused the temporary disappearance of Priors Copse, which extended to a mere three acres by this time, but this area has been completely replanted with indigenous trees. At the Dissolution of the Monastries Peasemore House was given to Cardinal Wolsey and when he was impeached it fell to the Abbot of Westminster, who subsequently sold it to a John Carlton.

The old church of St Paeda was of Norman construction but was demolished during the 19th century. The tower on the existing church of St Barnabas was built by Coward and dates back to about 1730, although the rest of the church was built during the last century. It does, however, boast a nice peal of six bells – possibly one of the best in the county.

In the mid-17th century a fire started at Drakes Farm destroying all the thatched cottages in the centre of the village, the church barns and rectory. A fine 17th-century thatched barn survives at Peasemore House and there are a number of flint and brick buildings, a few downland cob buildings and two granaries on staddle stones to be seen, one in the village and one at nearby Hill Green.

In the past Peasemore was a busy little place; the woollen mills, which served Jack O'Newbury, were destroyed in the fire, and more recently the village blacksmith, two shops, the school, the post office and bus service have gone – but there are positive signs of new enterprise. This has always been predominantly a centre of downland agriculture but with the decrease in the number of people employed on the land there is a danger that Peasemore might join the ranks of other dormitory villages. One new 'industry' is the recent development of a racehorse training establishment with its own all-weather gallop.

It is hoped that there will be active encouragement for other traditional rural industries in the future, providing local employment and topics for discussion in the Fox and Hounds.

🍁 PINKNEYS GREEN

This small hamlet on the north-western boundary of Maidenhead has been known as Pinkneys Green since about 1650 and has a population of 7,400, comprising 2,800 households according to the 2011 census. Probably its most notable feature is the magnificent Pinkneys Green Common which is managed by the National Trust and has seen a number of activities over the years. In the early part of the 20th century it was used by aviation pioneer Johnny Benton, who experimented with his man-lifting kites that led to him building early flying machines. It has since been home to kite boarders, model aircraft enthusiasts, horse riders, kite fliers, picnickers, and not to forget ramblers and dog walkers.

A notable long-term resident was Sir Nicholas Winton MBE, a British humanitarian who arranged the evacuation of 669 mainly Jewish children from Czechoslovakia in the lead up to the Second World War, in order to protect them from the influence of the Nazis. They were relocated to Britain where homes with foster families were found for them so they could be looked after. The press dubbed him 'England's Schindler'; he died in 2015 at the great age of 106. There is a memorial water garden in nearby Oaken Grove Park to commemorate his achievements and a sculpture of him at Maidenhead railway station.

The village has a cricket club situated on the edge of the green where their first match took place in 1885. Cricket was only permitted to be played on Saturdays due to the Lord's Day Observance Act of 1780. The field opposite is visited each May by Carters Steam Fair. The fair is powered by a number of steam engines, has steam powered rides and showman's road locomotives. At this venue it is totally operated by steam and is the only known travelling funfair still able to do this.

Pinkneys Green Scouts hold their annual fete here and their scout hut in Winter Hill Road is where the Ellington Morris dancers meet to practice. There is also a Youth Community Centre and an amateur football team who play home games in Oaken Grove Park. The first ever Girl Guide group was set up at Pinkneys Green by Agnes Baden-Powell, sister of Robert Baden-Powell founder of the Scout movement; her sister Teresa Del Riego was a talented violinist, singer and composer and at one time lived in Golden Ball Lane, not far from the scout hut.

The local children went to the C of E School at Stubbings until it closed in 1934, at which time Alwyn Road School was built and children transferred there. This school closed in 1992 with children moving to Courthouse School.

The church of St James the Less at Stubbings was built in 1850 by a wealthy local resident for use by his family and local people and is part of the Cookham Dean Ecclesiastical Parish. There is also St Mark's Crescent Methodist Church and Blenheim Chapel. The last remaining shop was the Post Office in Lee Lane which in 1871 had been in Pinkneys Road at Kents Corner, near the Waggon & Horses (now the Boundary Arms). There had been a butcher's shop/general store in Pinkneys Drive next to the flint house but this has long been closed.

The four local farms are Pinkneys farm, Hindhay farm, Hyde farm and Lee farm which has stabling for private riders to keep their horses.

There are four public houses, the Pinkneys Arms, the Golden Ball, the Boundary Arms and the Robin Hood.

In the 17th and 18th centuries, this area was the haunt of highwaymen such as the notorious Dick Turpin; they took rich pickings from travellers on the Bath Road by stopping their horse-drawn coaches and stealing from the occupants – or worse! Criminals, convicted of the most serious crimes were often sent to the gallows and a gibbet was situated at Hangman's Corner in

Winter Hill Road. This is where Winter Hill Road joins with the appropriately named Choke Lane. It has been known for horses to become distressed and refuse to pass this spot, so riders are advised to give it a wide berth just in case.

Major employers in past times were Coopers Brick & Tile Works; their products made from locally dug clay moulded and fired in the kilns at their Hindhay Lane site. The brickworks have long been demolished. The site has been redeveloped and a woodland trail incorporating the clay ponds has been created as a nature reserve, where you may come across a Spotted Orchid if you are lucky. Many houses in the area were built with local brick and tiles; some have elaborate panels, roof finials depicting dragons and other mythological beasts. The Cooper family also operated a Lime Works where they quarried chalk and converted it into lime for use in house-building mortar.

The popular film star Richard Todd lived in the village in a converted inn – the Old Shoulder of Mutton, which overlooked grassland leading towards The Thicket. He made many films including *The Dam Busters*, *The Longest Day*, *The Story of Robin Hood and His Merrie Men*, etc.

Another interesting resident was Raymond Bessone, 'hairdresser to the stars' and known to most as Mr Teasy Weasy. He was the first hairdresser to be featured in a television show and plied his trade at his salon in London's Mayfair where he trained Vidal Sassoon and in his local salon in The Colonade, Maidenhead.

🍁 PRIESTWOOD

Although Priestwood may not be considered technically a village these days, the rural spirit and interest remains. After all, Priestwood began in the wooded south-west section of the parish of Warfield, with a tributary of the Kennet, the Bull Brook, passing through it, fed by Warfield waters.

Today Priestwood is proud of its New Town amenities but has managed to keep its undulating contours and many well-established trees. There is now an attractive riverside walk to Binfield along the Bull. At first we were sad to see farms taken over and Priestwood Common woodlands bulldozed out of existence, but when the pleasant houses with their pretty gardens and wide, well-grassed spaces emerged, we were reconciled to our loss, especially when we saw erstwhile London children playing so healthily and safely in their new surroundings. The growth of neighbourliness has been encouraged by the shopping centre and the church. The church of St Andrew completed in

1888 was once a Gothic Revival building designed by the architect H.G.W. Drinkwater but was demolished 100 years after it was built. In its place stands an exciting new design allowing a spacious uncluttered nave where the altar is wholly visible and the priest is one with his congregation, and not segregated as in older churches.

Bracknell Street grew from a small settlement where paths crossed in Windsor Forest, into a sleepy but prosperous community of about 5,000 inhabitants. Horse fairs were held in April, August and October all through the 18th and 19th centuries when bull-baiting was popular. This sport was forbidden after 1835. The October Fair was also a Hiring Fair where anyone from a cook to a farm labourer announced their skills for hire. The cooks wore a red ribbon and carried a basting spoon, and the housemaids had a blue ribbon and carried a broom.

When the Windsor Forest Turnpike Trust was formed in 1759 Bracknell boasted several hostelries for the London stage coaches. Two of the turnpike milestones, proclaiming the distance from Hyde Park Corner, are still to be seen.

🍁 PURLEY

Purley is a split-level village, cut in two by the Western Region line of British Rail and the Reading/Oxford Road (A329) which runs parallel to it. The nearest railway station is Tilehurst, a mile distant in the east, and to the west are Pangbourne and other Thames-side villages. Four narrow red brick bridges cross the railway, taking you from the lower to the upper level. The River Thames curves round the northern and eastern boundaries, through Mapledurham Lock with its colourful flowerbeds in the warmer months. From here can be seen the wooded hills of the Chilterns on the opposite bank and the boats travelling upstream the 33 miles to Oxford or possibly all the 78 miles downstream to London.

The name Purley has been variously spelt as Porlaa, Porlei etc. and is said to mean 'a clearing in the woods for snipe and bittern' rather than an earlier suggestion of 'land of the pear trees'.

Purley village – the original Purley Street – is a mere quarter of a mile of pretty old cottages and the primary school, with Purley Lodge at the west end. In the 18th century John George Liebenrood, a Dutch merchant and local benefactor, who married a Purley girl, lived in this house, rumoured to have connections with Reading Abbey. In 1872 the Rector of Purley, Rev Richard Palmer, generously financed the brick and flint school building for 55 children (specified to be of 'the labouring, manufacturing and other poorer classes of

Purley'). His sister gave approximately three-quarters of an acre on which plot were 'two messuages (houses) together with gardens and orchards and the schoolhouse and buildings'.

The path leading onwards to the church of St Mary the Virgin is now a road of modern dwellings, with a boat marina. The church, for a long time isolated from the village, is again surrounded by houses, and like so many others was extensively restored in the 1870s by G. E. Street, to conform with the approved architecture of that time. In 1983 a hexagonal lantern-roofed north aisle, with knapped flint exterior walls, was added to accommodate the growing population, also to serve as a church hall.

Purley Magna manor house was once close to the church but in about 1800 the Storer family, Lords of the Manor at that time, built Purley Park, a fine mansion in the classical style on higher, dryer ground. Today Purley Park Trust provides services for people with learning disabilities there.

On the western side, standing well back from the main road, is Purley Hall, previously known as Hyde Hall and said to date from 1609. The boundaries of Sulham, Whitchurch and Purley meet in the dining room. The Hyde family was much persecuted for their Catholic beliefs.

The mortgaged estate was sold to Francis Hawes of the 'South Sea Bubble' scandal in 1720. The Wilder family bought it in 1773 and held it for nearly 200 years. During that time Warren Hastings rented the house while he prepared his defence against impeachment. His ghost, or that of his wife, is reputed to haunt the house. This side of Purley is shielded by a large area of beech and conifer plantations, maintained by the Forestry Commission, which provide secluded walks and the habitat of muntjac, fallow deer and other wildlife.

The population of Purley remained less than 200 until 1900, when numbers increased dramatically, especially after the influx of refugees from the London blitz during the Second World War. Many remained permanently in their holiday homes on the Purley Park River Estate.

The upper part of Purley, mostly residential, includes the recreation ground and sports pavilion, providing facilities for football, netball, cricket and tennis, with a thriving social club. There are no public houses in Purley. There is, however, a very nice hall, built by villagers as a memorial to those killed in the Second World War, which during the day houses the play group.

Like so many Thames-side villages, urbanisation and heavy vehicular traffic has blurred the old village outlines but every effort has been made to preserve trees. There are many noble beeches and the venerable oak in Long Lane. It is questionable whether this was ever part of the western boundary of Windsor Great Forest, as village tradition claims. New planting continues.

🍁 READING

High ground between the Kennet and Thames provided a good defensive site during Saxon times. Followers of Saxon chief Reada settled here, giving rise to the name Reading. The Anglo-Saxon Chronicle recorded the devastating raids by Norse invaders. In 871 'the army came into Wessex to Reading'. The Danes occupied the settlement and fierce battles were fought in the surrounding area in their attempt to conquer Wessex. The conflict continued for more than a century until in 1017 a Dane, Cnut (Canute) became King and Reading then became a Danish possession.

The throne returned to the English with the accession of Edward the Confessor and during his reign Reading became a borough. Reading is described in the Domesday Book as having 59 properties, with dues paid annually to the king.

In 1121 King Henry I founded Reading Abbey. Endowed with great wealth, the Abbey welcomed monks and pilgrims, many of whom were catered for by the Hospitium. At the height of its power, the Abbey contained 200 relics, including the hand of St James the Apostle. It dominated the spiritual and economic life of Reading for four centuries until the Dissolution of the Monastries in 1539.

Wealthy Reading Abbey was an important target. The Abbot, Hugh Cook Faringdon was tried for high treason and charged with denying the supremacy of the King. He was sentenced to be hung, drawn and quartered to set a bloody example of the price of disloyalty. The Abbey became the property of the King and all its valuables were removed. The Abbot's quarters were retained as a Royal residence for visiting monarchs. By 1549 the systematic dismantling of the abbey church and monastic buildings had taken place. Nothing which could be carried away or sold remained. Only the rubble interior of the walls survived.

The people of Reading suffered from the loss of the employment the abbey had provided. However, prosperity increased gradually during the following two centuries with trading in wool and leather using the two long-established trade routes and river links.

Reading was not left unscathed by the Civil War. In 1642, the Royalist garrison at Reading was besieged by the Parliamentarians, and epidemics ravaged the population. Charles I was imprisoned in the town in 1647. However, with good transport routes, Reading recovered, becoming an important market town and coaching stop between London and Bath. The George Hotel is a surviving example of a coaching inn. New industries were established in brewing, iron founding and brick making.

During the 19th century new transport links led to a rapid expansion. In 1810 the Kennet and Avon Canal opened, providing a direct link with the ports of Bristol and, via the Thames, with London. The arrival of Brunel's railway in 1840 enabled even easier transport of raw materials and finished goods. Reading became known for 'beer, bulbs and biscuits' as three industries dominated the town. The Simonds family established a successful brewery and a banking business. Suttons Seeds ran its headquarters from the town centre while Huntley & Palmer's factory, founded in 1822, sold their biscuits around the world. There was a rapid growth in population as people moved from the countryside to work in these prospering industries. By 1900 the population had trebled from just over 21,000 in 1850 to over 72,000.

This period produced several of Reading's iconic Victorian buildings: the Town Hall in 1875, the Concert Hall in 1882 and the Museum and Library in 1883, all designed by Alfred Waterhouse, noted architect and designer of the Natural History Museum and Manchester Town Hall. A 19th-century full-size replica of the Bayeux Tapestry takes pride of place in the museum. The prison, designed by Sir George Gilbert Scott in 1844, was where Oscar Wilde was imprisoned from 1895 to 1897. His experience there inspired him to write *The Ballad of Reading Gaol*. St James' Church was one of the first churches designed by Augustus Pugin while the Forbury Gardens, opened in 1873, were restored in 2005 and laid out with Victorian planting schemes to resemble the original designs. The gardens contain an unofficial emblem of Reading, the Maiwand Lion. This massive cast-iron sculpture is a memorial to the men of the 66th Berkshire Regiment who were killed at the Battle of Maiwand during the Anglo-Afghan War.

During the First World War Reading opened several temporary hospitals for wounded and convalescing troops. In the Second World War Reading was designated a 'safe town', judged to be sufficiently far from London. It received large numbers of evacuees and relocated government departments. The mansion at Caversham Park became the listening service for the BBC and the Ministry of Information. During the post-war years programmes of redevelopment and housing expansion began to change the nature of Reading.

In Reading today modern industries such as IT, accounting, finance and a huge Tesco depot have gradually established themselves. Green Park, built with its own wind turbine, 195 acres of parkland and water features to encourage biodiversity, is one of several business parks. Crossrail is scheduled to open bringing greener and faster train links while about 70% of our brightly coloured buses run on 'green fuels'.

Many people have been welcomed from the Caribbean, Pakistan and

India. There are also long-established Irish, Polish, Portuguese and Nepalese communities. An iconic mural of Black History has adorned a wall on Mill Lane for over 25 years. Reading is officially twinned with Clonmel in Ireland, San Francisco Libre in Nicaragua and Düsseldorf in Germany.

The Oracle, with its riverside location, offers shops and restaurants. Alternatively RISC has a fairtrade shop, Global Café, bar and roof garden. The Purple Turtle, a late-night bar and music venue first opened in the 1990s.

Madejski Stadium is home to Reading Football Club, and is also used by London Irish Rugby Club. There are two large museums – Reading Museum and the Museum of Rural Life (MERL).The Royal Berkshire Hospital houses a medical museum, while the Cole (zoology) and Ure (Greek archaeology) museums are in the University.

Cultural centres include the Hexagon theatre, Concert Hall, South Street Arts Centre, Progress Theatre and Rising Sun Arts Centre. Reading Symphony Orchestra give regular concerts. There are many established theatre groups; one of the most successful is Reading Between the Lines, with their productions of *Henry I of England* and *Matilda the Empress* – linked to Reading Abbey. Since 1971, one of the best known music festivals in the world has been held every August in Reading and a Waterfest also runs each year, on the River Kennet next to the abbey ruins. Other big community annual events include Reading Pride and a Beer and Cider Festival.

Many famous names have connections here: Mary Russell Mitford wrote *Belford Regis*, drawing on her knowledge of Reading; Amelia Dyer, *The Baby Farmer*, hanged for the murder of many babies in the 1890s; Phoebe Cusden, mayor in 1946, was responsible for the initial twinning with Düsseldorf; both Jane Austen and Kenneth Branagh attended schools in the town; Kate Winslet, Chris Tarrant, Lucy Worsley and Ricky Gervais were born here. Michael Bond survived the bombing of the People's Pantry in 1943 and was later inspired by evacuee children at Reading station, wearing luggage labels and carrying suitcases, to write *Paddington*. Trooper Fred Potts was awarded the VC following the heroic rescue of his colleague Arthur Andrews (also from Reading) at Gallipoli in the First World War.

In 1908 Edith Morley, was made the first woman professor of a British university, in Reading. Well known alumni include: Wilfred Owen, Michael Rosen, Tomasz Schafernaker, Cornelia Parker, Bob and Roberta Smith, Jamie Cullum, Pippa Greenwood and many Olympic athletes.

🍁 REDLANDS

When the *Readingas* established the settlement that was to become Reading, probably in the 5th century, the area now called Redlands had already been the scene of human activity for thousands of years. Archaeological finds in the area included flint tools used in hunting and in farming dating back to the Stone Age.

Further archaeological exploration found a burial ground on the edge of the Redlands area where the bones were identified as Romano-British. Some of these would have belonged to people who farmed the land around the very old route known to Saxons as Rudden Lane, in modern times now called Redlands Road.

In medieval times Reading Abbey had a leper hospital on land later known as the Spital Field which covered all of the area now known as Redlands. The name derived from 'hospital' and changed over time to Spittal Fields. After the Dissolution of the Monasteries the abbey lands were taken by the Crown and Spittal Fields was sold several times, eventually to Sir Francis Knollys, a prominent member of the Elizabethan court and an MP. Within the Spittal Fields was Red Lane Farm, first mentioned in a tenure agreement of 1604, and located near the present Royal Berkshire Hospital. This was held under tenure for many years until it was sold by Sir Francis' widow to a local wealthy woollen draper. Red Lane Farm's ownership for the next hundred years passed through the draper's family by inheritance until the late 1700s when it became part of the Earley Court Estate.

During this period the area of Spittal Fields had only two boundary roads – to the north, Ort Lane, the main route to London now called London Road and to the west, Red Lane, now Redlands Road. The latter was frequently used to avoid the turnpike tolls on the main route south from the town centre until a toll gate was put in at the top of Red Lane too.

Red Lane Farm was farmed by the members of the Shackel family but the estate on which the farm lay was, by the 19th century, owned by Lady Sidmouth. From the ridge at the top of Red Lane, part of which is now covered by Upper Redlands Road, there was a magnificent view across the Thames admired by the Marquis of Blandford who lived on nearby Whiteknights estate. He acquired land on the present Upper Redlands Road to construct a carriage drive on the edge of Whiteknights to take advantage of this.

In 1839 the Sidmouths were approached to sell a plot of land for the proposed Royal Berkshire Hospital. Instead they donated four acres of the farmland for the site which opened later that year. The farm in the mid-19th century had considerable land including a market garden next to the hospital and a hundred-acre field crossed diagonally by a footpath from Reading to Earley. The farmer lived in Red Lane House on the corner of what is now Addington Road and Redlands Road.

In 1865 Viscount Sidmouth then sold 126 acres of the farm for housing, evicting the Shackel family who had farmed the land for 200 years. The land was bought in 1865 by Peter Spokes, a local chemist who had formed the Redlands Estate Company to develop the land for housing for all the workers in the growing industries like Huntley & Palmers. In 1869 ten acres were bought to build Reading School, designed like the Town Hall by Waterhouse.

The footpath became Erleigh Road which by 1873 was planted with lime trees as were other neighbouring roads where larger villas were being built. Meanwhile the construction of terraced housing to rent to workers continued in nearby streets. By 1878 St Giles church noted that there were over 200 new houses in the area with occupants numbering a total of around 1,000, all living over a mile away from their parish church. So an iron church (tin tabernacle) was built on Erleigh Road, replaced four years later by the completion of the current St Luke's church in 1883.

By the time of the 1881 Census, Redlands housed many young families as it continues to do. They had come from rural areas in Wiltshire, Hampshire, Oxfordshire and Buckinghamshire. Almost a third of the population were children and the average age of adults was 34. There was no local school until Redlands School opened in 1891.

When the First World War came, both the school and the Parish Hall next to St Luke's Church became temporary hospitals for the casualties. Pupils were dispersed to schools in nearby areas and infants were taught part time in the Parish Rooms next door to the hospital in the Parish Hall.

There had always been areas of open space in Redlands, harking back to its origins as fields but at the outbreak of the Second World War much had disappeared under housing. However, there were still orchards near the original boundary roads as well as allotments. After the war many of the large villas in the western part of Redlands were converted from family homes to other uses such as nursing homes, guest houses and offices. Later, in the 1960s some were demolished to release land for flats or converted for multiple occupancy.

The inhabitants of Redlands became more multicultural as families from Pakistan and India began to move into the area. The purchase of the Whiteknights estate by Reading University in 1947 to establish a large campus meant that in more recent years there has been a huge increase in the student population of the area as many of the terraced houses have been rented to them.

Redlands School has for some years had pupils speaking as many as 25 languages, reflecting both the changing nature of the Redlands population and of Reading as a whole. Nearly all of the local traders whose shops once thrived in the area had disappeared by the 1980s. These included the local post office and, like many villagers, Redlands inhabitants have to travel to the town centre or other areas for many of their shopping needs and services if the local Cooperative supermarket cannot supply them.

The Parish Hall is well used by a number of local groups and in 2007 it was where Redlands WI began and continues to thrive with over 60 members of a wide age range. It has the distinction of being the only WI within central Reading, for such the area of Redlands has become. Nevertheless, with its strong community feel, its local school and church and much of its Victorian character intact in both its attractive housing and other buildings, it is very much 'a village within the town'.

🍁 REMENHAM

The River Thames defines much of the Remenham Parish boundary, flowing for about five miles in a horseshoe-shaped gorge cut into the 300-ft high chalk hills. This gorge is thought to have been formed at the end of the last Ice Age 10,000 years ago. Remenham is a rural village on the bank of the Thames and was first recorded in the Domesday Book as Ramenham (raven's home) in 1086 as a manor held by King William the Conqueror. It had a tax value of 1 mill and 1,000 eels. The population was 40, including four slaves. It just survived the plagues of the 14th and 17th centuries.

Touring through Remenham, you might start at the Little Angel public house on Remenham Lane. This has been a favourite rendezvous for local residents and other well-known names, including Kate Moss, Orlando Bloom, Liam Gallagher and even Prince Harry. Dating from the 18th century, it also has a resident ghost Mary Blandy. She was accused of poisoning her father because he did not approve of her choice of husband, and was chased out of Henley by a hostile crowd. She fled across the bridge and took refuge with her friend who was the landlord of the Little Angel. She was later arrested and executed in Oxford in 1772, but some say she still haunts the pub.

Travelling along the lane you leave Regatta Headquarters and Leander Club behind while travelling alongside the river and the Henley Regatta course. The Regatta was first held in 1839 and originally was held on one afternoon. However, its popularity down the years encouraged a longer event and by

St Nicholas' church, Remenham

1986 it had extended to five days. Prince Albert became the first royal patron in 1851.

Just before the Remenham Rowing Club you pass a large house on the left. This was where the actress Gladys Cooper lived. She started as a child model and starred in silent films in the twenties and was on the London stage for many years. She was made a Dame in 1967. Her sons-in-law were Robert Morley who lived in Crazies Hill and Robert Hardy who lived in Henley.

Passing a few riverside dwellings you will see in front of you St Nicholas church. This was mentioned in the Domesday Book in 1086 and the first rector was recorded in 1297. Originally it was a chapelry of Hurley and was served by the monks of Hurley Priory. On the north wall you will find a memorial plaque to Lord Hunt who lived in the parish for many years. There is a beautiful lychgate dedicated to Violet Noble of Park Place, who died aged 14 years from scarlet fever and look too, for the grave of Cable Gould, a lock keeper, who died in 1839, aged 92. Just next to the church is the brick and flint village hall which was given to the parishioners of Remenham by Viscount Hambleden in 1913 and which is the meeting place of Remenham WI.

It is not long before you will see Temple Island appearing, the start of the

Regatta Course and one and a half miles from Henley. This ornamental temple on the island was built in 1771 as a fishing lodge, designed by James Wyatt, who also designed the interior. The island and temple were purchased by the Regatta Stewards in 1987 and have been fully restored under the auspices of the Regatta Committee.

As you approach the end of Remenham Lane, you will come across the Flower Pot, at the junction with Ferry Lane – a short walk down to the site of the old hand-operated chain ferry across the river where boat mooring is still available. The pub is worth a visit, to see the eclectic collection of many glass cases of fish.

Turning the corner and starting up Aston Lane, you pass one of the entrances to Culham Court. This is an imposing house on the banks of the Thames, the present building dating back to 1770. King George III and his wife Queen Charlotte visited in 1804 and some special bread rolls were brought down from London, freshly baked, for their breakfast! The house is still privately owned and extensive work has been carried out on the estate over the past 10 years. Within the estate, a new chapel has been built by Culham Chapel Trust, in the style of a classical temple built by a team of British traditionally skilled craftsmen. A public mass is held on the last Sunday of every month.

Moving up Aston Lane, you pass the former house of Lord Hunt who became world famous as the leader of the first successful ascent of Mount Everest in 1953.

Temple Island, Remenham

Parish Hall, Remenham

Turn right on reaching the main road, back to Henley, you will see Remenham Place on the right. This was bought in 1920 by Sir Douglas Dawson, the Lord Chamberlain in charge of banning material deemed too obscene for public performance on stage and screen. The system collapsed soon after the *Lady Chatterley's Lover* trial. In the late 1960s it became a residential home for gentlefolk but was sold in 2011 and is now a private house again.

Further down on the left, is Park Place. This was originally a farm called Strouds and was purchased by Lord Archibald Hamilton. His son William married his mistress Emma who later became the mistress of Lord Nelson. In 1738, Lord Archibald sold the house to Frederick who was Prince of Wales and father of King George III. General Conway, veteran of the War of the Austrian Succession and of the Battle of Culloden, bought the house in 1751. More recently, it was run as a school for disadvantaged children but in 2011 it became Britain's most expensive house when it was bought by Andrey Borodin for £140 million.

🍁 RISELEY

Life in the small village of Riseley changed radically for its inhabitants with the opening of the Swallowfield bypass in 1981. Before that time, and upon the completion of the M4 motorway, heavy container lorries and other traffic had thundered through the village, barely negotiating the narrow bends of the notorious A33. What had once been a country road, through the middle of a small village, became a major link for all traffic going south and south-west.

Over many years various schemes to relieve the situation had been considered and rejected. One half of the village hardly knew the other half, separated as they were from each other by this continual stream of vehicles, but suddenly rural peace once more descended upon Riseley.

People could stand and gossip by the roadside, as they do in all small villages. Mothers no longer feared for the safety of their children as they set off on their bicycles to call on their friends, or just played the running, jumping and skipping games which children everywhere enjoy. Indeed, for the first few weeks after the opening of the new bypass, it was the sound of children's voices echoing about the village of which one suddenly became aware. And the older villagers, reminiscing about the days of their childhood, were reminded of how they had been able to play up and down the road, and had enjoyed maypole dancing on the village green.

Once again, Riseley has a village green and Riseley Memorial Hall which is now home to Riseley Village Tea Rooms. At the end of 2012 the pre-school, the main source of income, closed leaving the hall underused and falling into disrepair. A local resident, Pam Wright, researched ideas and came up with the plan of opening a not-for-profit tea room, staffed by volunteers. This provides an excellent place for locals to meet and has increased community spirit.

🍁 RUSCOMBE

About half a million years ago, an ancient Thames flowed eastwards over the gravel of Sonning Golf Links to Ruscombe, where it turned north. Many Stone Age flint implements have been collected from the gravel pits of Ruscombe Hill, and the present highway through the village was the old Saxon Road.

The first recorded history occurs in the foundation charter of the Cathedral of old Sarum in 1091. Among the original endowments is listed 'the church of Sunning (Sonning) with the tythes and other property thereto belonging, and ten hides of land in Rothescamp (Ruscombe)'.

The eastern part of the parish, known as the 'Lakes', was once a marshy swamp, flooded in winter, providing perch, pike and eel in abundance for the fishermen, and withies for the baskets were woven by industrious villagers. In 1820 the upper part of the Broadwater Stream was carried away by the Bray Cut, thus draining the lake. The land was enclosed and cultivated.

The Church of Saint James the Great, made of flint, has a long history, but the chancel is all that remains of the old structure. The 400-year-old Church Cottage is said to be the original Chaplain's House, but is no longer church property. Of the same date is the shooting and fishing lodge where George I was reputed to pause for a meal when out for a day's sport from Windsor.

William Penn, famous as the founder of Pennsylvania and a Quaker, lived in the parish from 1710 until his death in 1718. He used to drive through Twyford, in a coach and four on his way to Friends' Meetings in Reading. The house was pulled down in 1830, probably Ruscombe House which was in the field opposite Southbury Farm. The original bakehouse and dairy buildings were finally demolished a few years ago, revealing an unexpected stairway and attic room. Legend says that this was a highwayman's hideout. Penn's name lives on in the Rural District Council Estate of Pennfields.

🍁 SHAW-CUM-DONNINGTON

Shaw-cum-Donnington is a parish on the northern end of Newbury. The original villages of Shaw and Donnington lie on the River Lambourn and are both served by the parish church of St Mary's at Shaw.

The original church in Shaw was built about the year AD 1,000, but it became

Shaw House

Donnington Castle

so dilapidated that it was demolished and the present church was consecrated in 1842. A priory existed at Donnington in 1448 but was dissolved by Henry VIII in 1538. The site is now the sale rooms of Dreweatt Neate.

Two notable buildings in the parish are Shaw House and Donnington Castle. Shaw House is one of the finest Elizabethan mansions in the country, completed in 1581 by Thomas Dolman. The Dolman family were successful clothiers and landowners in Newbury. It is now in the possession of West Berkshire Council, who hold many events there.

Donnington Castle was built in 1386 by Sir Richard Abberbury. During the Civil War it held out for the King and was besieged for two years between 1644 and 1646. After its surrender, Parliament voted to demolish it and now only the gatehouse remains. The Second Battle of Newbury in 1644 took place in this area.

Donnington Hospital was originally built in 1393 by Sir Richard Abberbury as homes for thirteen poor men. These buildings were rebuilt after the Civil War and are still standing on the Oxford Road between the two river bridges. The Charity now has additional homes in the village.

Today the parish has grown considerably with many schools and new houses. It is also home to some large international companies. A favourite place for picnics is Snelsmore Country Park. It is one of the largest heathlands in southern England, and within easy walking distance of Donnington Castle.

The Village Hall is host to many groups and activities from Pre-School to Tai Chi, Gardening Club to Parish Council, Brownies and Guides, and, of course, the Women's Institute. The first meeting was held in 1919 but by the 1960s numbers had dwindled as many more women worked. The evening group began in 1966 and is still going strong today.

🍁 SHINFIELD

Shinfield gets its name from the shining fields, which are the flooded fields surrounding the Loddon River after heavy rain.

Shinfield has become much larger over the past 15-20 years, with housing now covering much of the farm and open land that was owned by the University of Reading. There is also more housing being built now and there will be even more in the future.

SANGs (Suitable Alternative Natural Greenspaces) and SSSIs (Sites of Special Scientific Interest) have been included on the boundaries of the new housing and are beginning to mature into safe, traffic-free places to walk the dog or take the children to ride their bikes among wild flowers and trees.

St Mary's church used to be on the outskirts of the village, but now is surrounded by new housing. The church will be celebrating its 950th anniversary in 2019. The old vicarage is now home to *L'Ortolan*, Reading's only Michelin starred restaurant.

Here is one of our Pound Green WI member's thoughts on Shinfield over the past 50 years –

We moved to School Green, Shinfield, when our son was 10 days old. He was 50 in September 2018.

The views from our house have changed dramatically. Before the building that is now Shinfield View, the luxury Residential Home, a local builder's yard Burrell's was opposite. It was nicely hidden by a hedge. A row of elm trees lined the little car park that led to the British Legion and the old, but much loved, Association Hall. We had lots of lovely parties there, especially on New Year's Eve. My children went to the Infant School on the green; the school recently celebrated its 300th anniversary. It was much, much smaller than it is now. They all loved it. There were two pubs on the green too. Both were popular before drink driving rules. The Bell and Bottle is still open, but the Royal Oak, famous for its large meals, is now a Co-op store.

The green outside the school is used for many village events, the May

Day Fun Run Fair, Shrove Tuesday pancake races, and St Mary's Church Summer Fete.

Chestnut Crescent was already built along with Cobham House. This used to be sheltered accommodation for the retired but is now for singles and couples who have lost their homes. The green at the junction with Hollow Lane and School Green was called Pound Green, which is now a roundabout the size of a 50 pence piece! Hence the name of our WI.

The house we live in is 111 years old and we have everything we need in our retirement within 200 yards: doctors, dentists, chemist, Post Office, an excellent bus service and of course the Co-op store. I won't mention the other changes such as the thousands of houses being built on our doorstep!

Shinfield is very fortunate to have many clubs and associations that encourage friendship and fellowship in the village, with villagers belonging to several of them.

There is also a well-used voluntary car service which covers Shinfield and the local villages.

🍁 SILCHESTER

Long before Silchester became the thriving Roman city which its name suggests, it was the important British town of Calleva Atrebatum. The name derives from the tribe of the Atrebates, whose kings ruled much of Southern England. Visitors to Silchester now can follow the perimeter of the Roman city by tracing the remains of the wall which enclosed this important centre and the gateways leading to London, Winchester and Old Sarum can still be seen. In the period between 1864–1892 the whole area was extensively excavated, displaying evidence of roads on a grid system and many very large and important buildings, chief of these being the Forum with the Basilica. Sadly, the ground had to be filled in again and it reverted to farmland, the lines of the former road system showing clearly in aerial photographs in the shading of the crops grown there.

New evidence has been discovered of a way of life in this Roman civilian town, for it was never a garrison, and the ruins of the amphitheatre which lies outside the wall near the East Gate have also been uncovered. The majority of the finds from the 19th-century excavations are in Reading Museum.

Just inside the Roman Wall at its eastern side stands the beautiful church of St Mary the Virgin. This is near the spot where the remains were found within the Roman City of what is thought to be the earliest known urban

Christian church anywhere north of the Alps. The earliest part of the present building dates from about 1180 and was added to by succeeding Lords of the Manor. There are some very early frescoes on the walls at the east end. When Oliver Cromwell's soldiers were desecrating so many churches, local legend has it that the original glass from the windows was removed and hidden somewhere for safe-keeping. Unfortunately legend does not recall where – so the parishioners of Silchester are still hoping to discover it intact! Certainly the carved chancel screen was buried in a dung heap at nearby Manor Farm and not restored to the church until early in the 19th century. This presented some difficulties to a local craftsman who was asked to repair the screen recently – how to match oak which has spent some years buried in a dung heap? Luckily he succeeded.

There is a tablet on a wall in the church recording the gift by a Mr Hyde in 1671, of four acres of valuable land to the poor of the parish. Hydes Charity still exists and is administered by trustees from the parish and the name is remembered in Hydes Platt, a small estate of houses in the village.

Although Silchester's history goes back to pre-Roman times it is by no means an old-fashioned village. In the Middle Ages the village moved from the Roman city area to the pound, where cattle were impounded when allowed to stray. Pound House was the pub, and Pound Cottage was the home of the pound keeper. There was also a smithy and a bakery near the corner. On its western boundary is situated what is probably the present hub of the place, Silchester Common. This is 160 acres of heathland and wooded areas, with parts designated as a Site of Special Scientific Interest, with rare plants, butterflies and birds. There are two playing fields for cricket and football, one of which is used by Silchester Church of England Primary School. Also on the edge of the Common is the Methodist Chapel and, close to the playing field, the local inn, the Calleva Arms and the Village Hall. The hall is the centre of numerous activities throughout the year.

Although nearby towns have experienced rapid development and the village is only 15 minutes' drive from both the M3 and M4, Silchester still enjoys a rural environment and peaceful setting.

🍁 SINDLESHAM

Sindlesham is widely known as an estate village in Wokingham Borough created by John Walter, father and son, who were proprietors of *The Times* within the extensive estate they created during the 19th century.

However, Sindlesham has a much longer history than this. It lay within the 'liberty' or jurisdiction of Winnersh, itself originally part of the Bishop of Salisbury's manor of Sonning. As an estate the 'liberty' was broken up probably before the 13th century and part of it became the manor of Sindlesham. This has been recorded as Scindlesham in the 12th century, Syndlesham in the 14th century, Sinsan in the 17th century and Sinsham in the 19th century.

In the 13th century the manor was in the hands of Robert de Sindlesham followed by his son, also Robert. But which was named 'Sindlesham' first, the family or the place is not clear!

A younger relative of Robert's, Margaret de Lenham and her descendants subsequently held the manor of Sindlesham until 1523. Within a period of sixty years or so from about 1585 to the start of the Civil War, the manor changed hands not by descent but due to religious or political allegiances. Sir Francis Englefield forfeited his estates including Sindlesham to the Crown after being found guilty of refusing to accept the Church of England, and a subsequent lord of the manor, John Backhouse, suffered in the Civil War for his loyalty to Charles I.

In the Middle Ages, extensive woods stretched from Ashridge in the north, east and west part of what became the Walters' estate. The Bear Wood part of it extended much further to the south and east than today. It became one of the administrative walks of Windsor Forest, such as Bagshotte Rails further south and was named Bear Wood Walke.

The keeping of deer and hunting took place strictly by permission of the Crown. The exclusive deer hunting reserve or chase of the Bishops of Salisbury in Bear Wood gave them the right to hunt here as Lord of Wokingham-cum-Yeyndon (Evendon), at least from 1316. The Bishop would stay, no doubt, in Sonning Palace with his guests and have enjoyed the sport of hunting fallow deer in Bear Wood.

However, there were several difficulties encountered by more than one Bishop of Salisbury, regarding Bishops Bear Wood during the 400 or so years between 1272 and 1645.

Bear Wood was not only a hunting paradise for the Bishops of Salisbury, but was of great importance to many local inhabitants. Part of it was described as 'being on the waste of the Manor of Evendons'. 'Waste' is always of importance to local people. A large part was common grazing for the animals of commoners of Wokingham (Evendons), Hurst, Barkham, Arborfield and Sindlesham, who had 'rights of herbage' and this had been so 'since time out of mind'. Their rights of common granted by the Bishop of Salisbury were jealously guarded. It seems they may also have grown crops there.

When James I, who was a fanatical deer hunter, came to the throne in 1603 he wanted to transfer a large number of his deer from other royal parks to Bear Wood. But there was no way of confining them. Initially the Commoners had bent over backwards to accommodate their new sovereign, even when his deer ate their crops.

However, in 1613 the Commoners found that the King had given permission to the two new Keepers of the Wood to raise a mound said to be seven feet high with a fence and hedge, around '60 to 80 acres' of land for 'the rearing and feeding of about 200 deer'. Part of the plan was to build a hunting lodge.

The Commoners' patience was at an end. Nearly 60 named Commoners and their children who lived in Barkham and Hurst, met at night on 9th February 1614, tore down the fences and hedge. Later, on 2nd June, their children broke up and scattered the building materials. Legal proceedings were instituted by the Crown in the Star Chamber against 13 or more Barkham inhabitants. The complaints and the case rumbled on.

The land, the Commoners said, was chase, not forest under forest law, and they had rights of herbage! The case continued until 1645, when the monarchy of King Charles I appeared doomed. The Commoners' difficulties were apparently resolved for there seems to be no mention of the case after that date.

Part of Bear Wood remained Crown land until 1830. In the process of creating a grand estate, John Walter II bought both it and much of the 'liberty' of Newland and built the first Walter house and the church.

John Walter III pulled down his father's house and built the mansion Bearwood House. Following his death in the 1890s and that of his son Arthur in 1910, the Canadian Red Cross ran Bearwood House as a hospital during the First World War.

From 1827, a public meeting had approved the foundation of the Merchants' Seamen Orphan Asylum. The number of orphans had risen during the First World War and when it ended Bearwood House was bought for The Royal Merchant Navy School. In 1961 the school began to accept fee-paying students and changed its name to Bearwood College. This has now been sold and has opened as one of the Reddam House schools which were first founded in South Africa.

An estate village is one which is wholly within the private estate, in this case Sindlesham on the Walters' estate of Bearwood. It consisted of several ornate cottages in part built as two terraces and includes a primary school, a pub and the church.

John Walter the elder (or second) built the present Anglican church in Sindlesham in 1830 in an elegant 14th-century style including a western tower which has an embattled parapet. It stands in the centre of a churchyard bounded by yew and laurel hedges. It is dedicated to St Catherine, the name of one of his daughters; in 1846 the ecclesiastical parish of St Catherine Bear Wood was created.

The Sindlesham Baptist congregation probably began to meet around 1828. The church was built in 1834 but was extended in 1868 and again in the 1980s and is of an unusual semi-circular plan.

Sindlesham House, formerly Sindlesham Lodge, was built after 1770 and is now the Berkshire Masonic Centre.

The present Sindlesham Mill which is a three-storey brick building is 19th century; it was listed Grade II in 1987. It was a watermill, active until about 1963 and produced *Homeland Flour* which was milled and packed at Sindlesham Mills. It was owned by part of the Simonds family.

🍁 SONNING-ON-THAMES

Sonning–on–Thames nestles on the banks of the River Thames, which forms the boundary between Berkshire and Oxfordshire. The ancient parish of Sonning once extended from Sonning Common in the north-west to Sandhurst in the south-east.

The Domesday Survey of 1086 shows that Sonning was a thriving community with a flour mill, fisheries, and a wide area of both pasture and woodland from which to prosper.

The importance of Sonning was established when a palace was built for the Bishops of Salisbury on the Holme Park estate. Visitors included Edward (the 'Black Prince') after campaigning in France during the Hundred Years' War and King John, who stayed whilst the Magna Carta was being drafted in 1215. In 1399 Henry Bolingbroke locked up the child bride of Richard II, Isabella de Valois, in the palace. After attempts to rescue her had failed, she was finally sent back to France whilst her husband was left to die in captivity. Local legend has it that the exiled young queen's disconsolate ghost still wanders the quiet banks of the river. In the 16th century the palace became the property of Elizabeth I who is said to have visited on several occasions. There is nothing to be seen of the palace now except uneven ground, however, artefacts were unearthed in an excavation during 1914 and are to be found at Reading Museum.

Holme Park, on Sonning Lane, has had many distinguished owners over the centuries, one of them being Robert Palmer, Tory MP for Berkshire in

Sonning

the 1830s. Palmer was a generous benefactor and his name is still associated with the cottages in Pearson Road and the first water pump in Sonning. Very close to the water pump is the Bull Inn, a timber-framed building dating back to the 16th century. It is said to have been a guest house for pilgrims visiting the relics of the mysterious St Sarik which were to be found close by at St Andrew's church. Originally owned by the Bishops of Salisbury, the inn is now owned by St Andrew's church.

The High Street once contained a variety of small businesses – a barber, a newsagent, a sweet shop amongst others. On Pearson Road, at the top of the High Street, is The Grove where the defeated Admiral Villeneuve was imprisoned in 1805 after the Battle of Trafalgar. Coincidently, General Eisenhower also stayed there briefly, whilst American and Canadian troops were billeted in Sonning before the 1944 D-Day Normandy landings.

At the other end of the High Street, behind a red brick wall, is The Deanery, a house designed by Edwin Lutyens with a garden originally created by Gertrude Jekyll. In Thames Street, as you walk down towards the river you pass the Red House, once home to the playwright Terence Rattigan. You then reach Sonning Bridge over which two-way traffic was permitted until the late 1960s. On the opposite side of the bridge is The Mill theatre (just in Oxfordshire). Originally a flour mill, it is mentioned in the Domesday Book and supplied flour locally for nearly 1,000 years until 1969.

On the Berkshire side of the river, in the summer months, you can enjoy a cup of tea at The Lock before wandering back up into the village through the churchyard. Some years ago there was a need to enlarge the churchyard and more ground was donated. The new burial ground was linked to the old one in 1948 by an archway built with bricks from bombed London houses.

In the heart of the village stands Pearson Hall named after the 19th-century vicar Canon Hugh Pearson. It was opened in 1889 and remains a popular venue for many village events. Next door is the Sonning Club, formerly the Working Men's Club – set up in 1876 to discourage excessive drinking!

There is a primary school within the village and Reading Blue Coat School now occupies the Holme Park estate. There is constant change within the village but it will always remain popular for both residents and visitors.

❧ SPEEN

On the road west just out of the town of Newbury, is the village of Speen. At first sight just a village cut in half by the A4, Speen has a history way back beyond the Romans, because it was a settlement and hillfort for the early Britons and is equalled by few other places for its rare archaeological association with the Celtic period, pottery and bronze spearheads having been dug up on Speen Moor. Such natural advantages led to the Romans selecting this site for the station they called 'Spinae'. It is also rare that the modern name of a place resembles that which it bore in Roman times, and Speen is a remarkable exception. It stood at the crossroads of all the Roman roads in this area. Saxons and Normans left their mark here too, with manor houses and parts of St Mary the Virgin, Speen's ancient church.

During the Civil War, there were two battles of Newbury during the period of strife between the Royalists and the Roundheads, and the second battle was fought at Speen Hill. During the Georgian era the nobility braved the bad roads and the highwaymen to take the waters at Bath. The Bath Road or A4 went right through Speen and the coaching inn, the Castle, stood at edge of the village. As time went on and traffic increased, Newbury had a bypass but the A4 still ran through Speen. Lorries grew bigger and speed limits were set. Then one day the M4 was opened and Speen returned to comparative quiet on the roads.

Take the Old Bath Road out of Newbury and you come to the start of Speen Lane. Look across the road at a Georgian building, once the coaching inn, now three houses known as Castle Houses. Right on the corner stands a stone monument to commemorate the Second Battle of Newbury during the Civil War. A little over 50 years ago, Speen Lane was still a lane with a few large old houses and a Jacobean house that became an hotel. These have gone, but the modern houses fit in well with the old lane. As we walk along, we can see that the houses on the left have a marvellous view over the Kennet Valley with the River Kennet bordering Speen Moor, where the Celtic pottery and bronze spearheads were found. Rare flowers and water birds can be found here. Further on we cross the deep cutting of the old railway. Dr Beeching put paid to that piece of railway. The only turning to the left takes us down to the church, past the Sextons Cottage, and pausing to lean on a gate and admire the view over ploughed fields, the Kennet and Avon Canal in the valley, and the hills away in the distance.

Then we see the church, nestling in the trees. St Mary the Virgin is the product of three churches on this site, each leaving its mark, the Saxon, Norman and 13th-century, and much is retained, despite Victorian restoration.

Out of the churchyard through the lychgate and up the grassy path, we find Our Lady Well, so named in dedication to the Blessed Virgin, the ancient church being under her special protection. The water was a spring of pure water held to have special healing powers for sore eyes, rickets, and measles. It is known locally as a Wishing Well, and it is said a ghost has been seen. We are back in Speen Lane and passing a 400-year-old farm and barn. We are almost at the end of Speen Lane, with its beautiful old houses, and finally the Village Hall and the War Memorial. The Victorian Village Hall built in 1886, sees many activities within its walls.

We have come out on to the A4 at the far end of the village, so let us turn back along the main road and complete our circle. On the corner of the turning on the left, is an old Toll House. The road is Station Road but there is now no station and the level crossing gates have long gone, but that is the entrance to an excellent playing field. Opposite the Toll House is the oldest pub, the Hare and Hounds, and further down the road on the edge of the village is the modern pub, the Starting Gate, a good name as many well known jockeys live in Speen. To complete our circle we arrive at the primary school.

The route we have just taken has changed very little over the years, with the exception of some modern houses at the beginning of Speen Lane. Speen has spread slightly on the northern side of the A4, but not much, and it remains an interesting place to visit and to live in.

Spencers Wood & Three Mile Cross

These two villages are just south of the M4 motorway and, like Shinfield, are rapidly increasing in size with new housing appearing all round.

Three Mile Cross is famous for a past resident – Mary Russell Mitford, the author of *Our Village*. Mitford Hall, where she lived for a time from 1820, has now been converted into offices. Next door to Mitford Hall is the Swan pub. There has been a public house on the site since before 1760 when it was known as the Globe Inn. In 1760 it was bought for 24 pounds and 10 shillings with a new name of the Three Sugar Loaves. It was used as a changing station for horses on the stage coach route from London to Portsmouth. It is still a popular and busy pub.

There are several old houses in the village. Wisteria Cottage, which dates from the 18th century, still has the most wonderful display of wisteria each year. Next door is Wheelwright's Cottage, where the wheelwright lived and on the far side of the road was the George and Dragon public house, now a private dwelling.

When I moved to Three Mile Cross in the 1960s the M4 had not been built, and Basingstoke Road was a country road into Reading, with hedges and grass verges. What a difference now! Our milk was delivered daily by the local farmer, Mr Beckingham, along with his two daughters, until he retired.

Spencers Wood's WI, which was formed in 1954, sadly closed in the 80s. St Michael's church now has a thriving café (Caf'Active) which is open every day serving drinks, cakes and light lunches. It has become a popular place for those on their own to meet up with others, as well as a place for young mums with their babies and toddlers to get together.

Spencers Wood Village Hall hosts toddler groups, badminton and other events. When I first moved to the village themed fancy dress dances were held there. Great fun.

There is a large recreation ground and in September it is the venue for an annual carnival run by local people. It also has a pavilion which houses a pre-school playgroup, an 'understanding computers' club and a youth club. Both villages have well used allotments.

There is a very busy voluntary car service and this covers most of the local villages. They are also served by a regular bus service into Reading. There are several small shops and a couple of garages, a primary school and secondary school. The old infant school is now the village library.

 # Stanford Dingley

Stanford Dingley is one of Berkshire's most beautiful villages and has a lovely setting in the Valley of the River Pang. It is as attractive as its name, the first part of which it owes to William Stanford, in 1224 Lord of the Manor, and the second part to Richard Dyneley, mentioned in 1428 as the son of Richard Dyneley Esquire, the bodyguard to Henry VI.

The village can be justly proud of its old buildings; its mill was first mentioned in the Domesday Book. It has a 15th-century coaching inn, several scheduled buildings and numerous attractive houses and cottages. The small village hall has recently been refurbished and brought up to date with modern equipment.

The new Globe Theatre was designed and assembled by a Stanford Dingley craftsman in the yard behind the church. The church is dedicated to St Denys, few churches in England bear his name.

Legend has it that he was martyred in Paris during the 3rd century by beheading. He has always been portrayed decapitated in medieval art, his head in his hands, and is indeed so represented on the lectern in the church.

This charming and picturesque church, screened by Spanish chestnut trees, has a wealth of interest.

Certainly a Saxon church was standing there before the Conquest. The present form is largely the result of building about 1200, but parts of the original masonry are contained in the walls at the west end of the nave. The font is plain, probably Norman, the roof is finely timbered, and a splendid 13th-century door, with contemporary iron work, is plainly part of the original scheme. Restoration work in 1870 revealed 13th-century wall paintings, which were stabilised and preserved in 2008 by specialists.

No self-respecting English village is without at least one ancient inn. Stanford Dingley can boast two. The Bull, a 15th-century coaching inn with a wealth of old beams, is famous locally for the game played there, Ring the Bull. The object was to swing a ring suspended from the ceiling by a cord onto a horn, certainly a game of some antiquity. The Old Boot Inn, though not so old, is reputedly haunted by a man who hanged himself in its orchard. Doors are said to close mysteriously at times.

Notable sons of the village were Thomas Teasdale, who made a fortune in the parish as a clothier, and later founded Pembroke College, Oxford. John Lyford, Citizen and Merchant and Merchant Taylor of London, was lord of the very ancient manor of Rushdens in the village, whose family also distinguished themselves as weavers and merchants in the clothing trade. Dr Richard Valpy was headmaster of Reading School from 1781. He had the Stanford Dingley patronage and made his brother rector. Three other Valpys also served the parish.

Throughout the ages, industries have thrived in the village. Alongside the brick and weatherboard mill mentioned in the Domesday records, was the tannery, one of the oldest industries in Berkshire, based originally on ample supplies of oak bark. One sad side effect is that the excellent asparagus from the Billington Farm is no longer available.

🍁 STOCKCROSS

Stockcross is situated just 2 miles west of Newbury on the old Roman road, Ermin Street, now the B4000 and has excellent access to the A4/A34 and M4. The village is part of the civil parish of Speen.

It is an attractive small village originally developed by the Sutton family in the late 19th century as a model village.

There have been two wealthy families connected to the area; the Cravens, who owned the Benham Estate from 1630 and the Suttons who purchased the estate in 1862.

The black and white fronted houses are iconic to the village and are managed by the Benham Estate (owned by Sir Richard Sutton Limited) although not many now house estate workers. Originally they had thatched roofs but over time some were rebuilt further back on their plots with tiled roofs and all had modern plumbing installed. The last thatch was replaced in 2013.

In the 1980s and 90s the estate sold off many of their other local properties and most of the modern housing in the village dates from this time.

Travelling to Stockcross from the Newbury direction on the right you pass Deanwood Golf Club which has 9 holes. Next door is the Vineyard which is a 5-star hotel and has about 50 rooms. A little further on is the turning to the BUPA Bayford House Care Home and Rookwood Farmhouse, a 4-star B&B, which holds a charity open gardens event each year.

In 1971 the old village school built in 1830 was demolished. The new school opened in Chapel Lane in 1965. Currently, there are around 100 primary pupils who come from a wide area around Stockcross and Newbury.

St John's Church is situated off Church Lane up a long drive. It was completed in 1839, built entirely at the expense of Rev Henry Majendie, a great local philanthropist. It became an ecclesiastical parish in its own right in 1844 and is now one of nine churches in the East Downland Benefice. It houses the work of acclaimed architect Sir Ninian Comper who, in 1905, was employed by Lady Sutton and her son Sir Richard to redesign the interior. Comper later added the Memorial Chapel (1922) and the chancel screen (1933). The last vicar to live in the village was Geoffrey Marsh. The vicarage was sold off in 1981. It is now named Stockcross House and the gardens can be visited under the NGS scheme. St John's has a small, regular congregation.

Up until the 1980s the village had three public houses but currently there are none. The Cricketers was demolished and replaced by housing in 1987. The Lord Lyon closed in 2016 and has been developed into flats. The Rising Sun closed its doors in October 2017 and the village awaits further news on its future.

Stockcross does have a popular and busy Post Office, shop and take away situated on the main road. Here you can not only post your parcel but also buy essential supplies and have a cup of tea with homemade cakes. Outside the Post Office stands the old red telephone box which was purchased by the Parish Council on behalf of the villagers.

The Sutton Hall is a very popular venue. Built by the Suttons, it opened in 1875, was extended in 1927 and upgraded again in 2000 with a modern kitchen and other facilities. It now consists of two halls that can be hired separately or together. An active committee encourages fundraising to keep the hall in good repair and support village activities. A harvest supper is well supported every September. The Stockcross Panto Players was formed in 2007. They rehearse at the Sutton Hall to produce three performances each December. Regular bookings include art, yoga, Pilates, tango classes and bridge. The Apollo Big Band rehearses there. The Grapevine is the village's quarterly newsletter and began in 1991. It is provided by the Sutton Hall Management Committee and is hand delivered around the village by volunteers.

Other groups are active in the village. Stockcross Two O'Clock Crowd (STOCC) was formed in 2002 and meets at the Sutton Hall for talks, tea and conversation on the last Wednesday of every month. No membership is needed; all are welcome with no restriction, just come if you can.

Stockcross and Surroundings History Association (SASHA) has been in existence since 2012 and meets at the Sutton Hall on the last Monday of every month. Originally it was formed to produce a book about the men remembered on the First World War memorial plaque in St John's church. It now has a website and is doing research projects and listening to visiting speakers.

Each August 'STOCKFEST', a community festival, makes its appearance for about 10 days. It is a celebration of local arts, music and culture with professional artistes from outside the area also invited to perform.

The Stockcross Bowls Club closed its doors around 2003 but the Billiard Club is still going strong.

Just as you leave Stockcross on the right you pass the Recreation Ground; it became a Field in Trust in 2012 during the Queen's Diamond Jubilee year. It is very pleasantly situated surrounded by woodlands and has a recently updated children's play area. It is home to Stockcross Tennis Club and also provides a venue for the football, playing boys and girls from the Newbury area.

Despite its proximity to major routes and other changes Stockcross retains a tranquil rural feel alongside its lively village activities.

🍁 STREATLEY

Streatley is a village right on the River Thames. The settlement developed where the ancient Icknield Way and Ridgeway tracks crossed the river at the Goring Gap between the Berkshire Downs and the Chiltern Hills. The original ford, which was turned into a causeway by the Romans, was replaced by a ferry. A wooden toll bridge was not built across the river until 1837. This was renewed in 1923 and the tolls were abolished. Until then it cost a penny to cross the bridge on foot.

The area around Streatley is extremely attractive with wooded hills running down to the Thames. Since Victorian times it has been popular with visitors who come to the village to walk, cycle, fish, take a boat trip or even paint the scenery. Now Lardon Chase and The Holies with their fine views across the countryside belong to the National Trust and are preserved for future generations to enjoy. Further protection is offered by Streatley's location in the North Wessex Downs Area of Outstanding Natural Beauty.

In the past farming was the main occupation but today most residents are commuters to nearby towns or London and many work from home. At one time Smallbones, a national building firm, was a big employer based in Streatley, founded by a village carpenter in the late 19th century. Boating also provided many jobs in the village, with craft being made, hired and repaired by the Saunders family at the waterside Swan inn. Sam Saunders, born in the pub in 1859, started as a boat builder, and went on to found the well-known aviation company of Saunders-Roe on the Isle of Wight. It survives today as GKN Aerospace.

Streatley has many lovely old buildings. There was once a famous corn mill, beloved by artists, but it burned down in 1926. The parish church of St Mary may have Saxon origins, but the present building is Norman, with extensive late-Victorian renovations. It is now part of a united benefice with the Oxfordshire parishes of Goring and South Stoke.

The two hostelries are long established. The Bull by the crossroads was a post house on the turnpike road from Reading. Horses were changed there for the stage coaches and were shod at the adjacent forge, now part of the pub. A yew tree in the garden allegedly marks the spot where a monk and nun were buried in 1440 after being put to death for misconduct! The Swan was originally a waterside inn for passing boatmen, but it became popular with visitors in the late 19th century, expanding into a hotel. During the 1970s the entertainer Danny la Rue owned it and many famous people came to stay there.

For nearly a hundred years the Morrell family, brewers from Oxford, owned most of the land and houses in Streatley. They lived in Streatley House on the High Street, a fine William and Mary building. Mrs Emily Morrell was an autocratic lady who ensured that little development took place in the village, contributing to its present unspoilt appearance. In 1938 after her death, the estate was sold off, but even so modern housing is restricted to The Coombe and a couple of small roads off the A329. In recent years the community saved Streatley Meadow on the High Street from developers and this valuable open space is now in trust for the benefit of all.

Mrs Morrell was instrumental in starting Streatley WI after refusing an invitation to join the newly formed WI in Goring (there has always been a rivalry between the two villages) and subsequently she became the first Berkshire Federation Chairman in 1920.

Streatley no longer has any shops; the nearest are within walking distance across the bridge in Goring where there is also a convenient railway station. Nevertheless, Streatley has good facilities run by a vibrant community. The Morrell Room is available for activities such as classes, clubs, entertainments and plays. There are playing fields and well-tended allotments. The golf club attracts players from miles around and also has facilities for functions. Most years (weather permitting) the Goring and Streatley Regatta takes place on meadows in the parish. The primary school, founded in 1830, is still going strong but in modern premises and there is a thriving pre-school. Streatley also has a youth hostel housed in a former large mansion which caters for many visitors including those from overseas. The latest innovation in the village is the conversion of the old red telephone box into a book swap.

With just over 1,000 residents, the population of Streatley has increased little over the past century. The picturesque High Street has not changed much in that period either, although alas it is sometimes blighted by traffic jams as motorists wishing to use the river crossing have replaced the peaceful horses and carts of yesteryear.

❧ SULHAM & TIDMARSH

Sulham and Tidmarsh are two pretty villages in the Pang valley about a mile south of Pangbourne. Sulham, sheltered by a fine ridge of beechwoods, is still very quiet, consisting of a few attractive old houses and cottages strung out along a narrow country lane. Tidmarsh has always been busier. The road running through it was a turnpike road in coaching days, and the old toll cottage can still be seen a short distance from the ancient Greyhound Inn and the village forge. Today the road is the A340, linking the A329 from Oxford with the A4 and the M4, and carrying a growing volume of traffic. The straight stretch which speeds motorists on their way south of Tidmarsh was built in 1855 by Mr Benyon of Englefield to replace the old twisting route through the hamlet of North Street to Theale.

The Pang valley, abundantly wooded and watered, has been a farming area for centuries. During construction of the M4 in 1970 the remains of a Romano-British villa and farmhouse were discovered near Maidenhatch Farm in Tidmarsh. Nunhide Farm in Sulham dates back to Domesday. There was a vineyard in Tidmarsh in the 13th century, by which time there was a mill, probably on the same site as the mill which only ceased to grind corn early in the 20th century. A rabbit warren was recorded in Tidmarsh in the 17th century, when James I granted the lord of the manor the right to keep deer, rabbits and pheasants.

St Laurence's Church at Tidmarsh was begun in the 12th century and has a 13th-century apsidal chancel. It has been well restored and retains its Norman font and south doorway. Sulham's 13th-century church was pulled down but was replaced in 1838 by the Reverend John Wilder with the present flint and stone church, with its tall spire and brilliantly coloured lancet windows. The Wilders were principal landowners in Sulham for over 300 years and members of the family served as rector.

John Wilder, rector 1836-92, also built several of the pretty thatched cottages (one of which was the Post Office until the 1960s), the village school (opened 1837, rebuilt 1892, closed 1970), and the round brick tower near Nunhide Farm known as Wilder's Folly.

In Tidmarsh Robert Hopkins of the Manor House built a school for 45 children in 1856. It was closed about 1905, but the tiny school house survives, as does Sulham school, as a private residence.

Farming and forestry are still the main occupations; and there is now also a breeze block factory, a stud, boarding kennels and riding stables. Tidmarsh has a small village hall which hosts numerous events.

🍁 SULHAMSTEAD

Sulhamstead is an oval-shaped scattered village, three miles across and more than twice as long, stretching from Burghfield Common northwards across the Bath Road, up to the wooded ridge of Englefield.

The present civil parish of Sulhamstead comprises the two ancient parishes of Sulhamstead Bannister Upper End and Sulhamstead Abbots. The word Bannister preserves the family name of the knight, John Banastre, whose family first held the manor in about the year 1120. Bannister Church was under the jurisdiction of Pamber Priory, and when that was suppressed the priory and much of its property was given by the king to The Queen's College, Oxford. From then until now the college has the right of appointment to the Rectory of Sulhamstead and some of the neighbouring parishes. Some of the flints from the demolished St Michael's Church were used in the building of the new vestry at St Mary's.

Sulhamstead Abbots is so called because it was once under the jurisdiction of the Abbot of Reading Abbey. All that is left of the original Norman church is the font. The church was first dedicated to St Bartholomew, but then came the Black Death, and the villagers, perhaps in a last ditch desperate plea for mercy, re-dedicated their church to the Mother of Our Lord and it became St Mary's.

The only remaining inn, formerly Three Kings Jack's Booth on the Bath Road, was once a busy coaching inn and there are many differing stories concerning the name. The most likely links it with Jack of Newbury, the wealthy cloth merchant, who undoubtedly would have spent a lot of time travelling the Bath Road to and from London. Nowadays it is named the Spring Inn, located opposite the pitches of the Sulhamstead Cricket Club, which is very successful and well supported.

St Mary's church, Sulhamstead

Sulhamstead House, a white Ionic porticoed house looking over the beautiful Kennet Valley, was built in the mid 18th century by Daniel May and the estate comprised 1,800 acres. In 1952 it was the Berkshire Constabulary County Headquarters, and in 1968, following the amalgamation of five forces, it became the Thames Valley Police Training College. The garden boasts a 600-year-old Cedar of Lebanon.

The village is fortunate in having a number of beautiful and interesting houses and gardens, among them Folly Farm, a fine example of a Lutyens house with a Gertrude Jeykll garden; the Old Rectory – a William and Mary house, and the ancient building Brazenhead, which was built around 1100. Sulhamstead Abbots is also home to Moathouse Cottage, a 16th-century cottage with the unusual feature of a chain of three fishponds.

The Village Hall, located on Sulhamstead Hill, was deliberately built on the parish boundary with Ufton Nervet so that it could readily serve both villages.

The Kennet and Avon Canal is now navigable from Reading to Bristol and provides moorings for many pleasure craft and residential narrowboats. Walkers and cyclists regularly enjoy the peace of the picturesque towpath.

❧ SUNNINGDALE

Sunningdale is a rather straggling area, the older village clustered round the church, and the newer part across the fields about a mile away, which grew around the London Road and the station.

Despite the boundary changes of 1974 the area was left unchanged, and the county boundary still divides the two parts and means that Sunningdale is administered by two county, three district and three parish councils.

The name is probably Saxon in origin, meaning 'the home of Sunna's people' and the land where the village grew was largely a marshy waste, part of Windsor Forest which formerly stretched from Windsor to Basingstoke. Evidence of early occupation was shown in the discovery of several Bronze

Age barrows. One, excavated in 1901, contained fragments of 23 cinerary urns, some of which are now in Reading Museum.

Throughout history, the main highway to the south west has passed through Sunningdale. The Roman Road from London to Silchester, known locally as the Devil's Highway, crossed the river at Staines, ran through the site of Virginia Water, Fort Belvedere and Coworth, then skirted the field behind Church Road, along the edge of the Recreation Ground and thence to Bagshot. Later the turnpike road from London, still marked by milestones, followed roughly the same route through, running to the east of the village. In the 18th century these roads through a wild and desolate Windsor Forest and Bagshot Heath made the area an ideal hunting ground for highwaymen. William Davis, Claude Duval, Captain Snow and Parson Darby are all known to have carried out their infamous deeds in this vicinity.

In 1828 a Baptist Chapel was built in the village but it was not until 1840 that a church was built in Sunningdale, on the site of an old gravel pit. Until then the village had been part of the parish of Old Windsor, although separated by six or seven miles of forest. Soon Holy Trinity Church was not big enough for the increasing population and was rebuilt in celebration of Queen Victoria's Golden Jubilee in 1887. The vicar at this time was Rev. Raffles Flint, nephew of Sir Stamford Raffles. Sadly, the Congregational Church, which celebrated its centenary in 1965, closed in 1980 and was converted for housing. Holy Trinity Primary School was built in 1842 on land given by St John's College, Cambridge. It provided education for all ages until Charter School, now comprehensive, opened in 1958, covering secondary education for the area.

Coworth Park was occupied as far back as Saxon times, but the present mansion, now a 5-star country house hotel, was built about 1800, the last private owner being Lord Derby. Coworth Park Farm is an excellent example of a Tudor farmhouse, the front being virtually unchanged since it was built.

Fort Belvedere was built as a folly in 1755 by the 2nd Duke of Cumberland, and enlarged and used as a hunting lodge by George IV. The ruins in the grounds, which we can see from the shore of Virginia Water, are part of an ancient temple transported here from Leptis Magna, near Tripoli. Queen Victoria was a frequent visitor and a royal salute was fired annually on her birthday from the guns mounted outside the house. As Prince of Wales, Edward VIII made his home here and modernised the interior. It was here that the abdication order was signed, and afterwards the King left through Coworth Park grounds in order to avoid the press and publicity.

There are several other large houses in the district, some still private residences, but many taken over for other purposes.

The few shops in the village centre have declined in number but there is a small selection near the station. There are two pubs, the Nag's Head and the Royal Oak.

The district is well known for its proximity to Ascot racecourse, which was founded by Queen Anne, and has Sunningdale golf course, which is the venue for many international meetings. Sunningdale Ladies' Golf Club is the oldest ladies' golf club in the country.

There are many magnificent trees in the area, some of which are quite rare specimens, and in the early summer the many coloured rhododendrons and azaleas in the gardens are worth admiring.

🍁 SUNNINGHILL

Sunninghill is not a picturesque village with thatched roofs, village green, manor house and smithy, although it had all these in the past. It lies 200 ft above sea level, about six miles from Windsor, in a wooded area with light heathland soil. The area was once part of a Royal hunting forest which ran south of the River Thames, and many roads nearby are still called 'rides'.

The Saxon tribe which lived here before the Norman Conquest were called the Sonnynes, hence Sonninghill and Sonnindale, and the daughter of the tribal chief, called Isabella, became abbess of a nunnery at Broomhall. In a little clearing where two rides cross, a church was built for the foresters or verderers. It was built in AD 890 and was replaced in the 12th century by a Norman church called St Michael and All Angels. The nuns of Broomhall were given the church by King John in the first year of his reign and held it until all monastries and nunneries were dissolved by Henry VIII, when it was taken over by St John's Cambridge, who hold it still. It was enlarged and altered in the 19th century and an original Norman arch, removed at this time, was later discovered built into a garden wall. This restored arch and a very ancient yew tree are probably the oldest sights in Sunninghill.

On the highest ground, surrounded by patches of bogland and dense forest, large houses began to be built. John and Joan de Sunninghill lived in the manor at Silwood Park in 1362 and since then the area has been a favourite place for large estates and well known names. Rumour has it that Nell Gwynne had a lodge there.

The founding of Ascot racecourse by Queen Anne and the popularity of the chalybete wells, which rivalled Bath in the 18th century, resulted in more houses being built and gradually the little cottages of the people serving them began to cluster south of the road to Ascot.

The Windsor Forest Enclosure Act in 1813 meant much hardship for the people. They could no longer wander freely to cut turf and wood for fuel and a man could be hanged for catching a hare to feed his children. The building of the South Western Railway from London to Wokingham in the 1850s, which passed through the village, made a difference and many houses carry the dates of the more substantial brick houses built during the next 40 years.

A mission hall was built in 1880 and both it, and the Salvation Army, suffered from the attentions of a group known as the Skeleton Army. These, paid by the brewers to stop the spread of the teetotal movement in the Non-Conformist churches, broke up meetings with fights, window-breaking and other activities such as releasing pigeons sprinkled with pepper through the windows. Later, this same building became a Music Hall and the inhabitants of Sunninghill were able to see London artistes like Little Tich and Albert Chevalier.

The village gained from the generosity of the land owners. One bought the land and had the first public school built, another the Reading Rooms, which now houses the village library. A fine village hall was built in memory of Thomas Cordes, who had lived at Silwood Park.

In the 1950s and 60s there was another upsurge of new building, when St Michael's school was enlarged, many of the open spaces and fields were filled with new houses, big houses were altered into flats or demolished and their gardens made into estates.

Some of the largest houses, where great house parties had gathered for Royal Ascot race-meetings, Henley and polo, became hotels, nursing homes, training centres for large firms or, in the case of the manor house, Silwood Park, part of Imperial College London.

Now there is a little light industry in the village, but most people work in London, Slough, Bracknell or Heathrow. The citizens of present-day Sunninghill live among the few remaining trees of the old hunting glades and the newer birches, pines and rhododendrons, with only the odd fox or squirrel to remind them of past days.

🍁 SWALLOWFIELD

Swallowfield, six miles south of Reading, is a large parish of 400 acres which includes Riseley and Farley Hill. A section of the Roman road from Silchester to London, now called The Devil's highway, runs along its southern boundary.

The whole district was once part of Windsor Forest and it still contains a good deal of woodland. The name of the village is derived from an old German word meaning 'rushing water' – an earlier name for the River Blackwater – one of three rivers which flows through the parish.

The old Manor House, now known as Swallowfield Park, has a long recorded history. A Norman lord, Sir John le Dispenser, one of its earliest owners, in 1256 built All Saints' Church in a corner of his park.

The estate has been owned by many distinguished families over the centuries and many notable people have been guests at their house. The names of some are written over doors upstairs – King Charles II, Queen Anne and John Evelyn are amongst these; other famous names are in the Visitors' Book – Henry James, Lord Curzon and Randolph Churchill for instance. Several of the Russells were interested in literature and they numbered amongst their friends and visitors Dickens, Thackeray, Charles Kingsley, Wilkie Collins, John Ruskin and Mary Mitford. This lady, who wrote *Our Village* and much else, lived for some years in a cottage in Swallowfield and died there in 1855. She probably got most of her material for her stories of country life at Three Mile Cross, where she lived before, and from Shinfield, but she makes passing references to Swallowfield, especially to its Parish Church, near which she is buried. Her grave is often visited by admirers of her writings. The house and surrounding grounds were sold to the Country Houses Association in 1964 – a body which bought and conserved large houses of historical and architectural interest and provides accommodation for retired and semi-retired people.

During the 1970s the usually quiet life at the Park was enlivened by visits from TV crews who used the mansion and its grounds as the back-cloth for incidents in films. How exciting it was to see Dr Who driving his old fashioned car about.

There is less traffic passing through since the Swallowfield bypass was opened; this benefits householders in or near the road to Reading. There is an interesting moated 16th-century house here, 'Sheepbridge Court' which is itself a listed building, while its moat is an Ancient Monument. The house was added to in the 17th century and has attractive unusual windows and brickwork.

To the east of the village, Farley Hill, a pleasant, well wooded district, relieves the flatness of the rest of the parish. It has its own church, St John the Baptist's – an attractive red brick building about 100 years old, the Victory Hall, a Junior School and several fine old houses. Farley Castle, formerly the home of the explorer, Mr Mitchell-Hedges, was bought in 1958 by Miss Woolley and adapted for use as a school for disabled children. Splendid work

Swallowfield Park

was done at Hephaistos School until its closure during the mid 1980s. Farley Court has been made into flats: Charles Kingsley lived there for a time while vicar of Eversley. Farley Hall is a handsome Queen Anne house.

🍁 TADLEY

Tadley is now a small town on the border of north Hampshire and Berkshire, with a population of around 11,500. Set within the Basingstoke, Reading and Newbury triangle, it is in easy reach of Aldermaston, Bramley and Basingstoke railway stations. You can drive through Tadley in 5 minutes on the A340, yet it is bursting with every kind of activity a visitor could want. From surprisingly good shopping to rambling across the common alongside Dexter cattle, from relaxing over coffee, swimming, working-out or singing in a community choir, there is never a dull moment! For local guides and information to peruse over coffee, head for the library on Mulfords Hill.

In the 11th century, Tadley would have been a tiny area of forest, with people living in huts. The main village was near St Peter's Church. Hatch Cottage nearby, built in the 15th century, is one of the oldest buildings, along with Burrell's Farm and Highway Cottage. Tadley Place in Church Road was owned by the Ludlow family. Henry Ludlow, who owned the property in the 1620s, was very unpopular when he ordered 12 houses on his land to be demolished and the occupiers turned out. Wyeford Place, also owned by the Ludlow family, became the home of Hugo Vickers, the Royal historian.

Tadley has famous aviation connections. In 1853, Henry Coxwell landed his hydrogen-filled balloon on the common and asked what this place was; the reply, by a terrified local, was 'Tadley, God help us!' Since then, Tadley is often referred to in that manner!

The cricketer, William Brereton Evans, lived at Fairlawn House. He was a passenger in Samuel Cody's 'Floatplane' which crashed on its test flight at Farnborough in 1913. He was killed and is buried at St Peter's Church.

During the Second World War, Spitfire fighter planes were assembled at 'Hangar 5' in Tadley, now Hangar Road. American troops lived in a hutted camp in Tadley, handy for Aldermaston Airfield, from where troops left for the D-Day invasion. The local war memorial remembers six Tadley people who gave their lives in this war, and 31 Tadley men killed in the First World War.

Since 1950, the Atomic Weapons Research Establishment (AWRE; now AWE) has been Tadley's main employer. Thousands of houses were built for staff, who came from Scotland, northern England, and London. Schools, churches and shops were built and Tadley changed for ever. William Penney, known as the 'Father of the British Atomic Bomb' became Director at the AWRE (1953-1959). He observed the second atomic bomb dropped on Nagasaki, and eventually helped to research and develop nuclear weapons under the authority of the UKAEA.

The Nash family has made traditional besom brooms in Tadley for over 300 years. Arthur Nash, manufacturer of besom brooms and pea sticks, was granted the Royal Warrant on 1 January 1999, famously providing brooms for the Queen, as well as the Harry Potter films.

The Loddon Valley Lions Club organises a Treacle Fair each June to raise funds for various charities. The 'Treacle Mine' began as an April Fools' Day joke on TV, but could be where American soldiers dumped their molasses cans during the war, or perhaps archaeologists found treacle tins buried when building work began on an old bakery site.

Tadley's Olympian, Kathy Smallwood, attended the Hurst School, took part in the 1980 and 1984 Olympics and won 23 major championship medals during her athletic career. Major George Conrad Roller (1856–1941) lived at Tadley Court. He was an artist known for restoring pictures damaged by the Suffragettes at the Royal Academy, and for illustrating advertisements for Burberry, the famous Basingstoke raincoat manufacturer, over 40 years.

Visitors can enjoy excellent specialist shops in several district shopping areas. Amongst them are Reading Warehouses (a department store with all manner of goods for the home and leisure), Doodles craft emporium, Kings DIY, famous Pedal On (cyclist heaven!) plus two charity shops offering great choice and value. Toucan Travel provides travel services to places far and wide. There is a large Sainsbury's/Argos and local Co-op, McColls, Budgen and Tesco stores. Tadley still has two banks represented!

Relax in Café Retreat or Sainsbury's Café after shopping or try the full range of pubs, restaurants and takeaways – too many to mention.

Or try Tadley's leisure facilities, you name it, you can do it! Visit Bishopswood Golf Course and restaurant, New Road's swimming pool, or Hurst Community College's leisure centre/gym, with sports and educational classes for all. There are football and rugby clubs for all ages. Tadley Common has tennis courts, football pitches and changing facilities at the Jubilee Centre. Or enjoy many country walks and park areas with playgrounds and park gym equipment.

Tadley's thriving Community Centre, and youth facility at The Point, offers current cinema shows, exercise classes, society meeting places and a café. The Tadley U3A has over 600 members and many different interest groups to join. The Burnham Copse Women's Institute meets at the Diamond Scout Centre, another resource well-used by local Scout groups. The Tadley Singers community choir has 100+ members, raising thousands of pounds for local charities. There are many other local groups to discover and join, as well as halls and venues – too numerous to mention here.

There are three primary schools. The oldest opened in 1877 (now Tadley Community Primary), and Burnham Copse and Bishopswood Schools opened in the early 1960s-70s. Besides the 12th-century St Peter's, there are seven other churches of various denominations, the oldest being the Old Meeting (now the United Reformed) Church dating from 1719. Many were built to support the influx of AWE workers.

Tadley is classed as a town yet still retains the friendly character of a village due to its location in beautiful countryside and its welcoming community.

🍁 Thatcham

Even with the recent spread of new houses, Thatcham preserves the heart of the old village at its centre.

St Mary's Church stands in a quiet area of trees, a high brick wall sheltering it by the alleyway on the north side; a low wall bordering the remainder of the churchyard and its tombs. Saxons first built a church on this site, of which nothing remains; the first stone building being constructed about 1141, its Norman doorway still preserved at the south side. Restorations and additions have been carried out through the years, including a church hall, and in 1970, two new bells completed one of the few ten-bell peals in Berkshire, which rings out on Sundays and festive days, and when visiting teams of ringers call at the tower.

Beyond the eastern end of the church, past a row of small cottages, is the Broadway Green. At its corner, the stump of the old butter cross still marks the site of a flourishing market where, in the 12th century, Newbury men, jealous of its success, attacked the stalls. There is still a market now and the green, with its small trees, rose beds and seats, is flanked by two supermarkets and other shops. Traffic passes constantly. The stocks, where Mrs Barfield, the Thatcham historian's wife and schoolteacher, sheltered an offender from the rain with her umbrella, have disappeared.

Where the Broadway joins the Bath Road at its northern end, stands the King's Head. This was one of Thatcham's old coaching inns and much of the early building and stables is still visible. It was due to its owner, Miss Fromont, who feared losing the coaching trade and who owned areas of land to the south of Thatcham that, when the railway came, it was only permitted to be built a mile away from the village.

The narrow High Street which turns off at this end of the Broadway, was once part of the old Bath Road, but has been bypassed for some time. The crooked lines of various roofs over its shops and still narrow pavements show the character of an old village street, although new frontages and windows have been added.

Kennet School, an academy secondary school, is available for local children, as well as several junior schools, among them Francis Baily Primary School along the Bath Road, named after the famous astronomer born in 1774.

The River Kennet, always full of swans here, curves towards Chamberhouse Farm, the house built on the site of the old Chamberhouse manor, once called a castle and surrounded by a moat, (the name coming from Roger de Chambre).

The Swan inn was once used by bargemen taking loads of meal, flour, coal, timber, iron and other heavy goods between Newbury and Reading, or from Bristol and Bath to London. Tables are still set out in its garden and it is full of visitors in the summer time. A lane runs beside the railway track by the site of the old Chamberhouse Mill, dating back to the early 15th century, and which produced flour until 1967. Further along at Colthrop Mills, the paper making industry flourished from 1805 when Fourdrinier, a Frenchman who invented paper making machinery, converted the old fulling mill to paper making.

Now a sprawl of new industry grows outwards along the Bath Road towards Woolhampton.

The canal itself is becoming busy again with pleasure boats, now that the locks between Reading and Newbury and even as far as Bath have been cleared.

At the western end of Thatcham, the old rubbish tip has been reclaimed and landscaped into a leisure park. A nature reserve lies along the footpath below this, beside the reed beds, home of the reed and sedge warbler. The gravel pits nearby have filled with water. Some of these belong to Thatcham and Newbury anglers. Swans and wild water birds come and go. It was near here that the first signs of habitation in Thatcham were found, with evidence of a Mesolithic site, and here where future residents may spend their spare time.

🍁 THEALE

The Parish of Theale situated in the Kennet Valley, extends as far east towards Reading as the Burghfield Road, the land being taken up by recent housing estates, but it has been separated from the actual village since 1972 by the M4 motorway. The A4 Bath Road, which was a coaching route from London to Bath is no longer in use as a main road and a bypass takes most of the heavier traffic away from Theale.

Theale can claim to be one of the oldest villages in the area, probably with continuous occupation for at least 2,500 years. During excavations for railway ballast in the 19th century, between The Green and the railway, many items of historical interest were found including pottery, tools and ancient burials. From these it is possible to assume that there has been a settlement in Theale from the early Iron Age (700 BC), through Roman and Saxon periods to the present day. Theale was the head of a Hundred, or administrative district, and as such was a place of importance through medieval times. The name Theale comes from the old English word for plank, possibly referring to a plank bridge over the River Kennet or the flood plain.

The Theale area was also the site of at least two battles. One, between the Saxons and the Danes at the Battle of Englefield in AD 871, is said to have taken place at a spot called Play Platt (the battleground). There was also a skirmish there during the Civil War.

Until 1932 Theale was a tithing of Tilehurst. Dr Martin Routh was the rector of Tilehurst from 1810, Tilehurst being the largest parish in Berkshire at the time. In 1832 his sister, Mrs Sophia Sheppard, donated funds for a church to be built in Theale and dedicated to The Holy Trinity. She died in 1848 and her memorial is situated on the north side of the chancel. It shows the lady engraved in brass, attired in a long gown with her head veiled. A dog lies at her feet.

In 1913 a Congregational Church (now renamed United Reformed) was built on land formerly occupied by an old Tudor tavern named the Angel and donated by William Cumber, farmer and alderman. A Hall of Memory was built in 1920 to house the Sunday School and Old Comrade's Club but it has since been replaced by a new hall named after its donor, John Cumber, son of William, and Justice of the Peace.

The Roman Catholic church of St Luke was built in 1969 and is served by monks from Douai Abbey.

The village once brewed its own beer, the name Blatch's Brewery being well known in the area. The buildings which remain the same are now used for other purposes. Theale has many inns compared with its population. In the old coaching days there were many more which gave it the name 'Little Sodom'. Now only the Bull, the Falcon, the Crown and the Volunteer remain. The 14th-century building which is now the Old Lamb Motel was the original Lamb Inn, the present one being built at the beginning of the 19th century and taking its name from the original one which for many years was known as the Old Lamb Teahouse. As a motel, the Old Lamb has retained its thatched roof and ship's timbers. A fine open fireplace and the original beer cellars are still there. Scratched on one of the leaded window panes is the date 1704.

Theale Grammar School was built in 1963 and is now Theale Green Community School with a very large catchment area. The Church of England Primary School has outgrown its site and a new school is needed for the increasing population.

A new Village Hall and Social Club were built in the late 1970s with help from the wartime Welcome Home Fund for servicemen and women of the village, public loans, collections and also government grants. These buildings have since been enlarged.

Theale village has grown with modern housing estates on either side of the main thoroughfare, and a golf course and industrial units to the south, probably due to its close proximity to the motorway and railway network. In 1901 the population of Theale was under 1,000. Now it is nearer 3,000. The future of Theale seems to be one of further industrial development and its consequent increase in housing accommodation.

🍁 TILEHURST

Tilehurst comes from the old Tigel, meaning Tile, and Hurst denoting a wooded hill, so Tilehurst was a wooded hill where tiles were made. Alas, today we have no kilns, the last one having been closed then pulled down. It is now a housing estate called The Potteries.

No history of Tilehurst would be complete without the mention of the 'Berkshire Lady', Frances Kendrick. She was a very high-spirited girl, so determined to marry the man she fell in love with, that she anonymously challenged him to a duel in Calcot woods. When Benjamin Child, the gentleman in question appeared at the appointed place he was a little put out to find that his opponent was a woman, and to add to his dismay Frances informed him that he must either fight or marry her. He was in a tight corner as he could not fight a woman, but if he refused he would be a laughing stock. They were married in 1706, and lived at Tilehurst Manor.

Tilehurst had many watering places and wells and ponds at one time. One such place is the Sheep Wash in Armour Hill. Many caused concern and had to be covered because of their unclean condition and several wells were taken out of use. A better water supply was provided by the Water Orders Confirmation Act of 1894. The present water tower in Park Lane was constructed in 1931-2 and is a very good landmark which can be seen from many miles around.

In School Road in 1910 there was an old forge with an adjoining shed which was used for the shooting of unwanted horses and ponies. They were then put into a cart with the help of a pulley-chain and drum and taken away, today in this place stand some modern shops and a bank.

St Michael's church is first mentioned as a gift to Reading Abbey in a charter of the Bishop of Salisbury from 1189-1193. The present church is of fairly recent construction with the exception of the south aisle which dates from the 13th century. The tower was built in 1737 and the spire was added when the church was rebuilt in 1854-6. The church houses the Vanlore tomb which is very elaborate and is thought to be the work of William Wright of Charing Cross who died in 1652.

🍁 TUTTS CLUMP

The hamlet of Tutts Clump was often called 'The Mayfair of Bradfield' because it was where people would retire to smart little homes. The Primitive Methodists purchased a piece of land and built the new chapel in 1879 moving from their old meeting place at the bottom of Rotten Row. A large youth club was formed here too and was run by Dorothy Wale in the 1950s, 60s, 70s and 80s where many met their future partners! At one time Tutts Clump would boast two shops, an undertaker, a fish and chip shop, a barber, a ladies' hairdresser, a large apple orchard adjacent to Green Lane and two pubs in Rotten Row!

Noah Wise broke away from the Methodist Chapel and built an independent chapel in the early 1900s (now the vets) and formed a brass band. This building was often called the Tin Top Tabernacle or Noah's Ark. Tin tabernacle churches were prefabricated and made from corrugated galvanised iron. It was also used as a small clothing factory during the Second World War called Greenbomes.

Mr Henwood was the local postman and also the grave digger for the chapel. Dr Watney (of brewery fame) built the reservoir (now owned by Thames Water) at Halleluiah Corner at the end of Bishops Road. Piped water and flushing toilets were eventually to replace the outhouse and cess pits. Alf Smith ran the kennels where the sound of dogs dominated. Also the sound of rooks that used to nest at the bottom of Rotten Row would break the silence.

The Woman's Institute meetings were held at Cherry Orchard in the early 1970s and had about eight members. In more recent years Tutts Clump has been put on the map by Tim Wale, who was born here in 1957 and who started a cider business in 2006 using unwanted local apples.

🍁 TWYFORD & RUSCOMBE

The two villages of Twyford and Ruscombe are indivisible now, but whereas Ruscombe dates back to the 11th century, Twyford was originally just a hamlet of Hurst. Its name is derived from the two fords that once spanned the River Loddon as it meandered on its way to the nearby Thames.

It was the Bath Road that first put Twyford on the map, and with trade and travellers making the journey to the west of England, coaching inns sprang up to cater for their needs. The A4 bypass which opened in 1928 curtailed this somewhat, but the railway had arrived in 1839, and this expanded the population and gradually transformed the area into today's vibrant community of businesses, shops and restaurants.

Despite its size, Twyford is still officially a village as it has its own Parish Council – as indeed does Ruscombe. Both villages have a parish church and are linked with two other local churches to form a local ecumenical partnership. St James the Great, Ruscombe, was built in the late 12th century. It has a Norman chancel, with the rest of the church, including the brick tower, being rebuilt in 1638-39. St Mary the Virgin, Twyford, was built in 1846. Further additions followed, including the construction of St Mary's Church Centre, comprising a hall, kitchen, toilets and offices.

Famous historical figures have connections with both villages. William Penn, the founder of Pennsylvania, lived in Ruscombe from 1710 until his death in 1718. Edward Polehampton, a poor boy who, legend has it, was taken in and cared for by the landlord of the Rose and Crown in Twyford around 1666, went on to make his fortune in London. By way of thanks he bequeathed money to a trust to build a school that would provide an education for ten poor boys from the village of Twyford. The present day school is divided between two sites, one for infants and the second for junior school pupils, both bearing the name of their generous benefactor.

Modern day Twyford displays a tremendous community spirit. Twyford Together is a not-for-profit volunteer organisation that aims to bring together local residents, businesses and groups. It is associated with many of the clubs and societies that cater for a very wide range of interests. For the young there are Scout and Guide groups, as well as a skate park. For the elderly there is a Day Centre run by Twyford & District Age Concern. Twyford Together has raised thousands of pounds for local charities and sponsors several major community events including the annual Charity Family Fun Run, the Christmas Fayre and the Living Advent Calendar, as well as Twyfest, a ten day long festival of community-based events covering music, drama, comedy and sport.

It has also published *Twyford Walking Maps* together with illustrated leaflets describing three of the walks in detail; Ruscombe Church, Charvil Country Park, and the River Loddon. The latter takes in the Loddon Nature Reserve (managed by the Berks, Bucks and Oxon Wildlife Trust), the lakes of which were formed by gravel extraction.

Twyford is fortunate in having two recreation grounds for its villagers to enjoy. King George's Field includes football pitches, tennis courts and childrens' playgrounds, whilst Stanlake Meadow has football pitches, a cricket square and a pavilion which doubles as a nursery school. Both provide the village with much needed green space to enjoy at a time when the area is developing rapidly.

The imminent arrival of Crossrail will no doubt bring further changes to this commuting community which is already enjoying the benefits of electrified trains up to London Paddington. Although the village has grown rapidly over the years, it has the reputation of being a very friendly place in which to live. It boasts many active clubs and societies, including a Women's

Institute which was founded in 1920, a local history society and a number of clubs for the retired, as well as an amateur dramatics society and horticultural association that puts on three horticultural shows a year. Twyford has much to offer. At the same time it has managed to retain its village atmosphere. Two small magazines, one monthly and the other bi-monthly, are delivered free of charge to local householders to keep them up to date with what is going on. In addition, in 2016 a local resident, Audrey Curtis, a former Secretary of the Twyford and Ruscombe Local History Society, wrote a book called *Twyford and Ruscombe through the Ages*. This is a fascinating and well researched read for anybody wishing to know more about the area from its very earliest times.

🍁 UFTON NERVET

The parish of Ufton Nervet occupies a strip of land four miles long and about one and a half miles wide in its broadest part, between Sulhamstead and Padworth, stretching from the Burghfield-Aldermaston road to beyond the Bath Road.

Ufton (Offetone) is mentioned in the Domesday Book. The church itself is modern, having been rebuilt by Mr Richard Benyon in 1861, but it contains many ancient monuments including memorials to the Perkins family of the 16th and 17th centuries. The ivy-covered ruin of the little chapel of Ufton Richard may be seen close to the old pound almost opposite the Dog and Partridge, which is now a private residence. Grim's Dyke or Ditch, an ancient earthwork, can still be found in Ufton woods where there are many walks and rides.

At the end of its lovely broad avenue of oaks stands Ufton Court, with its ancient great barn, outbuildings and cottages, and on the south side its terrace, old walled garden and fishpond.

Although it dates from the 15th century, the present Elizabethan house was built in the shape of a letter 'E' with a few later additions. From the 15th century until 1782 the property was owned by the Perkyns (later Perkins) family. They were Roman Catholic recusants, and in the days of Queen Elizabeth I many priests found sanctuary there. The famous priests' hiding holes still exist, and there is evidence of an Oratory. In 1838 the Ufton Manor was sold to Mr Benyon de Beauvon. The widow of Richard Perkyns remarried Sir John Marvyn of Fountell Giffard in Wiltshire, but maintained her connection with Ufton. She died in 1581 and in her will provided for an annual distribution to the 'poore' of Ufton of '… Good and Howshoulde Bread', 'canvas of twelve pence to the all', and 'bleweclothe of twenty pence the yards'. This bequest, known as the Annual Bread Dole, has been faithfully administered ever since. For almost 450 years, both bread and house linen have been given to the parishioners of Ufton by the trustees of the Marvyn Charity in mid-lent, through the same window in the hall of Ufton Court.

In 1715 a new young bride arrived at Ufton Court. Arabella Fermor, considered the most beautiful woman in London Society, had been the cause of society gossip and was reluctantly immortalised as Belinda, the heroine of Pope's long satirical poem *The Rape of the Lock*. Today, Ufton Court is home to an educational charity.

In the 1870s a school was founded at Ufton Nervet. A hundred years later Sulhamstead School closed, and the two were amalgamated on the Ufton site as one village school.

The countryside through which the River Kennet flows is still very peaceful; pheasants and partridges, dispersed with a flurry by the occasional skulking fox, forage for food, as they have always done, in Cow Pond Piece, Nan Pie and Rod Beds.

🍁 WALTHAM ST LAWRENCE

Aerial photographs to the north-east of Waltham St Lawrence show traces of an unusual Romano-English temple: Roman and pre-Roman remains can still be found and it is possible the area has been inhabited since Neolithic times. The original settlement was destroyed by raiding Saxons in the 7th century.

The church, mentioned in the Domesday Book, was part of the first Earl of Essex, Geoffrey de Mandeville's reward for supporting the Conqueror. The Advowson, regarded as a source of income, was passed over to the Prior of Hurley when the Earl decided to found a monastery as an act of piety.

An important family were the Newburys who lived in a moated manor house, Beenhams, and for 400 years ran a printing business in London. They gave to the village the 14th-century Bell Inn which stands near the church and Neville Hall. The Lordship of the Manor was bought originally from the See of Winchester and eventually sold to the Neville family in 1608.

During the Civil War the village was deeply divided, with the Neville brothers fighting on opposite sides, and though the principal families were Parliamentarians, the vicar remained a Royalist. According to the Parish Register there were burials of soldiers from both sides, and when Beenhams was demolished in the 19th century it is reputed that the skeleton of a Royalist soldier in full accoutrement was discovered. Sir Thomas Foote, a 17th-century Lord Mayor of London, rented the house at one time and set up a charity which still exists. A barn standing near the site of the old manor is said to be the oldest in Berkshire.

In the mid 17th century the population was around 300. Little is known of village activities apart from records of the ringing of the church bells for various accessions, coronations and royal birthdays. When Queen Victoria came to the throne in 1837 the population had risen to around 740. A small brick church was built in Shurlock Row in 1870 – this has a reredos in hand-carved oak on the wall behind the altar. The clock in the small bell-tower was put there after the First World War as a memorial to Mr Beale who lived in the old manor house (now demolished) which stood next to Manor Farm in Shurlock Row.

The Second World War brought great changes. Since 1952 many new houses have been built, some being council property. Barns were converted, old cottages renovated, large houses divided, others extended, and one public house, the Fox and Hounds on the Straight Mile became a private dwelling.

The majority of inhabitants derive their livelihood from surrounding towns or by commuting to London. Very few earn their living from the land as in times past. Of the nine farms in the parish only half remain, the rest having been divided among other estates, and the houses and buildings sold off. The large orchards and nurseries which once flourished have all gone apart from one, selling mainly alpine and rockery plants. In spite of all these changes there remain villagers who can trace their ancestry back many generations. The primary school at West End, built in 1910 to replace the two church schools still has children whose grandparents were themselves former pupils.

A small but important printing firm, the Cockerel Press, originated in Waltham but is no longer there. Various businesses flourish for a while, then disappear, but there is still a busy garage for car repairs and sales, and smaller concerns mainly of the building, odd jobs and garden supplies kind.

There is plenty of activity in the community including a Village Show, run originally by the Women's Institute and now by a Village Committee, which is held each summer. Occasionally everyone gets together as they did during Queen Victoria's reign to organise a fete or raise money for the village.

🍁 WARFIELD

Warfield was originally an Anglo-Saxon settlement, the name originally meaning 'open land by a weir'.

St Michael's church, still one of the best preserved churches in Berkshire, has been the Parish Church for the area for over 1,000 years. The Grade II listed building is home to some beautiful carvings and 'Green Men' sculptures. One newer feature in the church is the magnificent stained-glass window designed by Brian Thompson, OBE.

Rectory House was once the home of Sir William James Herschel. It was here that he published his book *The Origin of Fingerprinting*. He recognized that fingerprints were a unique and permanent way of indentifying a person and he is credited with being the first person to use fingerprints in a practical manner. His old-age hobby was coloured photography developed on glass. Miss Caroline Herschel, a descendant of the former – who lived in Warfield for many years, retired to Bath where she died, and where the Herschel Museum has been opened.

Church Farm was the home of Miss Dorothea Herschel, and during the 1920s she taught the village children country dancing and was the power behind almost every event held in the village. Her niece, the late Mrs Eileen Shorland, the local historian and author of *The Pish* published in 1967, lived at Meadons. There is an oak tree in the churchyard planted by Sir William Herschel and beneath this are ashes of the Herschel family.

Warfield Primary School, once in danger of closing, is the centre of activity with the number of pupils increasing each term.

🍁 WARFIELD PARK

The Park WI is situated on Warfield Park. I, Doreen Beale, feel very lucky to have lived here for the last 15 years. It has a lovely community atmosphere and a village sense of fun.

It all started a long time ago in December 1947 when Mr Ian MacLaren obtained permission for a maximum of 12 caravans to be sited on the Park. Now there are nearly 500 park homes on the 92 acres. Times have changed from when Mr MacLaren invited people to site their caravans on his land and mark out their own boundaries. These humble beginnings are why the Park is so unique with its unusual layout and varying sized pitches. When Mr MacLaren left Harrow and Cambridge, he began work as a stable lad and then joined the staff of the Racing Outlook. From there he started a garage at Colnbrook, landed in Normandy on D-Day as a Captain in charge of transport, started an Air Charter Service, went into pig farming and then started Warfield Park in a small way. He lived with his partner Helen on the Park until his death in 1969.

During the Second World War the Americans were stationed here in the Manor House and it was used as a listening station. They built maintenance and Nissen buildings, together with wooden accommodation cabins, around the Estate to house their servicemen and constructed tracks around the Park for their vehicles. The maintenance building and an accommodation cabin are still in use today as workshops. At the end of the war there was a severe shortage of housing and in the summer of 1946 the wooden cabins and Nissen huts were taken over by squatters. Most of them were ex-British army and airmen and their families. An instruction was issued by an officer of the War Department to provide them with gas and water and so they were able to stay on the Park. Over the years it has grown in popularity. The Park became very popular and so Mr MacLaren made a number of planning applications to expand. He obtained planning permission for a sanitary block with laundry and boiler house in 1963, a toilet building in 1966 and then a general store and an extension to the office in 1968. The park homes situated here now are a far cry from the caravans that were originally here. In fact, just like modern bungalows with all mod cons!

There is certainly a 'village' feel to living here. A beautiful large hall was built about 2004 where various clubs can meet throughout the week including WI, darts evenings, craft, line dancing, bowls, bingo, tai chi, garden club and many more. There is something for everybody. Twice a month there is a coffee morning held which is always very well attended. In August the Park residents have a Fete Day, which takes place on the green outside the hall where there are many stalls, tombola, bric-a-brac, coconut shies, beer tent, children's face painting and lots more. We all come together to make it a very special day and if the sun shines, even better! There is also a social evening held in the hall at least once a month, where we have a group playing, singers or a comedian which is always well attended and the dance floor is usually full.

The camaraderie feel to living here is very much in evidence, especially when someone is not well, there is snow on the ground or a cuppa and a chat is needed. Many dog owners live here and it is impossible to walk to the post box or just have a stroll around listening to the birds singing without meeting up with someone, everyone is very friendly. It is very quiet and peaceful and not having street lights at night gives it a definite country, rural feel.

Warfield Park is situated very close to the M3 and M4 with good access routes everywhere, and being once part of Windsor Great Park it has lots of lovely trees and is close to the town itself and castle. With the regeneration of Bracknell old town, there are now many eating places, large and airy shops and walkways. We are also situated within easy reach of Henley, Marlow, Maidenhead and anywhere along the River Thames itself.

Most of the people living here are retired and have downsized from where they lived before, which gives us all a great leveller. Amongst our WI members are some extremely good cake makers which is very handy when we have our meetings, and calling in on a friend there is always a cuppa and a piece of cake on offer.

🍁 WARGRAVE

The riverside village of Wargrave lies on the bank of the River Thames close to the confluence of the Thames and the Loddon. The A321 from Twyford to Henley-on-Thames passes along the village High Street. The name Wargrave is believed to be a derivation of weir-grove, and this is appropriate as Wargrave is close to a weir and in a wooded valley. Many houses enjoy beautiful riverside settings by both the Thames and the Loddon.

Wargrave has an annual regatta with the village of Shiplake which lies on the opposite bank of the Thames in Oxfordshire. The regatta has a long history of over 150 years. It is a great boating and family occasion.

Wargrave has a population of about 4,000 people; it includes Cockpole Green, Crazies Hill, Kiln Green and Hare Hatch. The centre of the village is very picturesque with a number of notable buildings. No fewer than 76 buildings or structures are listed. Timber Cottage in the High Street dates from the mid 14th century and is the oldest surviving building there.

To the west of the High Street is Mill Green, the village green. Here lies St Mary's Church, dating from the 13th century but largely rebuilt after being severely burnt in 1914 by suffragettes. Fortunately, some parts survived the devastation including the Norman north doorway. In a corner of the churchyard is an impressive columbarium (a storage area for cremated remains), designed by Sir Edwin Lutyens as the mausoleum for the Hannen family. Another Edwin Lutyens monument is the First World War memorial, with later Second World War additions. Next to St Mary's church is the early 16th-century Wargrave Court, once the manor house, and now a large private home.

Beneath this historic surface lies a vibrant village. Wargrave has at least 40 clubs and organisations catering for all tastes and ages including Royal British Legion, Theatre Workshop, History Society, Bridge, Boating, Tennis, Bowls, Football, Ramblers, Scouts and Guides (also Cubs, Beavers, Brownies and Rainbows); the list goes on. The commendable Luncheon Club and Pop-In Club give invaluable service to the elderly. They meet weekly and provide lunch and a sociable gathering. There are two Women's Institutes: Cockpole Green WI, formed in 1932, meets in Crazies Hill village hall and Mill Green WI, formed in 1973, was named after Wargrave village green.

Every two years Wargrave hosts a village festival which lasts two weeks and brings the village together. Events are held by most of the village clubs. The festival is masterminded by a hard-working festival committee. A large marquee is erected on Mill Green and there are numerous events including an open-air Shakespeare play, art and craft displays, dancing, concerts, a flower festival, tea parties, open gardens, village fete and a summer ball. On the last Sunday there is a church service in the marquee followed by lunch on Mill Green.

As with most villages, Wargrave does not have the number of shops that it once enjoyed. But it is better provided for than most villages. It still has a Post Office, chemist, library, newsagent and a well-stocked general store. Most importantly Wargrave has excellent medical care. The Wargrave Surgery has a team of doctors, nurses, a pharmacist and support staff. There are two churches: the Parish Church of St Mary's and the Roman Catholic Church of Our Lady of Peace.

In bygone days there were eighteen inns in the area. Today there are four: the Bull, the Greyhound, and St George and the Dragon in Wargrave, and the Horns at Crazies Hill. The Bull is the oldest inn dating from the 15th century. Like all good old inns it reputedly has its own local ghosts; and they are likely to remain, to enjoy the aromas of the delicious food served in the inn.

Wargrave has schools for all age groups. It is an unusual village: a child can be educated from early pre-school to age 18 years without having to leave the village. The senior school has superb sports facilities which serve both the school and the wider community. The Recreation Ground in Wargrave is maintained to a very high standard. In the summer cricket is played and in the winter football and hockey. There are also excellent floodlit tennis courts.

Wargrave has its own newspaper the *Wargrave News*. It is published each month by a dedicated team of volunteers and delivered to every house within the village – and it is free! We all look forward to the *Wargrave News* dropping through the letterbox. In its pages local issues are aired, events publicised, letters on a myriad of subjects are printed, school and club activities recounted; and all of this promotes a strong, healthy and informed village community.

People who move to Wargrave rarely want to leave; many have lived in a number of different houses within the village. This feeling of belonging and wanting to stay is not only because of the location but because they enjoy and appreciate the community spirit of this special village.

🍁 WASH COMMON

Wash Common lies to the south-west of the market town of Newbury, occupying high ground between the Kennet and Enborne valleys. In days gone by the area had a village feel but it is now swallowed up as a suburb.

In September 1643 during the Civil War, the first Battle of Newbury was fought here and many local roads are relevantly named; Charles Street, Essex Street, Battle Road, Falkland Road, Cary Close etc. This theme was taken up again in the early 1970s when a new estate was built and more thoroughfares were named after men caught up in the fighting; Villiers, Meyrick, Stapleton, Meldrum and many others.

Viscount Falkland (Lucius Cary) lost his life in the battle serving with the Royalist Cavalry and the Falkland Memorial (the first memorial to be taken over and still maintained by the National Trust) stands at the junction of Essex Street and the Andover Road. An information board has been located here giving excellent details of the battle. It was a key event in the war, and some 3,000 soldiers were killed.

Opposite the Falkland Memorial and next to the Gun public house, a row of retail establishments now inhabit an area that was once a pond!

The Falkland name lives on in the area – Falkland Primary School, Falkland WI and more recently, Falkland Surgery. Long before these, the well-known Falkland Cricket Club established its ground off Enborne Street. Today it has two grounds for First and Second X1s. The Club also hosts Minor Counties matches with Berkshire playing at least once during the season.

In the woodland adjacent to the Common, a Bronze Age site has been excavated and details are, once again, provided on information boards. The area has a long history!

St George's C of E church is Italianate in style and in the 1990s a huge fund-raising initiative was launched to raise money for a new Church Centre comprising a hall, annexe and office. The then Archdeacon of Berkshire, the Venerable Michael Hill, opened the completed project in January 1997. St George's has 'gone green' being the first church in the country to be self-supporting in green energy. Quite an achievement!

A number of groups meet under the umbrella of St George's and in the mid 1980s a committee organised an October Autumn Festival incorporating a competitive Garden and Craft Show. Eventually, this became The Wash Common Garden and Craft Show which now takes place annually on the second Saturday in September and is held in the Wash Common Community Centre.

The former St Luke's C of E church (in a corner of the church hall car park) is now home to the New Era Theatre and has recently been extended to provide an entrance foyer. The New Era Players produce several plays during the year which are very well supported. The theatre also offers exhibition space, mainly for local artists and artisans.

The Scout and Guide movements for all age groups are well established within the area, meeting in the Battery End Scout Hut and in St George's church hall respectively.

Sadly, there is no longer the Post Office/General Store which did a thriving business until the beginning of the Millennium and was quite a hub in the local community. However, despite the many changes that have occurred over the years, Wash Common is still a very pleasant place to live and the undulating countryside is very close to escape to, away from suburbia!

🍁 WELFORD

Welford is a rural downland parish comprising six settlements – Welford itself, Wickham, Weston, Easton, Hoe Benham and Halfway. It is rich in history and folklore, having been continuously inhabited since at least the Roman period.

In 686 Welford and Wickham were granted to Abingdon Abbey by King Caedwalla of Wessex, and Welford Park became the site of a monastic grange, much favoured for its abundant game and fish. There has been a church at Welford for over 1,000 years and evidence of the Saxon structure, including a silver coin of Edward the Confessor, was revealed during rebuilding in the 19th century. In 1394, Welford monks received an official warning from the Abbey for keeping their pigs in the churchyard! When the Abbey was dissolved by Henry VIII, Welford Park passed first to the King, who used it as a deer hunting lodge, before later being leased to Sir Thomas Parry,

Comptroller to the Royal Household. The church of St Gregory at Welford includes, amongst its many interesting features, a fine alabaster monument to Sir Thomas' widow, Lady Anne, with figures of her seven sons and twelve daughters.

A manor house was first built at Welford Park during the reign of Elizabeth I, evidence of which can still be seen in the cellars of the present house, which dates from the early Georgian period. Welford House has many fascinating tales to tell, including its use as a convalescent home for wounded soldiers during the First World War.

Weston and Easton on the Lambourn, or 'bottom' road also have a place in the history of the parish. At Easton, beer could be purchased at Olive Branch Cottage for consumption on a bench under the tree across the road, known as the 'public bar'; and it is said that a gibbet once stood at nearby Rood Hill, on the parish boundary with Boxford. Weston became involved in the agricultural Swing Riots of 1830, when the village constable confronted a mob intent on breaking the threshing machine at Weston Farm. It was also home to a group of mummers who performed their traditional Christmas plays around the area.

The secluded hamlet of Hoe Benham was the site of the old parish workhouse, which burned down in mysterious circumstances in the 1830s. From here also comes the local legend of the 'ghost pig' which is said to have haunted the area for many years, reputedly connected with the troubled spirit of an 18th-century farmer who came to a tragic end.

Situated on the busy A4, the Halfway Inn has for centuries welcomed travellers on this important route between London and Bath. During the heyday of coaching another inn, the Jolly Sailor, stood nearby. The Bath Road was 'turnpiked' in the 18th century and the old Halfway toll house, known as the Round House, was a familiar sight to motorists until it was demolished in the 1960s.

The War Memorial, a Celtic Cross on the road between Welford and Wickham, stands as a reminder of the high price paid by the parish in the two World Wars. RAF Welford, established in 1941, played an important role in D-Day, Operation Market Garden, and the Battle of the Bulge.

During the Second World War, 600 acres were commandeered to form Welford airbase to be occupied by the American 101st Airborne Division. On the night of 31st March 1944 a Lancaster bomber on its way back from a raid on the German town of Nuremberg crashed on the runway due to a misunderstanding by traffic control and the pilot. All the 8-man crew were killed. In the station garden is a memorial to the crew. An annual memorial service is held at the site. The base is now used jointly by British and US forces for the storage of conventional arms.

Welford House grounds are famous for the annual display of snowdrops that carpet a large area amongst woodland. The grounds are open to the public during February and takings are generously donated to local charities. The house has become famous for another reason – the venue for the television series *The Great British Bake Off*.

🍁 WEST ILSLEY

The village of West Ilsley sits nestled in the lee of the Berkshire Downs, bounded by two ancient roads, the Ridgeway to the north, (the neolithic path that runs from Avebury to Ivinghoe Beacon), and Old Street to the west which crosses the Ridgeway at Land's End along Copperage Road, (half way to Farnborough), where a Roman settlement called Old Newbury is believed to have been situated.

The Ilsley name is understood to be a derivation of *Hilde-Laege* or 'place of conflict' as it is believed that Prince (later King) Alfred defeated the Danes at the Battle of Ashdown in the area. The importance of this victory was paramount in England's eventually becoming one nation under his grandson Æthelstan, Ashdown itself being the seat of Alfred's Castle is only a few miles west. At the time of the Domesday Book, West Ilsley was part of the Hundred of Compton, and divided into two manors. One was valued at 40 shillings and the other 80.

Just outside the parish boundary on the Ridgeway is Schutchamer Knob which, in times past was a market of importance where great numbers of people would gather in order to buy, sell, barter and exchange grain and other goods. The Saxon Shire Moot, (equivalent to a County Council meeting), took place here monthly where the freemen of each Hundred would deal with crime, lawsuits and taxes under the Reeve (local Chief). These meeting places were often held near a distinguishing feature as is the case here with a large round barrow marking the place. In 1340 it was noted that the land was so barren that tenants were forced to relinquish their land and move away.

In 1644 the villagers petitioned King Charles I to express their concerns over the hardships his government was causing and requested exemption. He duly visited and was entertained by the rector Dr Godfrey Goodman who paid the price of his loyalty to the Crown by being ousted from his position two years later by the Roundhead authority. The Civil War itself brought undue hardship

Main Street, West Ilsley

to the farmers as the opposing factions took what food was available without a thought for the locals. On 12 August 1645 the knights, gentlemen, free-holders and other inhabitants of Berkshire arranged a general meeting on the Downs between Ilsley and Wantage. They declared that they had been 'for a long time over-pressed with the many insupportable burdens, and contrary commands of the many garrisons and armies both of the King and Parliament'.

Their leaders drew up the following petition:

'We the miserable inhabitants of the County of Berkshire, foreseeing famine and desolation will inevitably fall upon us, our wives and children, unless God of His infinite mercy, shall be graciously pleased to put a period to those sad distractions, are unanimously resolved to join in petitioning His Majesty and the two Houses of Parliament for a happy peace.'

The only result of this petition was that the High Constable of Reading was sent to prison for promoting the meeting.

John Moreland, a local farmer, started the Moreland Brewery in 1711 and his beers quickly gained popularity. The brewery remained in West Ilsley until relocating to Abingdon in 1887 and though the building is long gone his home, West Ilsley House, still stands.

In the mid 19th century, the village had its own witch. She was said to take the form of a hare running across the downs. She was chased by dogs and was bitten as she tried to get through her cottage door. Her neighbours found her sitting by the fire nursing the wound and that stopped any further magic.

Modernity has seen the demise of the bakery, (Sheppards Bakery closed in the early 1960s but was making 300 loaves a day at its peak), the school closed when a new one was constructed at East Ilsley. The post office, village shop, and Royal Mail post bus have all disappeared along with a radical change in the demographic. However, the Harrow public house still lords it over the hallowed cricket pitch, racehorse training is the new industry, the farms are run by those who respect the land and that unique quintessential village spirit remains as testament to those both past and present who call West Ilsley home.

❀ WICKHAM

Wickham stands on Ermin Street, the Roman road between Silchester and Gloucester, and many artefacts from that era have been found here. An archaeological survey has revealed evidence of buildings, suggesting that Wickham may have been a 'vicus' or small town on this important route. Roman masonry was re-used by the Saxons in building a watchtower at Wickham, later incorporated into St Swithun's Church.

This church is known for its intriguing Elephant Chapel, dating from Victorian times, with its set of large papier-mâché elephants – three of which were purchased at the Paris Exhibition to illustrate the virtues of Fortitude, Docility and Strength. Later, five copies were made in this country bringing the full troupe up to eight.

Two pew ends in the centre aisle were designed by Sir George Gilbert Scott, and the font cover was brought over from New Zealand, originally for a Crystal Palace Exhibition in 1862.

The Five Bells Inn at Wickham has served many generations of thirsty locals, and in the 18th and early 19th century also acted as a regular stopping-off point for Welsh drovers taking their flocks to market. In the 1830s a number of skeletons, supposedly drovers, were discovered here – allegedly the victims of a nefarious former landlord, Mr Fulbrook, acting in league with highwaymen who operated on Wickham Heath. The Five Bells was also the scene of an incident involving the well-known local Wizard, or Cunning Man, John Palmer, who put a spell on drovers staying at the inn so they were unable to get out of bed without his consent!

Wickham has often been the social hub of the parish; the school opened in 1857 and a Working Men's Club was established in 1875, with the present village hall opening in 1926. Wickham was also home to the well-known Welford District Brass Band, which was much in demand around this part of Berkshire for many years before the First World War.

The village school in Wickham was built in 1857 on land granted by Charles Eyre Esq. of Welford House and paid for by him and Rev William Nicholson. The school is still flourishing having been considerably extended and altered since those days. Over 100 pupils attend the school.

In 1969 the quiet country road through Wickham was widened to allow vehicles involved in the construction of the M4 to pass more easily. The road was designated the B4000 and was witness to a significant increase in traffic. Following a two-year campaign by local residents, West Berkshire Council approved an Environmental Weight Limit of 7.5 tonnes between Speen and Shefford Woodlands. This came into force in February 2003.

WINDSOR GREAT PARK

This small village hidden in the heart of Windsor Great Park is unknown to the many residents of nearby Windsor.

Until 1948 the small community living and working in the park, forestry workers, gamekeepers and gatekeepers lived in splendid isolation in a few houses clustered around Prince Consort Workshop. The workshops had been designed by the Prince Consort about 1850 and consisted of stabling for cart horses, a saw mill driven by water power, and carpentry and joinery shops. Over the years these workshops have further developed to employ motor mechanics, fencers and blacksmiths.

During and after the Second World War activities in the Park considerably increased; 1,500 acres of land were now being farmed and there was a large gardening area of 6,000 acres including the Savill and Valley gardens, and an ever-growing area of woodlands. The workforce increased considerably on the estate which meant that the men had to travel several miles by foot or bicycle from outlying villages.

King George VI, who was on the throne at the time, had always taken a great interest in the developments of the Park and the welfare of his employees. It was at his instigation that the first thoughts of a real village in the Park arose. The King's wishes were accepted by the Commissioner of Crown Lands who was responsible for the management of the Crown Estate. Architects were engaged to design The Village, which was to be sited near the main centre of activity, Prince Consort Workshop, where many of the men worked. They were instructed to vary designs and materials, roofline and aspect. These conditions were most successfully achieved, resulting in a village full of character.

To complete the village, a charmingly designed shop-cum-Post Office was built. This is still running and now provides the park's many visitors with light refreshments.

The garden is full of customers come rain or shine. The village also has a social centre now called The York Club. The WI meet here to hold their meetings in the hall. The club has many sections including bowls, football, golf and cricket. It was originally called The York Hall to commemorate the great interest in which the Duke and Duchess of York (later King George VI and Queen Elizabeth) had taken in the daily life of the park.

The village comprised 24 cottages and was completed in 1948. A few years later, with a further increase of staff, an additional 24 properties were added to the village. Recently a Biomass Furnace has been built and all the village properties and the York Club now get their heating and hot water directly from this site.

The children of the estate, and some lucky children from neighbouring villages, are educated at The Royal School. This was built on the instruction of Queen Victoria to educate the employees' children and many generations of these families have attended the school.

The pastoral welfare of the residents is taken care of by a resident Canon and services are held at the nearby church located within the grounds of Royal Lodge, the home of the current Duke of York.

The village has been thoughtfully designed and skilfully blends into the beauty of open spaces and old trees. It is a truly unique place to live and raise a family.

🍁 WINKFIELD

Winkfield is said to be the second largest parish in England and takes in a great arable area of Windsor Forst, with the widely separated hamlets of North Street, The Plain, Maidens Green, Brook Hill, Winkfield Row and Chavey Down.

There are some fine old buildings and interesting houses to see, including St Mary's church which dates from the 13th century, the old Court House, now the White Hart inn, the Old Rectory, the Abbey Farm and Abbey Gate House. Also there is the Knights Hall in Winkfield Lane, the old Forge and the Pump Room, plus Handpost Farm, Keepers Cottage and Tile Cottage at Winkfield Row.

Winkfield Place was, for many years, the Constance Spry School which not only had residential students but also ran day courses in the Constance Spry way of cookery, flowers and other domestic arts. It has now been divided up into private apartments.

Once farmers and foresters, the people of Winkfield now tend to work in the neighbouring towns or commute to London.

🍁 WINNERSH

Winnersh has changed, growing enormously over the last 30 years. It is a long village with the main road (A329) between Reading and Wokingham dividing it. Before the installation of traffic lights, the road was apparently known as 'The Murder Mile' because of the number of fatalities along this stretch. The crossroads where the Reading Road and the road between Arborfield and Hurst cross is often seen as the centre of the village. Originally a farm, the land was first sold to a company who dealt with and assembled tractors from America. After a few years they sold up and the Crimpy Crisp Factory was built. They also produced nuts and raisins and when they were bought out by a subsidiary of Pepsi the building was closed and demolished. Hewlett-Packard then had their UK headquarters there until they moved to Bracknell in 1997, and Sainsbury's purchased the site for their new supermarket. Over the years this building has been enlarged and the company bought the adjoining garden centre to enable the car park to be extended as the original had been partially used for the redevelopment.

There are a few shops in the area, convenience stores, a small post office, carpet shops, restaurants, hairdressers, a garage, the usual doctors and dentists and of course an estate agent! Surrounding farmland is being sold and applications for house building are being made – sometimes on land that those who have lived here for only a few years, know is unsuitable for the purpose.

At one end of the village is Winnersh Triangle, an area of businesses and hotels. The ease of access to the railway and motorway make this a busy area. Winnersh is well served by two stations, enabling a commute to Reading and to London, and buses from Reading to Bracknell also pass through very frequently.

There are three primary schools serving Winnersh, one of which opened two years ago, and a boys' secondary school which takes pupils from a larger area (the girls' equivalent is in Wokingham). The library opened in 2003 and is situated in the school grounds, which means that people no longer have to rely on the visiting mobile library. Various activities take place there, especially for younger children.

St Mary's Church, built in 1965, was originally in the parish of Hurst but since the boundaries changed it's now attached to St Catherine's at Sindlesham. When Winnersh WI was first formed in 1928, it used to meet in St Catherine's Lodge next to the church which was the Dower House of the Bearwood Estate owned by John Walter the owner of *The Times* newspaper. The church was dedicated to his daughter Catherine. Now, after various homes, the WI meet in St Mary's Church Hall along with various other organisations. There are three Rainbow groups who meet at St Mary's, two Brownie packs and a Guide unit. Another Brownie pack meets in the Baptist Church. There used to be a small Methodist Chapel in Winnersh but that closed in the 1980s.

Nearby is Dinton Pastures Country Park, which was developed by Wokingham District (now Borough) Council in the 1970s following gravel extractions for the building of the local motorway. Part of Dinton Pastures was originally in Winnersh until the boundary changes in 1986. It is a very popular place for walkers, joggers and cyclists and has an excellent play area for children. Of course the café is a welcome meeting place after walking round one of the lakes, or feeding the ducks. There is also a small country park with an orchard, wildflower meadow and a wetland which is home to the Great Crested Newt.

🍁 WOODLEY

Present day Woodley lies between the main roads from Reading to Wokingham on one side, and Reading and Maidenhead on the other, and has developed into a sprawling, thickly populated area, on land which until relatively recently was farmed. We probably owe this to the proximity of an M4 motorway intersection, and thus a swift passage to London.

However, the village first began to emerge in the 18th century as a series of 'Greens' or settlements lying on the routes to other villages or important buildings such as Sandford Mill which was mentioned in the Domesday Book. It still stands, though very few of the original houses remain and have to be sought for amidst present day housing estates. By the end of the 19th century another separate area emerged, known as Cobblers City – still referred to as 'the City'. The inhabitants of this group appear to have been independent of agriculture and developed other trades, and some even went into Reading for work.

At the turn of the 18th century much help came from the Palmer family who lived in nearby Sonning, but interested themselves in the welfare of their Woodley tenants (for they owned most of the land), and in others scattered throughout the Greens and Cobblers City. It was Robert Palmer who in 1871 built and endowed the church of St John the Evangelist, together with a school. Both buildings are very attractive examples of their period and are in active use.

The village hall, called the Coronation Hall as it was built in the year of our Queen's coronation (1953) was officially opened in 1956 by the late Sir Douglas Bader who was a member of the Woodley Aerodrome Flying Club in pre-war days. It is strategically placed in the Memorial Recreation Ground which commemorates the dead of the First World War.

A shopping centre incorporating a modern Chequers Inn stands on the site of an old coaching inn on a route through Windsor Forest. The Bull & Chequers remains at Woodley Green, and a modern public house, the Good Companions, caters for the needs of Wheelers Green.

WOOLHAMPTON & MIDGHAM

Both these villages are situated on the A4 Bath Road between Reading and Newbury. The village of Woolhampton has a railway station and the River Kennet and the Kennet & Avon Canal to the south. The church of St Peter and Douai Abbey are up the hill to the north together with three schools. The railway station in Woolhampton is called 'Midgham' to stop a misunderstanding with 'Wolverhampton' as happened in the early days!

Midgham proudly has the church of St Matthew as a landmark, seen from the main road on top of the hill. Much of the area has woodland providing beautiful bluebell walks in the spring. It is a hamlet and the church and village hall provide the community with meeting places. These two churches are part of a Benefice of six in the area, which include Beenham, Brimpton, Aldermaston and Wasing. Both churches were restored in the 1860s by the Blyth family and more recently have kitchen and toilet facilities. There are First World War memorials situated in each of the two graveyards.

The Roman Catholic School was taken over by monks who were expelled from Douai in France in 1903. On the adjoining playing fields a new pavilion is used for village sports and recreation. Douai Abbey is an impressive building and was finished in 1993, although the school has now closed, and residential homes have replaced some of the buildings. The Abbey presents some wonderful concerts as well as respite to travellers.

There are two pubs in Woolhampton having lost the Falmouth to dwellings and the Rising Sun. The Rowbarge enjoys its situation beside the River Kennet and hosts the Mikron Theatre Company in the summer who travel the country by their own barge transport.

The canal is busy, and mostly used for recreation. The Devizes to Westminster canoe race takes place annually over the Easter weekend. There was once a 'rope walk' alongside the river from the bridge to the present lock gates.

The Angel Inn is a landmark on the A4 in the middle of the village. In 1931 it was rebuilt because the road had to be widened due to the volume of traffic. The village shop is a busy centre and the corner shop opposite offers many delightful gifts. Sadly there is no longer a Post Office.

The Coach and Horses pub is along the road in Midgham – always busy! There are several interesting and historic buildings in Woolhampton. Coming from the petrol station in the east you will see the rod beds (reeds) which were harvested for basket-making for home and foreign markets until the Second World War. Further along is the fountain standing on the corner of Station Road. It was given to the village by Miss Charlotte Blyth to celebrate Queen Victoria's Diamond Jubilee, providing the village with clean drinking water from an artesian well 160 feet down. Originally there was a cast-iron trough at the back, but sadly this was stolen in 2000. Further along the road is a matching brick building known as the Gill Campbell Hall, also given by Miss Blyth for Christian fellowship in 1895. The original Woolhampton and Midgham WI had their inaugural meeting there in 1937. There were many

Kennet & Avon Canal at Woolhampton

restrictions to the use of the building so the King George V Hall was built in 1929 further along the road. This has since been replaced in 2006 with a new hall and allotments, which are well used – including WI meetings for ladies from both villages and beyond. The clock on the Gill Campbell Hall, now a private residence, still keeps perfect time. The Old Mill, built in 1820, in Station Road still has its wheel.

It is hoped that the old village fire engine will soon be returned after its safe keeping in the Blake's Lock Museum in Reading. It had been purchased in 1906 from a local mansion sale and was first used on a fire caused by sparks on the railway. It was kept at Brook Farm which was in Station Road between The Mill and the railway until the 1950s. Its new location is still to be decided.

With the railway electrification work taking place, scenery along the river and canal towpath will never be the same again. Such is progress …

🍁 WRAYSBURY

Wraysbury, formerly in Buckinghamshire, lies at one of the easternmost points in Berkshire. It is a village on the banks of the River Thames, and is full of history. It was formerly called Wyrardisbury, and an archaeological dig on higher ground where stands the parish church produced Mesolithic and Neolithic flints, and also some Saxon and Roman remains. In times past, although subject to flooding, Wraysbury was strategically placed for river traffic.

In medieval times, Wraysbury was part of the Crown Lands of Windsor, and royal parties would have hunted in the forests. At Ankerwycke, there are the ruins of an ancient priory, and at Place Farm, later known as King John's hunting lodge, can be found one of the best examples of scissor beams in this country.

Magna Carta Island is opposite the village, and it is here that the famous charter is reputed to have been signed. At Magna Carta House there is a stone tablet, found in the River Thames in Victorian times, believed be the original table on which the signing took place. This stone is now housed in a room in the older part of the house, surrounded by the shields of the Barons of the day.

In the grounds of the burnt-out shell of Ankerwycke House there is an ancient yew tree, under which Henry VIII was believed to have courted Anne Boleyn, and later waited with her successor, Catherine Howard, for the news of her death.

It is not known when the first church was built on the present site of the parish church of St Andrews, but it is almost certain to have been in Saxon times. Records show that in 1112 the living belonged to the Abbot of St Peter's in Gloucester. In 1327, in the reign of Edward III, it was given to the Dean and Canons of Windsor, in whose hands it remains today. The Chancery, which is the oldest part of the church, was probably built about the time of the signing of the Magna Carta in 1215. The church has six bells, the oldest of which is dated 1591.

Wraysbury has two pubs, the oldest, the George dating back to 1666. There are also several interesting houses and cottages in the village. One house, now known as the Barley Mow was built in Tudor times, and is thought to have been two cottages. By 1600 it became a beer house, known as the Papermakers' Beerhouse.

The papermakers worked at the mill in Wraysbury, which had previously been a copper mill; the copper ore came up the Thames on barges and was then taken by horse-drawn transport to the mill. One of the beams in the Barley Mow is reputed to be from one of the barges, and shows the rib marks. The age of some of the beams has been confirmed by experts as being from the Tudor period.

🍁 YATTENDON

Yattendon is a really beautiful old village, compact and immaculately cared for. It is set in lovely wooded countryside designated as an Area of Outstanding Natural Beauty (AONB). The centre is built round a wide road, almost a square, where a free-standing oak dominates the scene. This was planted to replace the old elm tree, which had succumbed to Dutch elm disease, by Lord Iliffe in 1977 to commemorate the 25th anniversary of the reign of Queen Elizabeth II. Around the 'square' is the very attractive Royal Oak, a good sized modernised village shop and post office, a well-used coffee shop and hairdressers.

The Manor House stands in a group of fine old houses along the village street as well as the church of St Peter and St Paul (built in 1450), the Village Hall, the Manor Wheat Barn, aka tithe barn and the village school. The Grange, the Old Rectory, and the Malt House, are also well worth looking out for.

In the days of Henry VIII the Manor House belonged to the Norreys family, who entertained the King and Queen – Katherine of Aragon with her lady-in-waiting, Anne Boleyn. According to legend, the young Henry Norreys picked up a handkerchief for Anne, and this set in motion the sad events which led to her death and his execution as one of her lovers.

Yattendon has a past association with Robert Bridges. Whilst living at the Manor House around 1896, he helped compile the *Yattendon Hymnal* for which

Yattendon

he wrote most of the hymns, fitting them to old tunes, and this is his best known legacy. Robert Bridges and his wife Monica also compiled the *Yattendon Psalter* which sadly is no longer in use. The ashes of Robert and Monica were placed under the terracotta cross – a memorial to his mother – which is in the front of the churchyard.

The church of St Peter and St Paul was built in the mid-15th century on an earlier foundation. The fine rood screen was made by local carvers and the enterprising members of the village class for copper-work made the copper font ewer and the brass candlestick behind the south door.

In 1956 a tragedy in the village led to the discovery of several deep and forgotten wells in old houses in close proximity to the Royal Oak. A Mrs Faithfull fell to her death, 134 feet down a well that suddenly opened in the floor. Many tons of flint were used to seal up this well, and several other wells in the village were also made safe.

Yattendon was the home of Ruth Mott, a WI member, who became a household name after appearing in the BBC series *The Victorian Kitchen*. Ruth, who lived in the village all her life, was a lifelong WI member having attended her first meeting as a young girl with her mother.

Yattendon Estates is the major land and property owner in the area and runs a 1450-acre Christmas tree business as well as farming in the locality. In recent years the Estate opened a small business park which is home to a variety of businesses. They include a wine shop, fitness centre, computer business, fine country clothing shop and a highly successful award-winning brewery ('Good Old Boy' ale is a particular favourite locally) supplying local and national outlets. It also has a shop, bar and bistro.

Annually, the village hosts a large fete which makes enough money to support many local activities for young and old.